KOSHER
on the
COAST

A unique blend of tastes

Proceeds from the sale of this book contribute to the fulfillment of Sisterhood's commitments to sponsor scholarships and educational enrichment programs, and to offer vital services and financial support to congregation and community projects.

WIMMER
COOKBOOKS

A CONSOLIDATED GRAPHICS COMPANY

800.548.2537   wimmerco.com

Introduction to Congregation Ner Tamid

Welcome to the Hill atop the lovely Palos Verdes Peninsula, overlooking the Los Angeles City lights and the blue Pacific. This is the home of Congregation Ner Tamid and our Sisterhood, which recently celebrated our 43rd birthday.

For many years, without a building to call our own, the Congregation and Sisterhood dreamed our impossible dream. As we gratefully accepted the hospitality of neighborhood churches, we worked for the day when we could build a permanent home-and, for Sisterhood, no home could be complete without a professional kitchen.

That day joyfully arrived, and today the beautiful synagogue warmly welcomes over 600 member families and countless guests. Having our own kitchen, Sisterhood can now do with ease all the things—and more—that we once did with only the sheer ingenuity of our women.

Sisterhood has always produced wonderful foods to enhance every occasion. Our weekly Oneg Shabbat features a variety of baked goods. Traditional fun foods are produced for Purim Carnivals; hamantaschen are baked in mass production for sale throughout the community and to help fill Purim baskets. Comfort foods are provided for the bereaved, and new Passover dishes are shared at tasting parties.

Although changing lifestyles may allow today's woman less time in the kitchen, enthusiasm for exchanging recipes remains constant. Over the years, Sisterhood has produced two sold-out editions of Kosher Kitchen Kapers, which combined recipes from varied Jewish traditions and the other ethnic-style dishes which constitute modern day "American," or "California" cuisine.

KOSHER ON THE COAST does all this, and more! It's been designed and organized with the active cook in mind. The recipes have been selected and tested so that the cook is sure to receive the applause and appreciation of family and guests. Cover to cover, you'll find it's the distinctive flavor of California that makes the difference.

The Artichoke

Artichokes were first cultivated in Italy around the middle of the 15th century. Gradually they were introduced to other sections of Europe and to the United States via French settlers in Louisiana and Spanish settlers in California. Today most of the world's artichokes are grown in California's fertile mid-coastal counties. The community of Castroville, just south of San Francisco, is known as the "Artichoke Capital of the World."

Artichokes can confuse the novice. At first glance, this member of the thistle family seems inedible. Just looking at the spiky leaves and the fuzzy chokes makes people want to dismiss them from their diets. Definitely take the time to prepare this food, as a delicious treat awaits you.

Artichokes come in all sizes, from very small to extra large. They are at their best in late spring. We find that the small to medium sizes have the best flavor. Just trim off the stem to make a flat bottom, then cut the spiky points straight across with a sharp knife.

Stand the artichokes upright in a deep saucepan, large enough to hold them snugly. Add ¼ teaspoon salt for each artichoke and 2 to 3 inches boiling water with a few drops of cooking oil to make the leaves glisten and a dash of lemon juice to prevent darkening. Cover and boil gently 35 to 45 minutes, or until the base can be pierced easily with a fork, adding a little more boiling water if needed. Lift the cooked artichokes and turn them upside down to drain. If artichokes are to be stuffed, gently the spread leaves and remove the choke (thistle portion) with a metal spoon, taking care not to remove any of the heart which is the ultimate taste prize. Don't forget, it's one artichoke per person.

If your preference is to stuff each artichoke for a more substantial dish, spread the leaves, opening a larger cavity and fill with your favorite chicken, tuna, rice or chopped, blanched fresh vegetable salad. Proceed to eat the artichoke as described below.

If not stuffed, pick off the outer leaves, one by one, and dip the fleshy end of the leaf into a sauce of your choice. Pull through your teeth and discard. When reaching the artichoke heart, you can then use your fork and knife.

Two Sauces:

Herb Mayonnaise: 1 cup mayonnaise, 1 cup watercress leaves, rinsed and dried, ¼ cup chopped Italian parsley and ¼ cup snipped fresh chives. Combine all ingredients and whirl in a food processor until smooth. Makes 1¼ cups. Place 1 or 2 tablespoons in the center of artichoke for dipping.

Yogurt Sauce: 1 cup plain yogurt (low-fat is fine), ½ cup mayonnaise, 1 teaspoon prepared mustard, 1 to 2 tablespoons freshly squeezed lemon juice and 1 teaspoon fresh dill (or the dry equivalent). Mix well. Makes 1¾ cups. Place 1 to 2 tablespoons in the center of each artichoke and serve.

Kashrut

Keeping a kosher kitchen provides a Jewish family the opportunity to make our own unique connection with our Biblical counterpart whose heritage we share. The ancient dietary laws, as presented in the Books of Leviticus and Deuteronomy and the various codes of Rabbinic Law, are timeless disciplines that have been followed throughout the generations. Basic laws deal with the separation of meat and milk, and permitted and forbidden meats and seafood.

Meat and milk products are never eaten together at the same meal. Separate sets of dishes for meat and dairy, as well as separate cooking and preparation utensils, are necessary components of a Kosher kitchen. They must be stored and washed separately, as well.

Permitted animals, such as cattle, sheep and goats, must all have cloven hooves and chew their cud. Domesticated fowl, including chicken, ducks, geese, turkey, pigeon and squab, are also permitted. All meat and fowl must be ritually slaughtered according to Jewish law, which adheres to the principles of reverence for life and ethics and compassion. Kosher butchers are the approved source of supply for meats and poultry. Additionally, various kosher products and poultry are now available in many supermarkets.

Fish that have fins and scales are permitted, and according to a ruling of the Rabbinical Assembly of America's Committee on Laws and Standards, swordfish and sturgeon are also kosher. All shellfish, such as lobster, shrimp, crab and oysters are forbidden.

Fruits, vegetables and eggs are considered neutral or pareve, and may be used with either meat or dairy.

There are many variations or interpretations of a law regarding the use of certain products or procedures. Sephardic and Askenazi practices may differ slightly, as may the conception of an individual rabbi. For that reason, "Kosher on the Coast" suggests a consultation with the rabbi of one's own congregation for answers to specific questions.

Sabbath

The Sabbath is considered the most important day in the Jewish week. It is welcomed each Friday evening with blessings recited over lighted candles, wine and challah. It is followed by a day of prayer, rest and renewal.

An effort is always made to create a Shabbat atmosphere, with a festive table setting and a menu that reflects the importance given to this most special of all observances.

Shabbat (The Sabbath) concludes with Havdallah after Saturday nightfall. This is a lovely ritual, which separates the day of holiness from the mundane.

The High Holy Days

Beginning with Selichot, which sets the mood, through Rosh Hashanah, until the final blast of the Shofar at the conclusion of Yom Kippur, this uniquely solemn period of High Holy Days is observed in homes and at synagogue services.

Rosh Hashanah

The taste of honey on a slice of apple brings with it the promise of a sweet year to come. This beautiful tradition, together with Kiddush, the blessing over the wine, and "Shehecheyanu", a prayer of thanksgiving, help to usher in Rosh Hashanah with warmth and hope, as each family gathers at the holiday table.

The theme of sweetness during the following days is incorporated into the festive menus, starting with a round raisin challah and accompaniments to the main course such as tzimmes, fruit kugel and honey cake.

Yom Kippur

Yom Kippur, The Day of Atonement, is the culmination of a period of serious self-examination, personal and spiritual fence-mending and sincere prayer for peace and well being in the coming year.

A day of fasting from all food and drink begins after the evening meal before sundown on the eve of Yom Kippur. With the Fast in mind, menus are usually planned avoiding highly seasoned foods.

At the conclusion of Yom Kippur, a traditional Break Fast meal is shared with family and friends. The customary preference is for a light dairy menu of juices, bagels, lox, herring and a wide variety of kugels and casseroles.

Sukkot and Simchat Torah

The harvest festival of Sukkot marks the conclusion of the reading of the Torah. It is celebrated five days after Yom Kippur, and it is also called the Feast of Booths. This refers to the temporary shelter, the Sukkah, which families customarily build for the holiday and decorate with seasonal produce.

Within the Sukkah, friends are invited to shared holiday meals, and a great family adventure can be enjoyed by sleeping in its shelter under the covering of palm fronds.

Immediately after Sukkot, the joyous celebration of Simchat Torah begins, marking the beginning of the Torah reading, starting with Genesis.

Fruits and nuts are ingredients featured in recipes used during these holidays. Symbolism is also found in serving stuffed cabbage, which is thought to resemble a rolled Torah scroll.

Hanukkah

In Jewish homes in most of our country, families prepare to place a Hanukkah menorah before a frosty windowpane, while Californians may possibly be experiencing a heat wave. Climates may vary, but the same air of excitement fills homes from coast to coast and in every corner of the world. The eager anticipation of the eight days of Hanukkah leads to its joyous arrival.

The Hanukkiah, a candelabra, specifically used at Hanukkah, is the focal point of the celebration that marks the victory of the heroic Maccabees over the Syrian-Greeks. When the ancient Temple was restored, the tale is told that there was found oil enough to last for only one day. The miracle that the oil burned for eight days is commemorated by kindling Hanukkah lights. Starting with one, an additional candle is lit each night until all eight lights are aglow.

Hannukkah songs, the dreidel game and exchanging of gifts have become part of the fun of celebration. Because they are fried in oil, potato latkes, served with apple sauce and sour cream, and Israeli Sufganiot, a jelly donut, are symbolic, if not dietetic, delicious holiday specialties.

Purim

When the wonderful aroma of freshly baked Hamantaschen permeates the air around our synagogue, we know that Purim is on its way. Hamantaschen making has been a Sisterhood project from the earliest days of our congregation. In recent years, the distribution of Purim baskets has also become a synagogue tradition.

The story of Purim, as told in the Book of Esther, is also called the Feast of Lots. It commemorates the saving of the Jewish people of Persia by Esther and Mordecai. The name of Haman, the villain of the plot, is blotted out by the stamping of feet and the noise of groggers during the reading of the Megillah in the synagogue. This joyous holiday is filled with fun and celebration, costume parades and carnivals.

Hamantaschen, with various fillings, and kreplach, filled with meat, are among the special Purim treats.

Pesach
(Passover)

The Exodus from Egypt and the transition from slavery to a life of freedom for the Jewish people is celebrated joyously at Passover Seder tables throughout the world.

The preparation for this holiday is, without doubt, the most labor intensive of all. In fact, there are those who have come to believe that spring-cleaning is a Jewish ritual devised by their ancestors. Every trace of leaven, or chomatz, must be removed from the home before Passover begins. Detailed instructions for kashering kitchen utensils and equipment and for lists of permitted and forbidden foods are made available at most synagogues. Sephardic and Ashkenazic customs vary, so it is advised to check with ones own rabbi. Classes are often held, offering instructions and suggestions in conducting both traditional and creative seders.

The eight-day celebration begins with two seder nights. The table is festively set, with the seder plate as its centerpiece, containing all the symbols of Passover. Matzoh, or unleavened bread, used exclusively throughout the holiday, reminds us of the haste with which our ancestors left Egypt, taking with them this flat bread which did not have time to rise.

The unique culinary challenge in using only kosher for Passover ingredients has been met in an assortment of delicious "Kosher on the Coast" holiday recipes.

Shavuot

Shavuot is the first spring festival that occurs forty-nine days after Passover. Shavuot commemorates the giving of the Torah at Mount Sinai.

Customarily, dairy dishes are prepared for this holiday, such as cheese-filled kreplach, borscht with sour cream, cheese blintzes and cheesecake.

Table of Contents

EDITORS IN CHIEF

Zelda Donin-Green
Esther Abramowitz
Sylvia Laxineta

FOUNDING COMMITTEE

Ruth Shults, whose idea for a
new cookbook was the
impetus for the project
Esther Abramowitz
Beverly Adler
Sandy Bernstein
Louise Colin
Jackie Devries
Cheryl Diamond
Jessica Feldman

Miriam Fierstein
Jan Gordon
Zelda Donin-Green
Julie Jensen
Jeanie Knell
Sylvia Laxineta
Estelle Markowitz
Susan Mathieu
Paula Reuben
Evie Rockoff

Judy Sanders
Mona Schoenfeld
Caryl Schwartz
Lila Shames
Robin Shulman
Carey Sommers
Toby Trabin
Eve Wechsberg
Barbara Zutz

RECIPE TESTING COORDINATOR

Zelda Donin-Green

WINE CONSULTANT AND EDUCATOR

Jerry Snyder

FUNDRAISING

Sharona Byrnes
Esther Abramowitz
Zelda Donin-Green
Sylvia Laxineta

TREASURER

Sylvia Laxineta

MARKETING AND PUBLIC RELATIONS

Sharona Byrnes

IN-HOUSE PUBLICITY

Esther Abramowitz
Sharona Byrnes

COVER AND PAGE DESIGN

A special Thank You goes to the Design Group and their teacher and coordinator, Amy Vansgaard, of the Otis College of Art and Design, in Los Angeles, for giving us the opportunity to work with the talented senior students on this project week after week, and for the good fortune to discover a most gifted artist and designer, Margaret Berg, whose work graces our cover.

With pleasure we thank both Cantor Sam Radwine and Christina Rosales of the Pasadena Culinary School for contributing recipes and holding a cooking demonstration for our sponsors, and to Robin and Steve Rome for opening their home for this event.

PROOF READERS

Esther Abramowitz	Barbara Gilson	Karen Marcus
Leslie Back	Zelda Donin-Green	Gerri Oshry
Sondra Bader	Jerry Green	Barbara Perless
Rose Berman	Marian Greif	Paula Reuben
Inga Cherman	Sylvia Laxineta	Celia Rothman
Judy Geminder	Roz Lefkowitz	

RECIPE SELECTION COMMITTEE

Esther Abramowitz
Zelda Donin-Green
Sylvia Laxineta
Evie Rockoff

RECIPE TESTING FACILITATORS

Appetizers: Zelda Donin-Green

Soups: Louise Colin

Salads: Susan Mathieu and Cheryl Diamond

Brunch and Breads: Julie Jensen

Pastas and Kugels: Jeanie Knell

Dairy: Lila Shames

Fish: Jessica Feldman

Poultry: Mona Schoenfeld

Meat: Ruth Shults

Vegetables: Miriam Fierstein

Vegetarian Main Dishes: Debra Schneiderman

Cakes: Esther Abramowitz

Pastry: Zelda Donin-Green

Cookies: Jackie Devries and Sandy Bernstein

Desserts, Fruit and Frozen: Shirley Yesnick

Traditional and Holiday: Eve Wechsberg

Outdoor Cooking – B.B.Q.: Barbara Zutz

Sauces: Zelda Donin-Green

Quick and Easy: Esther Abramowitz

JUDAIC WRITERS

Eve Wechsberg
Judy Sanders

WRITER

Judy Sanders

Note: Several categories were combined with each other for the final listings.

To all the cooks who contributed their favorite recipes to be a part of our Congregation cookbook legacy, we thank you wholeheartedly. We very much regret that we were unable to include every recipe submitted to us due to either similarities or the availability of space. We hope you will understand our need to develop a well-balanced selection in each category and if we have inadvertently omitted any contributors, please forgive us.

RECIPE CONTRIBUTORS

Esther Abramowitz	Jerry Green	Sherri Quillen
Bunny Alper	Rick Green	Cantor Sam Radwine
Leslie Back	David Green	Marilyn Rafkin
Sondra Bader	Marian Greif	Edna Rappaport
Amy Ball	Cheryl Gross	The Rees Family
Lillian Becker	Ruthann Grossman	Paula Reuben
Alice Berk	Sandy Gurewitz	Gail Robillard
Marcia Berk-Nimmer	Eileen Hecht	Evie Rockoff
Carol Berkowitz	Martha Hepner	Sally Rockoff
Doris Berkowitz	Adrienne Herman	Shelly Rockoff
Joan Bernick	Shana Abramowitz-Hoolihan	Christina Rosales
Ruth Blinder	Julie Jensen	Celia Rothman
Ida Bobrow	Joan Kagan	Bob Rothman
Myrna Chatow	Gila Katz	Naomi Savell
Inga Cherman	Ronnie Katz Gerber	Mona Schoenfeld
Laurie Cherman Gerstmann	Ruth Kisner	Lila Shames
Sheri Cohen	Miriam Knable	Robin Shulman
Rima Cohn	Jeanie Knell	Ruth Shults
Louise Colin	Marily Kritzer	Alan Siegel
Shirley Colodny	Alysse Laemmlie	Clara Simon
Myra Diamond	Estelle Langholz	Elsie Sirull
David Donin	Marcia Larson	Sherry Smith
Marcia Donin	Sylvia Laxineta	Shelley Snyder
Meredith Donin	Judy Levin	Renee Sokolski
Laura Dubrow	Eleanor Lindenbaum	Phyllis Spierer
Laurie Ladenheim-Dunbar	Henry Lurie	Lynn Srebnik
Judith Feldman	Sandy Lurie	Matsume Steadly
Miriam Fierstein	Judy Maizlish	Mercedes Stein
Dottie Fisch	Dora Majerovic	Sally Stember
Robin Franko	Eunice Marder	N. Sundberg
Judy Geminder	Doris Melnick	Ellen Tarlow
Laurie Cherman-Gerstmann	Shira Most	Toby Trabin
Pam Gershkoff	Sara Moulton	Fran Warner
Barbara Gilbert	Shulie Neumark	Eve Wechsberg
Barbara Gilson	Marcia Berk-Nimmer	Edna Wodnicki
Beth Goldfarb	Ellen Orenstein	Barbara Wurmbrand
Lilian Goldfarb	Gerri Oshry	Thelma Yellen
Pearl Gottlieb	Sheila Poncher	Barbara Zutz
Zelda Donin-Green		

RECIPE TESTERS

Esther Abramowitz
Miriam Ackermann
Barbara Adler
Beverly Adler
Karen Allman
Sondra Bader
Alice Berk
Doris Berkowitz
Rose Bernan
Mindy Bernstein
Sandy Bernstein
Ruth Blinder
Sharon Blumberg
Helene Buchman
Cindy Buckner
Monique Caine
Lola Chevlin
Grace Colin
Louise Colin
Marci Colin
Judith Daar
Jackie Devries
Jennifer Devries
Myra Diamond
Marcia Donin
Meredith Donin
Ray Lynn Duffy
Lonnie Dyner
Jessica Feldman
Miriam Fierstein
Marilyn Finklestein
Dottie Fisch
Jan Fisher
Dalia Frank
Robin Franko
Muriel Freed
Judy Freedman
Franky Friedman
Norma Furman
Ina Gartenberg
Judy Geminder

Cheryl Ginsberg
Beth Goldfarb
Jerry Green
Kelly Green
Rick Green
Zelda Donin-Green
Marian Greif
Ruthann Grossman
Martha Hepner
Shanna Abramowitz-Hoolihan
Julie Jensen
L. Johnson
Roberta Johnson
T.R. Johnson
Elaine Kagan
Joan Kagan
Marta Kanes
Claire Kaufman
Myma Kayton
T.S. Kessler
Jeanie Knell
Gigi Kramer
Lillian Kratz
Joan Kraus
Marilyn Kritzer
Sylvia Laxineta
Dottie Leach
Roz Lefkowitz
Judy Levin
Sharon Levine
Ellie Lindenbaum
Marilyn Linder
Sally Lux
Susan Mathieu
Ellyn Mogford
Susy Morrell
Mary Mortellaro
Shulie Neumark
Ellen Orenstein
Gerri Oshry

Rita Oster
Connie Passamanick
Carol Piocky
Donna Pollock
Toni Quinton
Rozi Raby
Carter Sam Radwine
Debra Resnick
Paula Reuben
Gail Robillard
Evie Rockoff
Ronnie Rotenberg
Cecily Ruben
Carol Rubin
Florence Sacks
Judy Sanders
Naomi Savell
Fritzi Schneider
Debra Schneiderman
Mona Schoenfeld
Dorothy Seidler
Elsie Sirull
Pam Shames
Robin Shulman
Ruth Shults
Clara Simon
Joyce Smith
Judy Stahl
Ricki Stajer
Natsume Steadly
Mary Sternson
Fay Strumff
Sheila Titlebaum
Toby Trabin
Carol Tufeld
Glenda Urmacher
L. Weber
Shirley Yesnick
Judy Yourman
Barbara Zutz

DIAMOND SPONSOR

Sisterhood of Congregation Ner Tamid
In honor of our 42nd anniversary

PLATINUM SPONSORS

In memory of *Judy Feldman*
Oh, how she loved to cook!

Esther and Sandy Abramowitz
In loving memory of our parents
Elizabeth & Salik Abramowitz and
Anne & Sam Pomarantz

Zelda and Jerry Green
In loving memory of our parents
Anna & John Green and
May & Max Donin

Sylvia and Bob Laxineta
In loving memory of our parents
Katie & Dave Laxineta
Anna & Barney Wolpert

Laura Dubrow
In honor of my girls, with love
Sandy Silver, Susan Dubrow and
Zoe Dubrow

Claire and Victor Kaufman
In honor of our children and
grandchildren

Leatrice Osofsky
In honor of my most accomplished
daughter-in-law, Joanne A. Osofsky

Groise Mispoche Havurah
In honor of our 30th anniversary

GOLD SPONSORS

Alice Berk
In memory of Howard Berk
Beloved husband, father, and
Grandfather

Evie and Bob Rockoff
In loving memory of Anna Miller and
Esther Rockoff

Judy and Dave Sanders
In loving memory of our parents
Paul & Selma Sanders and
Joseph & Ida Kahn

Ellen Tarlow
In loving memory of Gerald Tarlow

Eve Wechsberg
In loving memory of
Rabbi Bernard Wechsberg

Sharona Byrnes
In honor of my parents
Eunice & Barney Krinsky

Robin and Avi Franko
In honor of our children
Orrin, Elana, & Sharona

Myra Diamond
In honor of my daughters
Lynne, Susan, Cathy, Nancy,
Carol, and my daughter-in-law
Cheryl, each one in her own way
a great cook

Evalee Weiss
In honor of my brother Herb Gomberg

SILVER SPONSORS

Sondra Bader
Ilene Eisenberg
Marilyn and Jerry Finklestein
Lillian and Fred Kratz
Eunice and Barney Krinsky

Betty and Burt Rein
Bob and Celia Rothman
Marilyn and Frank Schaffer
Toby and Ed Trabin

ADDITIONAL THANKS

Abarbanel Wine Company
www.4kosherwine.com

Greg and Carolyn Thompson

Equivalents

1 cup	=	8 fluid ounces
3 teaspoons	=	1 tablespoon
2 tablespoons	=	1 fluid ounce
4 tablespoons	=	¼ cup
5⅓ tablespoons	=	⅓ cup
1 stick butter or margarine	=	½ cup
¼ cup egg substitute	=	1 egg
1 cup heavy cream	=	2 cups whipped
¼ pound Cheddar cheese	=	1 cup grated
1 cup cottage cheese	=	8 ounces
1 teaspoon dried, crumbled herbs	=	1 tablespoon fresh
⅛ teaspoon garlic powder	=	1 small clove
2¼ cups packed brown sugar	=	1 pound
3½ cups powdered sugar	=	1 pound
14 graham cracker squares	=	1 cup crumbs
6 ounces chocolate chips	=	1 cup
1 cup raw rice	=	3 cups cooked
1 large onion	=	1 cup chopped
1 medium lemon	=	2 to 3 tablespoons juice
1 medium lemon	=	1 tablespoon zest
1 medium orange	=	6 to 8 tablespoons juice
1 medium orange	=	2 tablespoons zest

To make some foods Pareve, or neutral, here are some substitutions:

Use non-dairy liquid creamer as a substitute for milk or cream.

Pareve margarine can substitute for butter.

Non-dairy whipped topping is a good substitute for whipped cream.

Vegetable broth can substitute for chicken broth.

For Passover

1 cup flour	=	½ cup matzo cake meal or ¾ cup potato starch
½ cup flour	=	2 tablespoons matzo cake meal or 6 tablespoons potato starch
1 cup powdered sugar	=	1 cup sugar minus 2 tablespoons, pulverized in a blender and sifted with 1½ teaspoons potato starch

Hors d'Ouevres

Hors d'Ouevres

Hot Artichoke Dip

1   can (7 ounces) chopped chiles
1   can (16 ounces) artichoke hearts in water, drained and chopped
1   cup mayonnaise
1   cup freshly grated Parmesan cheese

Combine all ingredients in a microwave-safe dish and mix well. Microwave on high 3 to 6 minutes or until bubbly. Serve with corn chips.

Serves 8.

Artichoke and Red Pepper Torta

Since California is the artichoke capitol of the world, it is no wonder that we who live here enjoy preparing recipes containing this wonderful edible flower head from a thistle plant with its amazingly unique flavor. In this simple-to-prepare spread, we alternate layers of cream cheese, ranch dressing with marinated artichoke hearts, scallions, parsley and red bell pepper. The mixture can be molded in a bowl, turned out and served with crackers.

2   packages (8 ounces each) cream cheese, softened (regular or light)
1   package (1 ounce) dry ranch salad dressing mix
1   jar (6 ounces) marinated artichoke hearts, drained and chopped
½   cup finely chopped fresh parsley
3   scallions with tops, chopped
1   medium-size red bell pepper, chopped, reserve a 1½-inch square for garnish
    Red leaf lettuce for garnish

In a mixing bowl with an electric mixer, blend cream cheese and dressing mix. In a medium bowl, stir together artichoke hearts, parsley, scallions and bell pepper.

Line a 3-cup bowl or mold with plastic wrap. Beginning and ending with cream cheese mixture, alternate layers of cream cheese and vegetables. If the cream cheese is difficult to spread, wet your hands to smooth. Refrigerate at least 4 hours or overnight.

To serve, line a serving plate with lettuce leaves. Invert torta onto leaves. Using a canapé cutter or knife, cut reserved pepper square into a small design or triangle and place on top. Serve with crackers.

Serves 10 to 12.

To create a "crudité basket", crumple sheets of cellophane paper to make a base in the basket, then cover with kale leaves. Cluster groups of vegetables together. Tuck a bunch of radishes with the leaves intact into one corner. Can be assembled in 5 minutes.

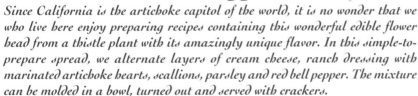

BARBECUED PECANS

2 tablespoons butter or margarine

¼ cup Worcestershire sauce

1 tablespoon ketchup

2 dashes hot pepper sauce

4 cups pecan halves or walnuts

Salt to taste (optional)

Preheat oven to 400 degrees.

Melt butter in a large saucepan. Add Worcestershire sauce, ketchup, and hot pepper sauce. Stir in nuts. Spread evenly in a greased glass baking dish.

Bake about 20 minutes, stirring frequently. Cool on absorbent towels. Sprinkle with salt. Store in an airtight container.

Baba Ghanoush (Eggplant with Tahini) Ⓟ

When Israelis abroad want to surprise their guests with a typical Israeli dish, they often serve them tahini and eggplant salad.

1	large eggplant	2	tablespoons lemon juice
1	medium onion, grated on largest holes and squeezed dry	2	cloves garlic, crushed
		2	tablespoons water, or as needed
½	bunch parsley, chopped	1½	teaspoons salt
½	cup tahini (sesame seed paste)		Dash of cayenne pepper

Place whole, unpeeled eggplant directly on a gas burner with flame set at medium. Turn eggplant as the skin chars and the inside becomes soft; or bake at 450 degrees for 30 minutes or until charred and tender. When done, cool slightly, cut in half lengthwise and scoop out the eggplant pulp with a wooden spoon, discarding the outer skin. Chop eggplant fine and place in a ceramic or wooden bowl. Add onion and parsley and mix well.

Blend tahini, lemon juice and garlic. Stir in water. Add to eggplant mixture and season with salt and cayenne. More lemon juice can be added for extra flavor. Garnish with parsley. Eat with pita bread or chips.

Makes 2 to 2½ cups.

Stuffed Mushrooms Ⓓ

Easy and a big hit with everyone-makes a lot!

2	ounces Monterey Jack cheese	¼	teaspoon black pepper
¼	teaspoon dried oregano	¼	cup bread crumbs
¼	teaspoon dried thyme	15-20	medium to large mushrooms, stems removed and reserved
¼	teaspoon garlic powder		Melted butter for drizzling
¼	teaspoon parsley		
¼	teaspoon salt		

Preheat oven to 350 degrees.

Combine cheese, spices, bread crumbs and mushroom stems in a blender or food processor fitted with a metal blade. Blend well. Spoon mixture into mushroom caps. Drizzle butter over filling and place mushrooms on a greased baking sheet. Bake 15 minutes.

Serves 8 to 10.

Barbecued Chicken Wings or Drumettes Ⓜ

5	pounds chicken wings	½	teaspoon dry mustard
1	cup brown sugar, firmly packed	¾	cup soy sauce
¾	cup Marsala or sherry wine	2	cloves garlic, minced

Preheat oven to 350 degrees.

Cut off and discard wing tips. Cut wings into 2 pieces at the joint. Place chicken on a baking sheet in a single layer. Bake 30 minutes.

Meanwhile, combine sugar, wine, mustard, soy sauce and garlic in a saucepan. Bring to a simmer. Pour mixture over chicken and bake, turning occasionally, for 30 minutes or until sauce has been absorbed and wings are deeply glazed.

Makes 50 to 60 pieces.

Belgian Endive Leaves with Hummus and Sun-Dried Tomatoes Ⓟ

2	large cloves garlic, minced	⅓	cup water
1	can (15½ ounces) garbanzo beans, rinsed with cold water and drained	½	teaspoon salt
			Dried red pepper flakes
1	sun-dried tomato, soaked in water if dehydrated	28	large Belgian endive leaves (from 3 large heads)
¼	cup lemon juice		Snipped fresh chives or minced parsley (optional)
¼	cup tahini paste		

Combine garlic and garbanzo beans in a blender or food processor and process until beans are puréed as smooth as possible. Add drained tomato, lemon juice, tahini paste, water, salt and pepper flakes. Purée 2 to 4 minutes or until very smooth. Adjust seasonings to taste. At this point, hummus mixture can be covered and refrigerated overnight.

Mix well before using. Fill each endive leaf with about 1 tablespoon hummus. Garnish with chives. Chill a few hours before serving.

Serves 28.

Hummus can be purchased already made, then add sun-dried tomato and red pepper flakes.

Freeze a peeled or unpeeled "hand" of ginger. While still frozen, grate or cut into small cubes and crush in a garlic press for spicy ginger juice. Freezing releases juices and makes the ginger easier to crush.

Brie with Sun-Dried Tomato Topping D

"Reminds us of foods eaten in Europe."

2 pounds Brie cheese, well chilled	2½ tablespoons oil from sun-dried tomatoes
5 tablespoons minced fresh parsley	12 cloves garlic, mashed
5 tablespoons freshly grated Parmesan cheese	2 tablespoons minced fresh basil
10 sun-dried tomatoes packed in oil, minced	3 tablespoons toasted and coarsely chopped pine nuts

Remove rind from top of chilled Brie and place Brie on a serving platter. Combine parsley, Parmesan, tomatoes, oil, garlic, basil and pine nuts. Spread mixture over top of Brie.

Refrigerate if prepared early in the day. Remove from refrigerator 30 to 60 minutes prior to serving for optimum flavor.

Serve with crackers. Offer small plates, as topping is a little messy.

Serves 16.

SAVORY FIGS

Cut a fig halfway and fill with a bit of blue cheese or smooth goat cheese which has been sprinkled lightly with cracked pepper and olive oil.

Cheese Boreka with Phyllo D

A delightfully rich and creamy appetizer to pop into your mouth.

1 pound phyllo dough	Chopped fresh parsley to taste
1 cup melted butter	
1½ pounds Monterey Jack cheese, shredded	1 egg, lightly beaten
	2 eggs, beaten
	1 cup milk

Preheat oven to 350 degrees.

Cut dough with a scissors to fit a well-greased 10 x 15-inch baking pan. Leftover strips can be placed inside at random. Using half the dough, brush melted butter on each sheet and layer in pan.

Combine cheese, parsley and 1 lightly beaten egg. Spoon evenly over dough. Cover with remaining dough, brushing each sheet with melted butter. Seal edges with butter, brushing all around the pan. Slice in small (about 1½-inch) squares.

Mix 2 eggs with milk and pour over top of dough. Bake 30 minutes or until golden. Cool before serving, or wrap tightly and freeze until ready to serve.

Makes about 100 squares.

Blini Cups with Caviar

Lovely and elegant for that special party. They have the look and taste of mildly tart pancakes.

Blini Cups

2	cups (1 pint) small-curd cottage cheese	3	tablespoons butter or margarine, melted
1	tablespoon sour cream	3	eggs
1	teaspoon vanilla	½	cup buttermilk biscuit mix
½	teaspoon sugar		

Toppings

1	cup (½ pint) sour cream	½	cup finely chopped onion (optional)
4-6	ounces red or black caviar		

Preheat oven to 350 degrees.

To make blini cups, mix cottage cheese, sour cream, vanilla, sugar and melted butter in a food processor fitted with a metal blade or with an electric mixer. Add eggs, one at a time. Mix in biscuit mix and beat until blended.

Spoon batter into greased nonstick 1½-inch miniature muffin cups, filling three-fourths full. Bake 35 to 40 minutes or until tops are golden brown. Remove from oven, loosen edges with a small knife and remove to a rack to cool.

Store in an airtight container at room temperature for up to 2 days, or freeze, but do not thaw before reheating.

When ready to serve, place blini cups on a baking sheet. Bake 10 to 15 minutes or until hot and crisp.

Place sour cream, caviar and chopped onion in small bowls. Serve blini cups with toppings on the side.

Makes 36 blini cups.

There is one rule a cook must always follow and that is, you should taste the food whenever possible before serving it to your family or guests. For an inexperienced cook, it may take a while to develop such a taste.

*During the summer,
if you have overripe
strawberries, just purée
them and add to
lemonade.*

Pesto Cheesecake

1	tablespoon unsalted butter, softened	½	cup freshly grated Parmesan cheese
¼	cup fine dry bread crumbs	¼	teaspoon salt
2	tablespoons freshly grated Parmesan cheese	⅛	teaspoon cayenne pepper
2	packages (8 ounces each) cream cheese, softened (can use low fat)	3	eggs
		½	cup homemade or store-bought pesto sauce
1	cup ricotta cheese	¼	cup pine nuts, toasted Basil sprigs for garnish

Preheat oven to 325 degrees.

Spread butter over bottom and up sides of a 9-inch springform pan. Mix bread crumbs with 2 tablespoons Parmesan cheese. Coat pan with mixture.

Using an electric mixer, beat together cream cheese, ricotta cheese, ½ cup Parmesan cheese, salt and pepper until light. Add eggs, one at a time, beating well after each addition. Transfer half of mixture to a medium bowl. Mix pesto with remaining half. Spoon pesto mixture into prepared pan, smoothing top. Carefully spoon plain mixture over pesto layer and gently smooth top. Sprinkle with toasted pine nuts.

Bake 50 to 60 minutes or until center no longer moves when pan is shaken. Cool completely. Cover tightly with plastic wrap and refrigerate overnight.

Run a small knife around sides of pan to loosen, if necessary. Release pan sides and transfer cheesecake to a platter. Garnish with basil. Surround with crackers or baguette rounds.

Serves 30 to 40.

Goat Cheese with Roasted Garlic and Sun-Dried Tomatoes Ⓓ

4   large whole heads garlic
2½ tablespoons margarine, thinly sliced
1   tablespoon olive oil
2½ cups vegetable broth
1   teaspoon dried basil
1   teaspoon dried oregano
1   teaspoon dried parsley

¼   teaspoon black pepper, or to taste
1   cup oil-packed sun-dried tomatoes, drained
5½ ounces goat cheese, sliced
½   cup fresh basil leaves for garnish
1   French baguette, sliced, or sliced cocktail bread

Preheat oven to 375 degrees.

Slice ¼-inch off tops of garlic heads and remove as much outer skin as possible. Place garlic head, cut-side up, in an 8-inch square baking dish. Arrange margarine slices evenly over garlic. Drizzle oil over margarine. Add 2 cups broth to dish and sprinkle with basil, oregano, parsley and pepper.

Bake 75 minutes or until garlic is tender. Baste with broth every 15 minutes, adding more broth if needed. Transfer garlic to an ovenproof serving dish. Baste with ¼ cup of remaining broth from baking dish.

Reduce oven to 325 degrees. Arrange tomatoes and cheese around garlic. Bake 10 minutes or until cheese melts. Garnish with basil. Serve with bread slices.

Use small cocktail forks to remove garlic from skin and small spoons for the sauce.

Roll a log of goat cheese in fresh herbs of your choice to give the cheese a "kick".

Chinese Chicken in Lettuce Leaves

This is a favorite of so many of us Southern Californians. Serve it as a starter for any Chinese-inspired dinner you have planned.

3	tablespoons oil, preferably peanut	1½	tablespoons soy sauce
1⅓	cups finely chopped chicken breast	3	tablespoons water
1	cup finely chopped green or red bell pepper	1	tablespoon fresh lemon juice
½	tablespoon sugar	1	large scallion, sliced
1-2	teaspoons salt, or to taste	½	cup chopped walnuts or peanuts
	Freshly ground black pepper to taste	8-12	iceberg lettuce leaves, washed, dried and chilled
2½	tablespoons minced fresh ginger		Dipping Sauce (recipe below)

Heat oil in a skillet or wok over medium-high heat. Add chicken, bell pepper, sugar, salt and black pepper. Cook, stirring constantly, for 3 to 5 minutes or until bell pepper turns a deeper color and chicken is cooked. Add ginger, soy sauce, water and lemon juice and stir well. Cook 1 minute longer. Remove from heat and sprinkle with scallion and nuts. Set aside and keep warm.

To serve, place 2 to 3 tablespoons of chicken mixture on each lettuce leaf. Roll up and place in a serving dish. Serve with Dipping Sauce on the side. Recipe can easily be doubled.

Dipping Sauce

½	cup rice wine vinegar	Dash of hot pepper sauce or chili oil
1½	tablespoons soy sauce	
1	teaspoon sesame oil	

To make dipping sauce, mix all ingredients in a small bowl until well blended.

Serves 4.

Corn and Scallion Pancakes Ⓓ

This pancake batter incorporates puréed corn as well as whole corn kernels for a wonderful layering of flavors and textures. Topped with guacamole, these tender cakes may be served as a special hors d'oeuvre or a light lunch, Southwest style.

1½	cups fresh or frozen corn kernels, blanched	½	jalapeño pepper, seeded and minced (optional)
2	tablespoons unsalted butter	1	tablespoon minced fresh basil
3	scallions, chopped	¾	cup flour
3	tablespoons dry white wine (optional)	¼	cup yellow cornmeal
½	cup half-and-half	½	teaspoon baking powder
3	eggs	½	teaspoon salt
1	tablespoon honey	½	teaspoon black pepper
			Guacamole (see page 94)

Purée 1 cup corn kernels in a food processor. Set puréed corn and remaining ½ cup whole corn aside.

Heat butter in a skillet over high heat. Add scallions and sauté 2 to 3 minutes or until tender. Add wine and continue to cook 3 minutes or until most of wine has cooked away. Transfer scallions to a medium bowl and allow to cool slightly. Add half-and-half, eggs, honey, jalapeño, basil and puréed and whole corn to scallions. Mix well.

In a separate bowl, combine flour, cornmeal, baking powder, salt and pepper and stir to blend. Add corn mixture to dry ingredients and stir until relatively smooth; do not overmix.

Heat a griddle or cast iron skillet over medium-high heat. Grease lightly. For each pancake, ladle about ¼ cup batter onto the griddle. Cook pancake on first side until the edges begin to look set. Flip pancake and cook on second side for 2 minutes or until golden brown. Serve immediately.

Top with Guacamole.

Serves 8 to 10.

To brew clear iced tea, fill a pitcher or jar with cold water, add tea leaves or bags and cover. Refrigerate 24 hours, or let stand in sun for 4 hours. Then remove tea bags or leaves, strain if needed through a coffee filter and serve over ice.

Eggplant Salad

A Mediterranean favorite.

½-¾	cup olive oil	1	can (8 ounces) tomato purée
1	large eggplant, unpeeled and cut into small cubes	½	cup chopped ripe olives
1	cup chopped onion	⅓	cup red wine vinegar
1	cup chopped celery	2	tablespoons sugar
1	cup chopped green bell pepper	1½	teaspoons salt

In a large skillet, heat ½ cup oil over medium-high heat. Add eggplant and sauté 10 minutes or until nicely browned. Add onion, celery and bell pepper. Cook and stir until vegetables are crisp-tender, adding more oil if needed. Stir in tomato purée, olives, vinegar, sugar and salt. Simmer, uncovered, for 10 minutes, stirring occasionally.

Remove from heat. Cool and refrigerate several hours or overnight. May be refrigerated up to 1 week, or frozen. Serve with pita bread that has been cut into eighths.

Makes 4 cups.

WANT A DELICIOUS HORS D'OEUVRE USING POTATO SKINS?

Store leftover potato skins in the freezer. To use, cut frozen peels into 1½-inch squares and arrange on a microwave platter. Sprinkle with Parmesan cheese, shredded Gruyère cheese and herbes de Provence. Microwave 15 to 30 seconds or until cheese melts.

Better Than Gravlax

Unbelievably delicious and with so little effort.

2	tablespoons sugar	1	tablespoon liquid smoke
2	tablespoons plus 2 teaspoons salt	2½	pounds salmon fillet, cut into 2 equal pieces

Combine sugar, salt and liquid smoke. Rub over all sides of the salmon. Place salmon in double Zip-Lock bags. Refrigerate in a flat glass baking pan, weighting the salmon down with unopened cans or jars of food. Turn salmon twice daily for 5 days.

Remove salmon from bags and rinse off salt. Dry with paper towels. Use 1 piece and freeze the other for future use.

For easier slicing, freeze salmon for 2 hours and be sure to use a very sharp knife in order to cut thin slices. Serve with sliced cocktail pumpernickel.

Kasha and Mushroom Knishes in Puff Pastry Ⓓ

This classic knish has a modern twist – puff pastry!

1	cup diced onion		Salt and pepper to taste
1	tablespoon safflower oil	1	package (10 ounces) frozen puff pastry, thawed
3	cups coarsely chopped mushrooms	2	tablespoons liquid egg substitute
½	cup liquid egg substitute	1	teaspoon water
1	cup kasha	1	tablespoon poppy seeds
2	cups vegetable broth		

Preheat oven to 350 degrees.

Sauté onion in oil in a large skillet until lightly browned. Add mushrooms and cook until mushrooms are lightly browned; set aside.

Place ½ cup egg substitute in a bowl. Add kasha and toss. Return skillet to heat. Add kasha to skillet and cook over high heat, stirring with a fork to separate kasha. Remove from heat. Bring broth to a boil. Slowly pour broth over kasha in skillet and cover tightly, cooking over low heat for 10 minutes or until all liquid is absorbed. Remove from heat. Stir in vegetable mixture and season with salt and pepper. Cool to room temperature.

Roll a pastry sheet into a 14 x 11-inch rectangle on a lightly floured board. Cut into 3-inch circles. Place 2 teaspoons filling into the center of each circle. Pull edges up around filling, completely enclosing it. Pinch dough together to form a tight package. Turn packages over and place, seam-side down, on a greased baking sheet.

Beat 2 tablespoons egg substitute with 1 teaspoon water to make an egg wash. Brush egg wash over each knish. Sprinkle with poppy seeds. Repeat with remaining sheet of dough. Bake 30 minutes or until golden brown. Serve warm or at room temperature.

Makes about 30.

Knishes and Several Fillings

Knishes are a favorite of Ashkenazi Jews. This modern version is smaller than the old, familiar knish. In Israel, one can find knishes sold by street vendors.

Dough

2½	cups sifted flour	2	eggs
1	teaspoon baking powder	⅔	cup salad oil
½	teaspoon salt	2	tablespoons water

Preheat oven to 375 degrees.

Sift flour, baking powder and salt into a bowl. Make a well in the center. Add eggs, oil and water to center. Work moist ingredients into flour mixture with hand and knead until smooth.

There are 2 ways to fill the knishes. In either case, divide dough in 2 and roll as thin as possible. Brush with oil. Spread filling on one side of dough and roll up like a jelly roll. Cut into 1½-inch slices. Place on a greased baking sheet, cut-side down, pressing down lightly to flatten. Or cut rolled dough into 3-inch circles. Place a tablespoon of filling on each. Draw the edges together and pinch firmly. Place on a greased baking sheet, pinched-edges up. In either case, bake 35 minutes or until browned.

Serves 24.

Potato Filling

1	cup chopped onions	1	egg
6	tablespoons margarine or butter	1	teaspoon salt
		¼	teaspoon black pepper
2	cups mashed potatoes		

Brown onions in margarine. Beat in potatoes, egg, salt and pepper until fluffy.

Cheese Filling

1½	cups diced scallions (preferred) or onions	1	egg
		½	teaspoon salt
4	tablespoons butter	⅛	teaspoon black pepper
2	cups farmer or hoop cheese	2	tablespoons sour cream

Brown scallions in butter. Beat in cheese, egg, salt, pepper and sour cream until smooth.

Meat Filling Ⓜ

½	cup minced onions	½	cup cooked rice
2	tablespoons cooking oil	1	egg
1½	cups ground cooked meat (leftovers are fine)	1	teaspoon salt
		¼	teaspoon black pepper

Lightly brown onions in oil. Add meat, rice, egg, salt and pepper and mix well.

Chicken Filling Ⓜ

1½ cups ground cooked chicken
¾   cup mashed potatoes
1   egg

1   teaspoon salt
¼   teaspoon black pepper

Mix all ingredients well.

Mushroom, Broccoli and Cheddar Bundles (Mini-Knishes) Ⓓ

Using frozen puff pastry makes this less time consuming. We can all use shortcuts.

1   package (10 ounces) frozen puff pastry (2 sheets)
1   egg
1   tablespoon water
1   tablespoon vegetable oil
1   package (10 ounces) frozen chopped broccoli, thawed and drained

2   cups sliced fresh mushrooms
1   small onion, chopped
2   cloves garlic, minced
1   cup shredded sharp Cheddar cheese
    Salt and pepper to taste

Preheat oven to 400 degrees.

Thaw pastry sheets at room temperature for 30 minutes. Beat together egg and water.

Add oil to a heated skillet. Add broccoli, mushrooms, onion and garlic and cook until mushrooms are tender and liquid evaporates. Remove from heat. Stir in cheese and season with salt and pepper.

Unfold pastry on a lightly floured surface. Roll each sheet into a 12-inch square and cut each into 16 (3-inch) squares. Place 2 teaspoons of vegetable mixture in center of each square. Brush edges of squares with egg mixture. Fold corners to center over vegetable mixture. Press edges together to seal and twist.

Place bundles 2 inches apart on a baking sheet. Brush with egg mixture. Bake 15 minutes or until golden brown.

Serves 32.

Chopped Liver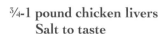

¾-1 pound chicken livers
    Salt to taste
3   tablespoons vegetable oil or
    chicken fat
2   medium onions, chopped

1-2 hard-cooked eggs, coarsely
    grated or chopped
    Freshly ground black
    pepper to taste
    Lettuce leaves and tomato
    slices for serving

Preheat broiler with rack placed about 3 inches from heat source. Rinse livers and pat dry on paper towels, cut off any green spots. Place livers on foil on broiler pan and sprinkle with salt. Broil 3 minutes or until light brown on top. Turn livers and sprinkle salt on top. Broil 3 to 4 minutes or until cooked through and color is no longer pink (cut to check). Discard juices from foil. Cool livers slightly.

Heat oil in a large heavy skillet over medium-low heat. Add onions and sauté, stirring occasionally, for 15 minutes or until tender and starting to turn golden.

Chop cooked livers in a food processor. Add onions and pulse on and off until blended. Transfer to a bowl and lightly mix in eggs. Season well with salt and pepper. Mixture can be refrigerated, covered, for up to 2 days. Serve cold, in scoops, placed on lettuce leaves and garnished with tomato slices.

Serves 4 to 6.

Faux Chopped "Liver"

3   onions, chopped
4   tablespoons margarine or
    cooking oil

1   (16-ounce) can peas or
    green beans, drained
3   hard-boiled eggs
1   cup chopped walnuts

Sauté onions in margarine or oil for 15 minutes. Combine onions with peas or green beans, eggs and walnuts in a food processor fitted with a metal blade. Process until smooth. Serve on thinly sliced bread or crackers.

Serves 12 to 15.

Cucumber and Smoked Salmon Rolls Topped with Caviar or Toasted Sesame Seeds Ⓟ

These can be made using other types of smoked fish. The very thin slices of cucumber makes this appetizer crunchy and beautiful. You can taste the Asian flavors.

1	English cucumber, peeled	1	ounce, or as desired, black
10	narrow slices smoked		or red caviar for garnish,
	salmon		or toasted sesame seeds
2	tablespoons wasabi powder		Scallions, thinly sliced
2	tablespoons water		lengthwise, about 1 inch
1	small jar pickled ginger,		long for garnish
	sliced		

Slice cucumber lengthwise with a cheese or vegetable slicer (a mandolin will make these perfect), about ⅛-inch thick. Cut cucumber and salmon slices into 4- to 5-inch lengths. Mix wasabi powder with water in a small bowl to make a paste. Spread a very thin layer of wasabi paste on each cucumber slice. Top with a salmon slice. Place a few slices of pickled ginger at one end of the cucumber. Roll up, pressing firmly. Use toothpicks to secure the rolls. Serve on a platter with spirals facing upward. Sprinkle with caviar or sesame seeds and garnish with scallions.

Makes about 20 rolls.

Spinach Balls Ⓓ

2	packages (10 ounces each) frozen chopped spinach, thawed and well drained	½	cup freshly grated Parmesan cheese
2	cups seasoned bread crumbs	½	cup margarine, melted
1	large onion, chopped	4	eggs, beaten
		¼	teaspoon black pepper

Preheat oven to 350 degrees.

Steam or microwave spinach; drain well. Mix spinach with bread crumbs, onion, cheese, margarine, eggs and pepper. Refrigerate about 1 hour or until able to handle. Form mixture into balls, about 1¼ inches in diameter. Place on a baking sheet and freeze. When frozen, balls can be stored in a plastic bag in freezer until ready to serve.

To serve, bake 20 to 30 minutes on a greased baking sheet.

Makes about 100 to 110 balls.

Low fat margarine and egg whites can be substituted to reduce fat and cholesterol.

For a novel presentation on a buffet table or when passing around hors d'oeuvres, use a 12-inch colored ceramic tile, place the food directly on the tile, and garnish with a flower from the garden.

FRESH HERBS AND DRIED HERBS

When a recipe calls for herbs, remember that in general, 1 teaspoon of dried equals 1 tablespoon fresh. This is because dried herbs have a more intense, concentrated flavor than fresh.

Avocados are one of our favorite fruits. To make it easier to remove flesh, don't remove the peel if at all possible. Instead, cut fruit from top to bottom with a paring knife, then twist halves apart and remove the pit. Slice flesh in the shell crosswise or dice, cutting lengthwise. This way, with a small spoon and gentle pressure from your fingertips on the outer peel, you can easily scoop out the sliced or diced fruit.

Taco Cheesecake Cabo San Lucas

2	packages (8 ounces) cream cheese (regular or low-fat), softened	1	container (16 ounces) sour cream (regular or low-fat), divided
8	ounces shredded sharp Cheddar cheese	3	eggs
1	package (1¼ ounces) dry taco seasoning mix	½	cup salsa
		2-3	avocados
			Lemon juice to taste
			Onion powder to taste
			Diced and drained tomatoes

Preheat oven to 350 degrees.

Beat cream cheese, Cheddar cheese and taco mix with an electric mixer until fluffy. Stir in 1 cup sour cream. Beat in eggs, one at a time, beating well after each addition. Pour mixture into a 9-inch springform pan. Bake 40 to 45 minutes or until center is just about firm. Cool 10 minutes on a wire rack.

Combine 1 cup sour cream with salsa and spread over top of cheesecake. Bake 5 minutes longer. Cool on rack 30 minutes. Refrigerate several hours or up to several days.

Peel and mash avocados and blend with lemon juice and onion powder. Spread mixture over cheesecake. Sprinkle with diced tomatoes to cover.

Run a knife around edges and release sides of pan. Place on a serving platter. Serve with lots of tortilla chips and crackers.

Serves 40 to 50.

Leftovers do not keep well, so save this recipe for a large group or party.

Tortilla Pinwheels

Can serve a crowd.

2	packages (8 ounces each) cream cheese, softened	1	package (10 ounces) frozen chopped spinach, thawed and well drained
½	cup chopped scallions	1	can (4 ounces) ripe olives, chopped
1	can (4 ounces) diced green chiles	1	package large flour tortillas

Mix cream cheese, scallions, chiles, spinach and olives. Spread mixture over each tortilla and roll up. Wrap tightly in plastic wrap and refrigerate until ready to serve.

To serve, remove plastic wrap and cut crosswise into ½- to ¾-inch thick slices.

Soups

Soups

Asparagus Soup

2	tablespoons butter or margarine	3	pounds asparagus, tough ends removed, cut into 1½-inch pieces
1½	large onions, chopped	1	large leek, white and pale green parts only, minced
3	cloves garlic, chopped	8	cups vegetable or chicken broth
1	tablespoon minced fresh basil	1½	teaspoons salt
1½	teaspoons minced fresh oregano	½	teaspoon white pepper

Melt butter or margarine in a large saucepan over medium heat. Add onions, garlic, basil and oregano and cook 5 to 7 minutes or until onions are translucent. Add asparagus and leek and cook 1 minute. Add broth and bring to a boil. Add salt and white pepper and reduce heat to a simmer. Partially cover saucepan and simmer 45 minutes or until asparagus and leeks are very soft.

Purée soup in batches in a blender. Serve hot or chilled in soup bowls.

Serves 6.

In soup-making, before adding vegetables to the pot, toss them with a little flour to keep them from sticking.

Avocado Gazpacho Soup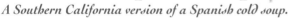

A Southern California version of a Spanish cold soup.

1	large cucumber, peeled, seeded and diced	¼	cup red wine vinegar
1	large avocado, diced	2	cups beef or vegetable broth
1	large tomato, diced	4	cups canned crushed tomatoes
1	medium green bell pepper, diced	1	tablespoon chopped fresh cilantro
1	medium red bell pepper, diced	1	teaspoon salt, or to taste
1	cup diced celery	½	teaspoon black pepper, or to taste
¼	cup sliced scallions		Dash of hot pepper sauce, or to taste
¼	cup white wine		

Combine all ingredients in a large glass or porcelain bowl and mix well. Cover and refrigerate overnight.

Serves 6 to 8.

USING FRESH HERBS

If you are using herbs from your garden, be sure to cut whole stems, not just individual leaves, so that the plants will continue to grow. To store fresh herbs, wrap them in barely damp paper towels, seal in a plastic bag and refrigerate. They will keep for about a week. For longer storage, place herbs in a glass with enough water to immerse stems only, cover with a plastic bag and secure with a rubber band. They should keep up to 2 weeks this way.

Butternut-Corn Chowder with Goat Cheese Croutons

4	ounces soft fresh goat cheese (such as Montrachet), chilled and cut into 1-inch thick rounds	4½	cups canned vegetable broth
2	eggs, beaten	2	teaspoons minced canned chipotle chiles
½	cup yellow cornmeal	1	bag (16 ounces) frozen sweet white corn, unthawed
	Salt and pepper to taste		
1	medium onion, chopped	2	tablespoons olive oil
1	butternut squash (2¼ pounds), peeled, seeded and coarsely chopped	2	teaspoons minced fresh sage

Cut each cheese round into 8 wedges. Pour eggs in a small bowl. Place cornmeal in a separate bowl and season with salt and pepper. Working in batches, dip cheese wedges into eggs, then into cornmeal, turning to coat. Press cornmeal gently to adhere and place on a baking sheet. Freeze 1 hour.

Sauté onion in a saucepan for 4 minutes or until just tender. Add squash, broth and chiles. Simmer 20 minutes or until squash is tender, stirring occasionally. Mix in corn and simmer 8 minutes longer or until corn is tender. Transfer 3½ cups of soup to a blender and purée. Mix purée into remaining soup in pan. Season with salt and pepper. Soup can be made 8 hours ahead. Chill uncovered until cold, then cover and keep cold until ready to serve.

Heat oil in a large nonstick skillet over medium-high heat. Add frozen cheese. Cook about 1 minute per side or until browned well.

Meanwhile, bring soup to a simmer. Mix in sage. Ladle into soup bowls and top with cheese croutons.

Serves 8 to 10.

Chipolte chiles can be found in Latin American markets, specialty food stores and some supermarkets.

Russian Cabbage Soup 🅜

1	can (28 ounces) tomatoes	2	pounds cabbage, coarsely shredded
6	cups water	2	tablespoons coarse salt
3	pounds beef brisket (optional)	¾	cup sugar, or less to taste
2	soup bones with meat		Juice of 1 lemon
1	can (6 ounces) tomato paste		Dash of cayenne pepper
			Dash of paprika

Combine tomatoes and water in a large stock pot and bring to a boil. Trim all but a thin layer of fat from the brisket. Cut brisket into chunks and add to stock pot along with bones, tomato paste, cabbage, salt, sugar, lemon juice, cayenne pepper and paprika. Stir to blend and bring to a simmer. Simmer, partially covered, for 2 to 2½ hours or until meat is tender. Remove bones before serving. Serve hot.

Serves 10 to 12.

If desired, beef may be removed and served separately as boiled beef, or soup can be made without the brisket.

Cold Cucumber Soup with Fresh Dill 🅟

1	tablespoon unsalted margarine		Freshly ground white pepper to taste
½	leek, white part only, chopped		Vegetable seasoning to taste
¼	medium onion, chopped	1	tablespoon chopped fresh dill
2	cucumbers, peeled, seeded and chopped	⅓	cucumber, seeded and cut into four (2 x 1½-inch) rectangles for garnish
1	quart vegetable broth		
½	cup non-dairy creamer	4	sprigs fresh dill for garnish

In a 3-quart saucepan, melt margarine over medium heat. Add leek, onion and chopped cucumber and sauté 2 minutes. Add broth and bring to a boil. Reduce heat to a simmer and cook, uncovered, for 20 minutes. Cool slightly.

Purée soup in a food processor or blender in several batches (the hot liquid will increase in volume dramatically as it is puréed). Pour soup into a large bowl and cool to room temperature. Cover and refrigerate 90 minutes or until cold. Soup can be prepared ahead to this point.

To serve, stir in non-dairy creamer, pepper, vegetable seasoning and dill. Ladle soup into 4 soup bowls and garnish with cucumber rectangles and dill sprigs.

Serves 4.

To add zip to minestrone soup, add a spoonful of pesto sauce.

Roasted Eggplant and Red Bell Pepper Soup Ⓜ Ⓟ

A low calorie soup.

6   large Japanese eggplants, or
      3 regular eggplants
      Salt and pepper to taste
      Extra virgin olive oil
2   red bell peppers
1   tablespoon olive oil
1   large onion, sliced
4   cloves garlic, crushed
1   quart chicken or vegetable
      broth
1   bunch fresh basil, stems
      discarded, diced small

Preheat oven to 400 degrees.

Wash eggplants and split lengthwise into halves. Lightly season with salt and pepper and sprinkle with olive oil. Roast eggplants for 25 minutes or until tender and golden brown. Purée flesh and skin in a blender or food processor. Set aside.

Place bell peppers under a broiler until charred on all sides. Place in a plastic bag 10 minutes to soften, then peel and remove seeds. Purée flesh in food processor until smooth. Set aside.

Heat 1 tablespoon olive oil in a skillet. Add onion and garlic and sauté until tender. Cover to sweat over low heat for 5 minutes. Add eggplant purée and broth and cook over low heat for 15 minutes or until flavors blend and mixture is heated through. Purée mixture in blender or food processor until smooth; then strain into a clean bowl. Season to taste with salt and pepper.

To serve, ladle eggplant mixture into individual deep serving bowls. Spoon red pepper purée into center and swirl into soup. Drizzle lightly with olive oil, if desired. Sprinkle with basil.

Serves 6.

Lentil Soup Ⓜ Ⓟ

Begin this soup in the morning; it should simmer all day.

3	cups dry lentils, rinsed		1½	cups chopped fresh tomatoes
7	cups water or chicken or vegetable broth		2	tablespoons dry red wine
2	teaspoons salt		2	tablespoons lemon juice
2	teaspoons minced garlic		1½	tablespoons brown sugar or molasses
1	cup chopped onion		1	tablespoon wine vinegar, plus extra for serving
1	cup minced celery			
1	cup chopped carrot			Chopped scallions for garnish
	Margarine for sautéing			
	Black pepper to taste (lots of it)			

Combine lentils, water and salt in a soup pot. Cover and simmer 3 to 4 hours.

Steam or sauté garlic, onion, celery and carrot in margarine. Add cooked vegetables to pot after lentils have cooked 3 to 4 hours. Continue to simmer over low heat.

About 30 minutes before serving, add pepper, tomatoes, wine, lemon juice, sugar and vinegar. Sprinkle extra vinegar and chopped scallions onto each serving.

Serves 4 to 6.

If desired, fresh herbs such as thyme, oregano or basil can be added with the tomatoes.

COOKING TIPS FOR BEANS:

1. To cook beans without bursting their skins, keep the heat low and the pot uncovered.

2. To keep long-cooked beans from turning to mush, add a bit of sugar to the recipe.

3. To soften up tough, slow-to-cook beans, add baking soda to the cooking water, starting with ½ teaspoon and increasing as needed.

Canadian Leek Soup Ⓓ

A wonderful soup for Yom Kippur break fast.

3	tablespoons butter or margarine		2	cups peeled and diced potatoes
2	leeks, white part only, cut into 1-inch pieces			Salt and pepper to taste
3	cups chopped onion		3	tablespoons flour
4	cups boiling water		½	cup milk
			½	cup sour cream
			1	tablespoon dried dill

Melt butter in a large pot over medium heat. Add leeks and onion and sauté until lightly browned. Add boiling water, potatoes, salt and pepper. Cook 25 minutes or until potatoes are soft.

Mix flour with milk until smooth. Stir mixture into soup and simmer until thickened. Add sour cream and dill. Remove from heat and purée, in batches, in a food processor or blender.

Makes about 6 cups.

Iranian Meatball Soup (Gundi)

Our recent large addition of Iranian Jews to Los Angeles brings us this wonderful traditional soup for Shabbat.

Broth

1½	pounds chicken wings or legs		Salt and freshly ground pepper
1	medium onion	7	cups water

Meatballs

¼	cup parsley sprigs	½	large onion, cut into chunks
1	can (8 to 9 ounces) chickpeas (garbanzo beans), rinsed and drained	½	pound lean ground beef
		¼	teaspoon salt
		¼	teaspoon black pepper

Soup

2	large boiling potatoes (about 4 ounces each), peeled and cut into large cubes	½	teaspoon dried red pepper flakes, or cayenne pepper to taste
2	large carrots, diced	2	tablespoons chopped fresh parsley
1	tablespoon tomato paste	1-1½	cups long-grain white rice, basmati preferred, cooked
1	teaspoon ground cumin		
¼	teaspoon turmeric		

Combine all broth ingredients in a large pot. Cook, partially covered, for 1 hour. Discard onion. Remove chicken and reserve for a different use. Reserve broth in pot.

Meanwhile, to make meatballs, mince parsley in a food processor; remove and set aside. Add chickpeas to processor and chop; remove and set aside. Mince onion in processor. Combine parsley, chickpeas and onion with beef, salt and pepper. Shape tablespoons of mixture into small meatballs. Squeeze each well so it will be compact, then roll between palms of hand to smooth ball. Refrigerate meatballs on a plate.

For soup, add potatoes and carrots to reserved broth. Cover and cook 20 minutes. Add tomato paste, cumin, turmeric and pepper flakes. Stir to blend. Add meatballs, cover and simmer over low heat for 30 minutes. Soup can be refrigerated at this point for up to 2 days.

Add parsley to hot soup. Adjust seasonings as needed.

To serve, spoon a generous amount of rice into each bowl. Ladle soup and meatballs over rice.

Serves 4 to 6.

Mushroom Barley Soup

This is an old-fashioned, hearty soup which originally came from Eastern Europe.

8	ounces fresh mushrooms, sliced	4	cups chicken broth
1	tablespoon margarine	⅓	cup dry pearl barley
1	cup chopped celery	3	carrots, diced
1	medium onion, chopped	¼	cup chopped parsley
2	tablespoons olive or vegetable oil	1	bay leaf
			Salt and pepper to taste
		½	cup non-dairy creamer

Sauté mushrooms in margarine in a small pan; set aside. In a medium soup pot, sauté celery and onion in oil over medium heat for 20 minutes or until softened. Add broth, barley and carrots to pot. Bring to a boil. Stir in parsley and bay leaf and season with salt and pepper. Cover and simmer 1 hour, stirring occasionally. Add mushrooms to pot and simmer, covered, for 30 minutes longer. Remove bay leaf and stir in creamer. Serve hot.

Serves 6.

West African Peanut Soup

When you want to serve something deliciously different.

2	cups chopped onion	4	cups chicken or vegetable broth
1	tablespoon peanut or vegetable oil	2	cups tomato juice
½	teaspoon cayenne pepper	1	cup smooth all natural peanut butter
1	teaspoon grated fresh gingerroot	1	tablespoon sugar (optional)
1	cup chopped carrot		Chopped scallions for garnish
2	cups chopped sweet potato		

Sauté onion in oil in a soup pot. Stir in cayenne and ginger. Add carrot and sauté 2 minutes longer. Mix in potato and broth and simmer 15 minutes or until vegetables are tender.

In a blender or processor, purée vegetables with cooking liquid and tomato juice. Return purée to pot and stir in peanut butter until smooth. Add sugar, as needed, if the carrots and sweet potatoes do not give the soup enough natural sweetness. Top with scallions and serve hot.

Serves 6 to 8.

Purée of Pumpkin Soup Ⓜ

A nice soup for Thanksgiving.

4	tablespoons margarine, melted	1	teaspoon salt
1	large onion, chopped	½	teaspoon curry powder
1	medium leek, chopped, use white part only	¼	teaspoon nutmeg
1	can (16 ounces) puréed pumpkin	¼	teaspoon white pepper
		¼	teaspoon ground ginger
4	cups chicken broth	1	bay leaf
		1	cup non-dairy creamer

Melt margarine in a medium saucepan. Add onion and leek and sauté, stirring occasionally, until softened. Stir in pumpkin, broth, salt, curry, nutmeg, white pepper, ginger and bay leaf. Bring to a boil. Reduce heat and simmer, uncovered, for 15 minutes, stirring occasionally. Remove bay leaf. Purée mixture in batches in a blender for a smoother texture or in a food processor fitted with a metal blade. Soup can be refrigerated up to 2 days or frozen at this point.

Return soup to saucepan. Add creamer and cook over medium heat, stirring occasionally, until heated through.

Serves 8.

You may use half-and-half instead of creamer, but you must substitute "pareve chicken broth bouillon or powder."

Cream of Summer Greens Soup Ⓓ

A family favorite and a must for the "break-the-fast".

1	pound fresh spinach, stems removed	1	tablespoon sherry
1	cup water	1	teaspoon dried basil
1	medium zucchini, chopped	1	teaspoon soy sauce
½	cup water		Dash of nutmeg
1	small head sweet leaf lettuce, chopped		Salt and pepper to taste
		¼	cup chopped fresh parsley for garnish
1	quart buttermilk	¼	cup chopped scallions for garnish
⅛	teaspoon dried dill		

Steam spinach in 1 cup water for 5 minutes. Steam zucchini separately in ½ cup water. Purée spinach and zucchini with their cooking liquids. Purée lettuce with about half of the buttermilk.

Combine all puréed vegetables, remaining buttermilk, dill, sherry, basil, soy sauce, nutmeg and salt and pepper. Mix well. Chill until very cold. Garnish with parsley and scallions.

Serves 6 to 8.

Tomato Soup with
Lemon-Rosemary Cream Ⓓ

A gourmet tomato soup that will feed a large group.

1	cup olive oil	2	bay leaves
2	yellow onions, minced	2	cans (28 ounces) diced tomatoes (fire-roasted preferred)
3	carrots, minced		
3	stalks celery, minced		
2	tablespoons minced garlic	2	quarts vegetable broth
1	teaspoon dried basil	1	cup tomato purée
½	teaspoon dried thyme		Salt and pepper to taste
½	teaspoon dried red chile flakes		Lemon-Rosemary Cream (recipe below)

Heat oil in a large stockpot. Add onions and sauté 4 to 5 minutes. Add carrots and celery and sauté 5 minutes. Add garlic, basil, thyme, chile flakes and bay leaves and cook 5 minutes or until garlic is softened.

Purée tomatoes with broth in a food processor or blender. Remove bay leaves and add tomato/broth purée and 1 cup tomato purée to soup. Bring to a simmer. Cook over low heat for 30 to 45 minutes. Season with salt and pepper. Top individual servings with Lemon-Rosemary Cream.

Lemon-Rosemary Cream

½	cup heavy cream	1	teaspoon minced lemon zest
½	teaspoon minced fresh rosemary	1	teaspoon fresh lemon juice
			Salt and pepper to taste

Whip cream until firm peaks form. Fold in rosemary, lemon zest and lemon juice. Season with salt and pepper. This topping can be prepared ahead of time and rewhipped.

Serves 16 (1 gallon).

To make this into a tomato bisque, stir the ingredients for the Lemon-Rosemary Cream into the soup.

To make "wheels" of corn on the cob, remove the husks and silks from 1 or 2 ears of corn. Use a sharp, sturdy knife to cut the corn into 1-inch lengths. Drop into chicken broth or a stew and cook several minutes. This method works particularly well with Southwestern dishes.

Southern California Tortilla Soup Ⓜ

A taste of Mexico.

1½	tablespoons olive oil		¼	cup chopped red bell pepper
1	large onion, chopped		½-¾	cup whole kernel corn
2	cloves garlic, minced		4	cups chicken broth
1	cup chopped cooked chicken		¼	cup chopped fresh cilantro, or about 1 tablespoon dried
1	can (28 ounces) Italian plum tomatoes, undrained		2	tablespoons chili powder
			1	tablespoon ground cumin
¼	cup canned diced green chiles		1	tablespoon fresh lime juice
				Corn tortilla chips

Heat olive oil in a large saucepan. Add onion and garlic and sauté until softened. Add chicken.

Process tomatoes with juice in a blender or food processor until smooth. Add tomatoes, chiles, bell pepper, corn, broth, cilantro, chili powder and cumin to saucepan. Simmer 30 minutes. Remove from stove and stir in lime juice.

To serve, ladle soup into individual bowls and top with tortilla chips.

Serves 4 to 6.

Chilled Zucchini-Cumin Soup Ⓓ

1	teaspoon olive oil		⅓	cup chopped fresh basil
1	large onion, chopped			Salt and pepper to taste
1½	teaspoons ground cumin		4	tablespoons plain nonfat yogurt
1½	pounds zucchini, cut into ¾-inch pieces			Sliced fresh basil for garnish
2	cans (14½ ounces each) vegetable broth			

Heat oil in a heavy medium saucepan over medium heat. Add onion and sauté 5 minutes or until tender. Add cumin and cook and stir 30 seconds or until aromatic. Mix in zucchini. Add broth and bring to a boil. Reduce heat and simmer 30 minutes or until zucchini is very tender. Cool slightly.

Mix chopped basil into soup. Working in batches, purée soup in a blender until smooth. Transfer to a bowl and season with salt and pepper. Cover and refrigerate 3 hours or until cold, or up to 1 day ahead. Ladle cold soup into bowls. Top each serving with a tablespoon of yogurt and sliced basil.

Serves 4.

Summer Vegetable Soup Ⓓ

2   large potatoes, diced
2   cups water
1   cup fresh peas
2   ears sweet corn, kernels removed
3   tablespoons butter
1½ cups diced onion
1½ teaspoons salt, or to taste
2   medium carrots, diced
1   cup diced broccoli

1   green bell pepper, diced
2   zucchini (5 to 6 inches long each), diced
1   quart milk, warmed
¼   teaspoon black pepper
½   tablespoon chopped fresh thyme, or ½ teaspoon dried
¼   teaspoon nutmeg

The easiest way to purée soups is by using a hand-held blender.

Cook potatoes in 2 cups water until soft. Mash potatoes, or purée in a blender, with cooking liquid. Add peas and corn kernels to potato purée.

Heat butter in a heavy skillet. Add onion and salt and cook 8 minutes. Add carrots, broccoli, bell pepper and zucchini in order listed, sautéing about 8 minutes after each addition. When all vegetables are tender and brightly colored, add to potato mixture.

Slowly add warm milk to the soup. Season with pepper, thyme and nutmeg. Gently heat soup, but do not boil. Serve immediately with a good dark rye bread.

Serves 4.

Try adding green beans, summer squash, or a variety of fresh herbs such as basil or marjoram.

Sisterhood's Favorite Low Calorie Soup Ⓜ Ⓟ

1   carrot, chopped
2   stalks celery, chopped
1   medium onion, chopped
3   tablespoons olive oil
2   cloves garlic, minced
⅛   teaspoon ground cloves
1   can (35 ounces) peeled tomatoes, puréed in a blender

4   cups vegetable or chicken broth
⅓   cup dried lentils
¼   cup red wine
    Salt and pepper to taste
    Chopped fresh parsley for garnish (optional)

Sauté carrot, celery and onion in oil until vegetables start to soften. Add garlic and cloves and cook 3 minutes longer. Add puréed tomatoes, broth and lentils. Bring to a boil. Reduce heat and simmer 20 minutes. Add wine and season with salt and pepper. Simmer 20 minutes longer. Garnish individual servings with parsley.

Serves 8.

When broiling peppers, first cut peppers in half and remove seeds. Place pepper halves, cut-side down, on a pan and broil about 7 minutes or until charred. Cool in plastic bag and peel. This method shortens cooking time and makes the peppers easier to peel because there are no seeds to deal with.

Turkey Corn Chowder

Corn, roasted peppers and potatoes give this post-Thanksgiving turkey soup an extra hearty flavor.

2	tablespoons margarine	1	large baking potato, diced
1	small red onion, chopped	2	cans (14¾ ounces each) creamed corn
1	large carrot, diced	1	red bell pepper, roasted, peeled and diced
1	stalk celery, diced		
6	cups chicken broth	2-3	cups leftover cooked turkey, cut into 1-inch pieces
2	leftover turkey bones (optional)		Salt and pepper to taste
2	leftover turkey wings or wing tips (optional)		

Melt margarine in a saucepan. Add onion, carrot and celery and cook 10 minutes or until softened. Add broth, bones and wings and bring to a boil. Reduce heat to a simmer. Add potato and simmer 15 minutes or until potato is tender.

Remove bones and wings. Add corn, bell pepper and turkey. Simmer 5 minutes. Season to taste with salt and pepper. Serve hot.

Serves 6.

Chilled Sweet Potato Soup Ⓓ

This is a variation of vichyssoise.

1	large onion, diced	½	teaspoon dried thyme
2	tablespoons butter	2	cups milk
2	pounds sweet potatoes, peeled and thinly sliced		Salt and pepper to taste
2	cups vegetable broth	¼	teaspoon curry powder (optional)
2	cups water		Chopped parsley for garnish
¼	teaspoon ground ginger		

Sauté onion in butter in a soup pot over medium heat until softened. Add sweet potatoes and cook 1 minute. Add broth, water, ginger and thyme and bring to a boil. Reduce heat to a simmer and cook 20 minutes or until all ingredients are softened. Carefully purée soup, in small batches, using a blender or food processor.

Return soup to pot and whisk in milk. Season with salt and pepper and curry powder. Chill thoroughly. Serve cold garnished with parsley. It is also good served hot on cold days.

Serves 6 to 8.

Salads &
Salad Dressings

Salads & Salad Dressings

Grilled Albacore Tuna Salad Ⓓ

This is a favorite salad served at some of our popular Southern California grills. Great all year around, especially with the mesclun greens.

1½ pounds fresh albacore tuna, cut into 4 pieces	1 tablespoon extra virgin olive oil
¼ cup balsamic vinegar-olive oil salad dressing, plus extra for drizzling	2 cups freshly sliced white mushrooms
Kosher salt and freshly ground black pepper	4 thin slices red onion
	20 kalamata olives, pitted
10-12 ounces mesclun salad mix	¼ cup Greek feta cheese, crumbled

Place tuna in a flat glass dish. Pour ¼ cup salad dressing over tuna and cover with plastic wrap. Marinate 1 to 3 hours, turning fish once. Remove tuna from marinade and season on both sides with salt and pepper. Place on a hot grill and cook 2 minutes on each side for medium-rare. Cool slightly, then cut into thin slices.

Divide salad mix between individual serving plates. In a medium skillet, heat olive oil. Add mushrooms and sauté until tender. Arrange sliced tuna on salad mix. Top with sautéed mushrooms, sliced onion and olives. Drizzle extra salad dressing over salad. Garnish with feta cheese.

Makes 4 servings.

Drain a jar of marinated artichoke hearts, chop coarsely and fold into your favorite potato salad.

Potato and Pea Salad Ⓟ

To save time, cut potatoes before steaming.

1½ pounds red potatoes	3 hard-cooked eggs, chopped (optional)
1 small red onion, finely chopped	1 package (10-ounces) frozen peas, thawed
½ teaspoon sugar	3 tablespoons minced fresh parsley
¼ cup cider vinegar	
2 tablespoons vegetable oil	
1 tablespoon Dijon mustard	

Cut potatoes into small cubes and steam 8 minutes or until tender. Transfer to a bowl and mix with onion. Whisk together sugar, vinegar, oil and mustard and pour over vegetables. Fold in eggs, peas and parsley.

Makes 6 servings.

Bottled vinaigrette dressing can be used instead of making your own.

Add a few spoonfuls of balsamic vinegar to potato salad or coleslaw or sprinkle over tomato salad with mozzarella and chopped fresh basil.

Baby Greens and Fruit
with Honey-Lime Vinaigrette Ⓟ

You will note that the unique dressing adds both sweet and tart taste to this refreshing salad. Avocados and oranges add a Southern California touch.

Dressing

⅓	cup vegetable oil	1	teaspoon sesame oil
¼	cup rice vinegar	1½	teaspoons minced red bell pepper
¼	cup honey	1	teaspoon minced onion
2	tablespoons Dijon mustard	¼	teaspoon freshly ground black pepper
1	tablespoon chopped fresh cilantro		Salt to taste
2½-3	teaspoons fresh lime juice		

Salad

8	cups mixed baby greens	2	cups jicama, peeled and cut into ½-inch pieces
5	kiwis, peeled and cut into wedges	1	cup thinly sliced red onion
4	oranges, peeled, white pith removed, sliced into rounds	1	cup pine nuts, toasted
		2	avocados, peeled and diced

Combine all dressing ingredients together in a small bowl until well blended.

Mix salad ingredients in large bowl. Add half of dressing to salad and toss to coat. Pass remaining dressing on the side.

Serves 6.

Chicken-Couscous Salad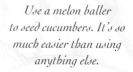

2	cups chicken broth	1	small cucumber or zucchini, cut into ¼-inch slices	
¾	teaspoon cinnamon			
2	teaspoons ground ginger	1	small Granny Smith apple, diced	
½	teaspoon ground cumin			
¼	teaspoon turmeric	⅓	cup currants or raisins	
1½	tablespoons olive oil	1	cup canned chickpeas, rinsed and drained	
½	pound boneless, skinless chicken breast			
1	cup couscous	1½	tablespoons olive oil	
1	medium carrot, cut into ¼-inch dice	¼	cup fresh lemon juice	
		½	teaspoon salt	
1	small red bell pepper, diced	¼	teaspoon pepper	

Whisk together broth, cinnamon, ginger, cumin, turmeric and 1½ tablespoons olive oil in a heavy, medium saucepan. Bring to a boil. Reduce to a simmer and add chicken breast. Poach 15 minutes or until meat is white throughout but still moist. Remove chicken and set aside to cool.

Return broth to a boil. Add couscous in a slow steady stream, stirring constantly. Continue to cook and stir 1 minute. Cover tightly, remove from heat and let stand 15 minutes. Fluff couscous with a fork, breaking up any lumps that may have formed.

Dice chicken into ½-inch cubes and add to couscous. Add carrot, bell pepper, cucumber, apple, currants and chickpeas. Toss to mix.

In a small jar with a lid, combine 1½ tablespoons olive oil, lemon juice, salt and pepper. Cover and shake until well blended. Pour dressing over salad and toss well. Cover and refrigerate several hours, or up to 3 days. Season to taste with additional salt, pepper and lemon juice.

Serves 6 to 8.

You can eliminate chicken, if desired.

Use a melon baller to seed cucumbers. It's so much easier than using anything else.

Poaching chicken is easy. Just cover with water into which you have added a little salt and pepper. Add a few slices of onion and simmer about 20 minutes. You can then remove the chicken, allowing it to cool before using in a recipe.

Chicken Salad with Red Grapes and Green Apple Ⓜ

If making salad as a sandwich filling, add a washed, dried and stemmed bunch of watercress and place on pumpernickel bread.

1	teaspoon salt	1	teaspoon freshly chopped tarragon
½	teaspoon black pepper		
1	pound boneless, skinless chicken breast	1	Granny Smith apple Juice of ½ lemon
¾	cup regular or low fat mayonnaise	1	cup finely diced fennel
		½	cup finely diced celery
1	tablespoon Dijon mustard	2	cups red seedless grapes, halved
2	tablespoons finely chopped chives		

Combine salt and pepper in a bowl. Heat a large skillet over medium-high heat. Coat skillet with cooking spray. Sprinkle chicken with some of salt mixture and place in hot skillet. Reduce heat to medium and cover. Cook 12 minutes or until chicken is cooked through, turning once halfway through cooking time. Remove from pan and set aside.

In a bowl, combine mayonnaise, mustard, chives, tarragon and remaining salt mixture.

Core apple and dice into ¼-inch pieces. Place apple in a medium bowl with lemon juice and toss to coat. Add fennel, celery and grapes.

Cut reserved chicken into ½-inch pieces. Add chicken and mayonnaise dressing to apple mixture. Stir to combine.

Serves 6.

Chinese Chicken Salad

The recipe can be made ahead of time if the ingredients are not combined until ready to serve. This a delicious, classic luncheon dish.

4	boneless, skinless chicken breasts	¾	cup diagonally sliced celery
½	package wonton skins, cut into ¼-inch strips	1	medium green bell pepper, thinly sliced
	Safflower oil	½	cup sliced scallions
⅓	package rice sticks (optional)	6	radishes, thinly sliced
1	cup sliced almonds, toasted	1	small head romaine or endive lettuce, broken into leaves
2	cups shredded lettuce		

Marinade

¼	cup soy sauce	1	large clove garlic
¼	cup sugar	1	tablespoon white wine

Dressing

⅓	cup red wine vinegar	1	teaspoon sesame oil
½	cup safflower oil	1	tablespoon sesame seeds
1	teaspoon salt	1	large clove garlic, crushed
¼	cup sugar	1	tablespoon soy sauce

Preheat oven to 375 degrees.

Marinate chicken in soy sauce, sugar, garlic and wine for 3 hours or longer. Place chicken and marinade in foil and seal well to make a pouch. Bake 1 hour. Cool and shred (do not cut) into bite-size pieces.

Deep fry wonton skins in hot safflower oil, watching carefully to avoid burning. Remove with a slotted spoon and drain on paper towels. Repeat process with rice sticks (if being used), drying well after frying.

Combine chicken with almonds, shredded lettuce, celery, bell pepper, scallions and radishes. Toss to combine. Add dressing and toss to coat salad. Serve on a bed of lettuce leaves. Sprinkle wonton skins and rice sticks on top.

To make dressing, combine all ingredients and mix well.

Serves 6 to 8.

FRESH AND CRISP LETTUCE

The best way to prolong the freshness of lettuce and prevent moisture loss is to soak the leaves for 5 minutes in cold water right after purchase, filling the lettuce cells with water, promoting maximum crispness. Spin dry or pat between a kitchen towel and seal in a plastic bag. Store in the most humid part of the refrigerator. This will keep the lettuce fresh and crisp for up to 5 days.

Coronado Salad Ⓓ Ⓟ

This refreshing and interesting-textured salad was created by a committee made up of several members of one of our large families. You'll like the results.

Dressing

½	cup olive oil	¼	teaspoon salt
3	tablespoons red wine vinegar	½	teaspoon dry mustard
1	tablespoon fresh lemon juice	1-2	cloves garlic, crushed
2	teaspoons sugar, or less if desired		

Combine all dressing ingredients in a jar and shake well to blend.

Salad

2	tablespoons butter or margarine	2-3	scallions, finely chopped
½	cup shelled sunflower seeds	1	can (10-ounces) Mandarin oranges, drained
½	cup slivered almonds	1	ripe avocado, sliced just before serving
1	head romaine lettuce, washed and drained well		

Heat butter in a skillet. Add sunflower seeds and almonds and sauté until golden brown. Drain very well on paper towels and cool. Combine lettuce, scallions, Mandarin oranges and avocado in a bowl. Add cooled seeds and nuts. Toss salad with dressing and serve immediately.

Makes 8 to 10 servings.

Confetti Orzo Salad Ⓟ

1½	cups dry orzo	¼	cup each finely diced red, green and yellow bell pepper
⅓	cup light olive oil		
3	tablespoons fresh lemon juice	½	cup peeled, seeded and finely diced cucumber (can use Persian cucumbers which do not need to be peeled or seeded)
½	teaspoon lemon zest		
½	teaspoon salt		
⅛	teaspoon coarsely ground black pepper		
1	clove garlic, crushed	¼	cup finely chopped scallions
1	medium carrot, diced into ⅛-inch cubes	¼	cup finely chopped red onion
		¼	cup finely chopped Italian flat-leaf parsley

Cook orzo in plenty of boiling salted water for 10 to 12 minutes or until tender. Drain in a wire mesh strainer and rinse under cool water. Whisk oil, lemon juice, lemon zest, salt, pepper and garlic until blended. Toss carrot, bell peppers, cucumber, scallion, onion, parsley, drained orzo and oil dressing together. Serve warm or at room temperature.

Makes 4 servings.

Jicama Carrot Salad ♣

Almost a relish, this salad is delightfully crunchy and refreshing. Serve small portions on a lettuce leaf.

2	carrots, grated	1	jalapeño pepper, seeded and minced
3	cups peeled and grated jicama (about 1¼ pounds)	2	teaspoons minced garlic
1	red bell pepper, diced	½	teaspoon red pepper flakes
¼	cup chopped onion	¼	teaspoon salt
½	cup rice wine vinegar	10-12	lettuce leaves
3	tablespoons chopped cilantro		

Combine carrots, jicama, bell pepper and onion in a large bowl.

For dressing, whisk together vinegar, cilantro, jalapeño, garlic, pepper flakes and salt in a small bowl or food processor. Pour dressing over vegetables and toss. Refrigerate 2 hours to allow flavors to blend.

Serves 10 to 12.

Curried Turkey Salad with Cashews ♣

This is a wonderful use for leftover turkey breast.

2	turkey breast halves (2 pounds each), with skin and bones	2	tablespoons curry powder
	Olive oil	1	tablespoon fresh lemon juice
	Salt and pepper to taste	½	teaspoon ground ginger
1½	cups mayonnaise	3	scallions, chopped
⅓	cup dry white wine	2	stalks celery, chopped
¼	cup mango chutney	½	cup raisins
		⅔	cup roasted salted cashews

Preheat oven to 375 degrees.

Place turkey in a baking pan and brush with oil. Sprinkle with salt and pepper. Roast 1 hour or until a meat thermometer inserted into the thickest part of the meat registers 180 degrees. Cool. Remove skin and bones and cut meat into ½-inch cubes.

Whisk together mayonnaise, wine, chutney, curry powder, lemon juice and ginger in a large bowl. Add turkey, onions, celery and raisins and toss to coat. Season with salt and pepper. Mix in cashews. Cover and chill. Can be made a day ahead.

Serves 6.

Lemon Rice Salad with Chicken, Capers and Pine Nuts Ⓜ

This tantalizing salad features an added texture for the palate.

¾ cup pine nuts
6 cups cooked rice
2 cups ½-inch diced roasted chicken
½ cup minced fresh parsley, Italian if possible

1 small red or orange bell pepper, cored, seeded and cut into ¼-inch dice
⅓ cup thinly sliced scallions
¼ cup capers, rinsed and drained
   Zest of 1 lemon

Dressing
⅓ cup lemon juice
½ cup olive oil
1 teaspoon salt
¼ teaspoon sugar

Freshly ground pepper to taste
6-8 leaves butter or leaf lettuce

Toast pine nuts in a medium skillet over medium-high heat, stirring frequently, until nicely browned. Set aside to cool. Combine rice, chicken, parsley, bell pepper, scallions, capers, lemon zest and cooled pine nuts in a large bowl. Toss lightly to combine.

Whisk together lemon juice, olive oil, salt, sugar and pepper in a small bowl. Add dressing to rice mixture and toss to mix. Place a lettuce leaf on each individual serving plate. Top with a mound of rice salad and serve immediately.

Makes 6 to 8 servings.

Orange and Onion Salad ⓟ

This is a Sicilian recipe. Beautiful when served in a glass bowl. May be prepared in the morning of serving.

Dressing

⅔	cup olive oil
¼	cup freshly squeezed lemon juice
2	tablespoons tarragon wine vinegar
¾	teaspoon salt
⅛	teaspoon pepper
¼	teaspoon dried oregano, crumbled (optional)

Salad

1	head romaine lettuce, washed, dried and chilled
1	small head iceberg lettuce, washed, dried and chilled
4	large naval oranges, pared with all white pith removed, or use blood oranges
2	kiwi fruit, peeled (optional)
1	large cucumber, peeled, seeded and patted dry
½	small red onion
	Italian black olives (optional)
	Freshly ground black pepper

Combine all dressing ingredients. Beat well and set aside.

Tear lettuce into bite-size pieces, place in a plastic bag and refrigerate until serving time. Thinly slice oranges, kiwi, cucumber and onion and place in a large salad bowl. Add dressing and refrigerate 45 minutes or until serving time.

To serve, combine marinated fruits and vegetables with lettuce. Toss to coat evenly. Top with black olives. Serve on well-chilled salad plates and top with freshly ground black pepper.

Makes 6 to 8 servings.

Pear, Walnut and Blue Cheese Salad

A bit labor intensive, but worth the effort.

Salad

4   cups (5 to 6 ounces) lightly packed untrimmed watercress sprigs, rinsed and crisped

4   cups (8 ounces) butter lettuce, rinsed, crisped and torn into bite-size pieces

2   small firm ripe pears, cored and thinly sliced

Candied Walnuts (recipe below)

Shallot Dressing (recipe below)

½   cup crumbled blue cheese

In a large bowl, combine watercress, lettuce, pears and some of Candied Walnuts. Add some Shallot Dressing and mix gently.

Divide mixture among 6 salad plates. Sprinkle with cheese and remaining Candied Walnuts. Drizzle remaining Shallot Dressing on top.

Candied Walnuts

2   tablespoons sugar

1   tablespoon water

½   cup halved walnuts

Pour sugar into an 8-inch skillet over medium-high heat. Shake often until sugar melts and turns an amber color. Add water (at first, the sugar will harden). Cook and stir until sugar melts.

Add walnuts. Cook and stir until all of the sugar syrup clings to the nuts. Spread nuts out on a piece of foil. Cool.

Shallot Dressing

2   teaspoons lemon juice

½   cup olive oil

1   large shallot, minced

½   teaspoon pepper

½   teaspoon sugar

Combine all dressing ingredients and mix well.

Serves 6.

Radicchio and Arugula Salad with Warm Mushroom Dressing Ⓟ

Both of the leafy vegetables for this salad are identified here by their commonly used Italian names. Radicchio is also known as "red chicory", arugula is widely cultivated as "rocket".

¼	cup pine nuts (optional)	2	teaspoons Dijon mustard
1	small head radicchio, leaves separated	1	small clove garlic, finely chopped
2	bunches arugula, trimmed	¼	teaspoon salt
¼	cup red wine vinegar	⅛	teaspoon freshly ground black pepper
¼	cup water	2	tablespoons olive oil
1	teaspoon fresh lemon juice	8	ounces fresh mushrooms, wiped clean and trimmed, thinly sliced
1	teaspoon Worcestershire sauce		
2	teaspoons sugar		

Preheat oven to 350 degrees.

Spread pine nuts in a pie pan. Toast in oven for 5 minutes or until lightly browned; cool. Keeping greens separated, wash radicchio and arugula, spin or pat dry and tear into bite-size pieces.

Dressing

To prepare dressing, combine vinegar, water, lemon juice, Worcestershire sauce, sugar, mustard, garlic, salt and pepper in a screw-top jar with a tight-fitting lid. Add oil, close jar and shake vigorously.

At serving time, pour dressing into an 8- or 10-inch nonreactive saucepan and set it over medium-high heat. When dressing is hot, add mushrooms. Cook, stirring occasionally, for 5 minutes or until mushrooms are tender. Divide radicchio leaves among 4 salad plates. Top with arugula. Spoon mushrooms and dressing evenly over greens and sprinkle with toasted pine nuts.

Makes 4 servings

Purple Cabbage Salad Ⓟ

Dressing

¼ cup brown sugar
¼ teaspoon black pepper
¼ teaspoon salt
¼ cup red or white wine vinegar
1 teaspoon reserved Mandarin orange juice (from salad)

½ cup vegetable oil
1 teaspoon pareve chicken bouillon powder
   Dash of garlic powder

Salad

1 pound purple cabbage, shredded
8 ounces shredded carrots
1 can (11-ounces) Mandarin oranges, juice reserved

2 handfuls dried sweetened cranberries
⅓ cup chopped green onions
⅓ cup pine nuts

Combine all dressing ingredients in a jar and shake well.

For salad, combine cabbage, carrot, oranges and cranberries in a large bowl. Pour dressing over salad at least 1 to 2 hours but not more than 24 hours before serving. Add green onions and pine nuts, toss and serve.

Makes 8 to 10 servings.

24-Hour Slaw Ⓟ

You'll have everyone asking for the recipe.

½ cup sugar
1 large head cabbage, shredded

2 large red onions, thinly sliced
   Hot Dressing (recipe below)

Combine sugar with cabbage and place half of cabbage in a large bowl. Cover with onion slices. Top with remaining cabbage.

Pour boiling Hot Dressing slowly over cabbage. Do not stir. Cover and refrigerate at once. Chill 24 hours. Stir well before serving.

Hot Dressing

1 teaspoon celery seeds
1 teaspoon sugar
1 teaspoon dry mustard

1½ teaspoons salt
1 cup cider vinegar
1 cup oil

Combine celery seeds, sugar, mustard, salt and vinegar in a saucepan. Bring to a rolling boil. Stir in oil and return to a rolling boil.

Serves 8 to 10.

Salmon Niçoise Salad ⓟ

A favorite sisterhood salad. This will make an elegant "Hollywood Bowl picnic".

Salmon

2	pounds skinless whole fillet of salmon	1	lemon, sliced
	Salt and pepper to taste	3-4	tablespoons balsamic vinegar

Vinaigrette Dressing

⅔	cup balsamic vinegar or red wine vinegar	1	teaspoon minced shallots
½	cup olive oil	4	cloves garlic, crushed
2	tablespoons Dijon mustard		Sugar to taste
			Salt and pepper to taste

Salad

2	pounds red-skin potatoes, cooked and quartered	¾	cup kalamata olives
2	pounds fresh green beans, blanched	½	cup thinly sliced red onion
8	cups Romaine lettuce, sliced	6	hard-cooked eggs, cut into wedges
4	marinated artichokes, quartered	2	tablespoons capers
2	pints cherry tomatoes, halved	2	teaspoons snipped fresh tarragon (optional)

Preheat oven to 450 degrees.

Place salmon filet on a sheet of foil. Season with salt and pepper. Cover filet with lemon slices and drizzle vinegar around fillet. Tightly fold foil around fillet to seal and place on a baking sheet. Bake 20 minutes. Cool in foil until warm. Salmon can be prepared up to 1 day ahead.

For dressing, combine vinegar, oil, mustard, shallots and garlic in a screw top jar. Cover and shake well. Season with sugar, salt and pepper.

To prepare salad, toss potatoes and green beans with 3 tablespoons Vinaigrette Dressing. Place lettuce on a platter or divide among individual serving plates. Place cooked salmon in center of platter or cut into individual portions and divide among plates. Surround salmon with potatoes, green beans, artichokes, tomatoes, olives, onion and egg. Sprinkle with capers and tarragon. Serve with crusty rolls.

Serves 8.

BLANCHING

Plunge vegetables or fruits into boiling water for 2 to 3 minutes to either maintain the bright color of vegetables or to remove the skins of stone fruit or tomatoes.

When making a salad using broccoli stems, peel the stems and cut into the salad.

Spinach and Roasted Beet Salad with Ginger Vinaigrette Ⓟ

There are many new ways to serve spinach. This lively dressing lends a little zip to this fresh tasting, colorful salad. Beets, when roasted, become sugary sweet.

4	medium red beets, ends trimmed	2	teaspoons low sodium soy sauce
½	medium-size red onion, thinly sliced	2	teaspoons minced fresh ginger
3	tablespoons rice vinegar		Salt and pepper to taste
2	tablespoons vegetable oil	8	cups fresh spinach leaves (about 8 ounces)

Preheat oven to 450 degrees.

Wrap beets in foil. Roast beets 75 minutes or until tender when pierced with a skewer. Cool slightly, then peel and cut into wedges. Place in a medium bowl. Place onion slices on top.

Whisk together vinegar, oil, soy sauce and ginger in a small bowl to blend well. Season with salt and pepper. Pour half of vinaigrette over vegetables and toss to blend.

Place spinach in a large bowl. Drizzle remaining vinaigrette over spinach and toss to coat. Arrange beet mixture on spinach.

Serves 4 to 5.

Tofu Taco Salad Ⓓ

An ingenious adaptation from the classic Mexican salad, especially for the kosher cook.

1½	blocks extra firm tofu, drained and cut into small pieces	1	cup shredded Monterey Jack cheese
	Olive oil for browning	2	large tomatoes, diced
1	package (1¼ ounces) taco seasoning mix	1	medium-size sweet onion, diced
1	medium head iceberg lettuce, chopped	1	green bell pepper, diced
1	can (15 ounces) pinto beans, drained	1	can (2¼ ounces) sliced black olives, drained
1	cup shredded Cheddar cheese	1	bag (13 ounces) tortilla chips
		1	jar (8 ounces) salsa (optional)
		1	pint sour cream (optional)
			Guacamole (optional)

Brown tofu in olive oil. Add taco seasoning and prepare according to package directions. Cool.

Place lettuce, beans, cheeses, tomatoes, onion, bell pepper and olives in a large serving bowl. Just before serving, add tofu and chips to salad. Serve with salsa, sour cream and guacamole on the side, if desired.

Serves 6.

To desalinate overly salty brined black olives, simmer about 10 minutes in water and drain well.

Tortellini Salad with Pine Nuts Ⓓ

Prepare for everyone who tastes this to ask you for the recipe.

Salad

2	pounds fresh tortellini pasta, cooked al dente and drained	½	cup pine nuts
½	cup each chopped green and red bell peppers	¼	cup chopped fresh basil
		¼	cup chopped fresh dill
1	cup chopped scallions	¼	cup freshly grated Parmesan cheese

Dressing

¼	cup balsamic vinegar		Freshly ground black pepper to taste
1	large clove garlic, minced		
¼	teaspoon salt	¾	cup peanut oil

Combine all salad ingredients in a large bowl. Chill until ready to serve.

To make dressing, combine vinegar, garlic, salt and pepper in a small bowl. Whisk in oil until well combined. Add dressing to salad just before serving and toss.

Serves 8.

Flavor your olive oil with crushed garlic or basil before drizzling over a simple sliced tomato and fresh mozzarella salad.

Salt won't dissolve in oil, so when preparing a vinaigrette, always dissolve the salt in the vinegar or lemon juice, then whisk in the oil.

Our Favorite Vinaigrette Salad Dressing

You may use any fresh herbs of your choice.

1	tablespoon prepared Dijon mustard	½	teaspoon salt
¼	cup red wine vinegar	½	teaspoon black pepper
1	teaspoon sugar		Minced parsley
		½	cup olive oil

Mix mustard, vinegar, sugar, salt, pepper and parsley in a blender. With motor running, add oil slowly until dressing is thick.

Makes 1 cup dressing.

You can use a whisk instead of a blender with good results.

Recipe doubles easily.

Chili-Cumin Salad Dressing

This is always a big hit with any green lettuce salad. Double the recipe so that you may share it with friends. Spicy! So serve with milder Mexican dishes.

1½	teaspoons cumin seeds	2	teaspoons honey
2	cloves garlic, halved	⅓	cup apple cider vinegar
1	teaspoon Dijon mustard	⅔	cup canola oil
1	teaspoon mild red chili powder		Salt and freshly ground pepper to taste

Toast the cumin seeds in a small, dry skillet over medium heat, shaking the pan often, until seeds release their aroma. Grind toasted seeds in a spice mill.

In a blender, blend ground cumin seeds, garlic, mustard, chili powder and honey to a paste. With motor running, slowly pour in vinegar and oil. When incorporated, season with salt and pepper. Store in a covered container in refrigerator. Shake before using.

Breads
& Brunch

Breads & Brunch

Blueberry Streusel Muffins

⅓ cup sugar
4 tablespoons butter or
    margarine, softened
1 egg
2⅓ cups all-purpose flour
1 tablespoon plus 1 teaspoon
    baking powder

1 cup milk
1 teaspoon vanilla
1½ cups fresh blueberries
    Streusel Topping
    (recipe below)

Preheat oven to 375 degrees.

In a large bowl, cream sugar and butter until light and fluffy. Add egg and mix well.

In a small bowl, combine flour and baking powder. Alternately add dry ingredients and milk to butter mixture, stirring well after each addition. Stir in vanilla. Fold in blueberries. Spoon batter into paper-lined 2½-inch muffin cups. Sprinkle with Streusel Topping.

Bake 25 to 30 minutes or until a wooden pick inserted in the center comes out clean. Remove from pan.

Streusel Topping
½ cup sugar
⅓ cup all-purpose flour
½ teaspoon cinnamon

4 tablespoons butter or
    margarine

Combine sugar, flour and cinnamon in a small bowl. Cut in butter until mixture resembles crumbs.

Makes 16 to 18 muffins.

Focaccia Bread

This is an old family recipe from Italy. One bite and you can't stop eating it.

1 packet yeast
1 tablespoon sugar
1½ cups warm water
4 cups flour

2 teaspoons salt
½ cup finely chopped onion
    Oil to taste
    Rosemary and salt to taste

Preheat oven to 400 degrees.

Combine yeast, sugar and warm water in a large mixing bowl. Stir until dissolved. Add flour, 2 teaspoons salt and onion. Knead until smooth. Place dough in a greased bowl and cover with plastic wrap. Let rise in a warm place for 1 to 1½ hours or until doubled in size.

Punch dough down. Remove from bowl and flatten dough to about 1-inch thick on a greased baking sheet. Brush oil over top of dough. Let rise until doubled in size. Sprinkle with rosemary and salt. Bake 20 to 25 minutes.

Makes 1 loaf.

Cheesy Muffins with Scallions Ⓓ

A nice complement to a luncheon salad.

1¾ cups all-purpose flour
4 teaspoons baking powder
1 tablespoon sugar
1 teaspoon salt
3 cups rice cereal squares, crushed to 1 cup
2 eggs, beaten

1¼ cups milk
⅓ cup vegetable oil
½ cup chopped scallions with tops
1 package (3 ounces) cream cheese, cut into ¼-inch cubes

Preheat oven to 400 degrees.

Combine flour, baking powder, sugar and salt in a large bowl. In a medium bowl, combine cereal, eggs, milk, oil and onions. Add cereal mixture, all at once, to dry ingredients and stir just until moistened. Separate cream cheese cubes into mixture and fold in. Spoon batter into 18 (2½-inch) greased muffin cups. Bake 20 to 25 minutes or until a wooden pick inserted in the center comes out clean. Remove from pan.

Makes 18 muffins.

Pecan Peach Muffins Ⓓ

1½ cups all-purpose flour
½ cup sugar
2 teaspoons baking powder
1 teaspoon cinnamon
¼ teaspoon salt
½ cup butter or margarine, melted (8 tablespoons)

¼ cup milk
1 egg
2 medium peaches, peeled and diced (1 cup)
Topping (recipe below)

Preheat oven to 400 degrees.

Combine flour, sugar, baking powder, cinnamon and salt in a large bowl. In a small bowl, mix together butter, milk and egg until blended. Pour milk mixture into dry ingredients and stir until just moistened. Fold in peaches. Spoon batter into 12 paper-lined 2½-inch muffin cups. Sprinkle Topping over batter. Bake 20 to 25 minutes or until a wooden pick inserted in the center comes out clean. Remove from pan.

Topping
½ cup chopped pecans
½ cup brown sugar, packed
¼ cup all-purpose flour

1 teaspoon cinnamon
2 tablespoons butter or margarine, melted

Combine pecans, sugar, flour and cinnamon in a small bowl. Stir in butter until mixture is crumbly.

Makes 12 muffins.

Tex-Mex Pumpkin Corn Muffins

1 cup yellow cornmeal
1 cup all-purpose flour
2 tablespoons sugar
4 teaspoons baking powder
½ teaspoon salt
½ teaspoon chili powder
2 eggs

1 cup solid pack pumpkin
1 cup milk
2 tablespoons vegetable oil
1 cup (4 ounces) chopped green chiles
¾ cup shredded Cheddar cheese

Preheat oven to 400 degrees.

In a large bowl, combine cornmeal, flour, sugar, baking powder, salt and chili powder.

In a small bowl, beat eggs. Mix in pumpkin, milk, oil and chiles. Add pumpkin mixture to dry ingredients and stir until just moistened.

Spoon batter into 18 greased or paper-lined 2½-inch muffin cups. Sprinkle cheese on top. Bake 20 to 25 minutes or until a wooden pick inserted in the center comes out clean. Remove from pan and serve warm.

Makes 18 muffins.

Chocolate Chip Pumpkin Bread

1 can (16 ounces) pumpkin
2 cups sugar
2 eggs
1 cup vegetable oil
3 cups flour
2 teaspoons cinnamon

1 teaspoon salt
1 teaspoon baking soda
1 teaspoon baking powder
½ teaspoon nutmeg
1 package (12 ounces) chocolate chips

Preheat oven to 350 degrees.

Combine pumpkin, sugar and eggs. Mix in oil. Stir in flour, cinnamon, salt, baking soda, baking powder, nutmeg and chocolate chips. Mix thoroughly to blend. Pour batter into 2 greased 9 x 5-inch loaf pans. Bake 1 hour or until a wooden pick comes out clean.

Makes 2 loaves.

Pineapple-Zucchini Bread

3	eggs	3	cups flour
2	cups sugar	3	teaspoons baking soda
1	cup cooking oil	½	teaspoon cinnamon
2	teaspoons vanilla	1	teaspoon salt
2	cups coarsely shredded zucchini	½	teaspoon baking powder
		¼	teaspoon nutmeg
1	can (8 ounces) crushed pineapple, drained	1	cup chopped walnuts
		1	cup raisins

Preheat oven to 350 degrees.

Beat together eggs, sugar, oil and vanilla. Add zucchini and pineapple and mix well.

In a separate bowl, combine flour, baking soda, cinnamon, salt, baking powder and nutmeg. Mix in walnuts and raisins. Blend dry ingredients into egg mixture. Divide batter between 2 greased 9 x 5-inch loaf pans. Bake 1 hour.

Makes 2 loaves.

You can make the following healthy variations with very nice results:

1   cup applesauce for the oil
1   cup egg substitute for 3 eggs
    Reduce sugar by ¼ cup

Zucchini-Cheddar Bread

Nice to serve with soup and salad.

3	cups flour	¼	cup chopped scallions
4	teaspoons baking powder	3	tablespoons chopped fresh parsley
½	teaspoon baking soda		
1	teaspoon salt	1	tablespoon snipped fresh dill
1	cup coarsely shredded zucchini	2	eggs
¾	cup shredded sharp Cheddar cheese	1	cup buttermilk
		4	tablespoons butter, melted

Preheat oven to 350 degrees.

Whisk together flour, baking powder, baking soda and salt in a large bowl. Add zucchini, cheese, scallions, parsley and dill and toss to separate and coat.

In a separate bowl, beat together eggs, buttermilk and butter. Add to flour mixture and stir until just moistened; do not over mix. Pour batter into a greased 9 x 5-inch loaf pan. Bake in center of oven for 55 to 60 minutes or until a pick inserted in the center comes out clean.

Makes 1 loaf.

Mushroom-Spinach Frittata

2	tablespoons oil	2	tablespoons freshly grated Parmesan cheese
2	tablespoons butter or margarine	1	tablespoon dried parsley, or 3 tablespoons fresh
½	pound mushrooms, sliced	¾	teaspoon salt
½	cup minced onion	½	teaspoon oregano
1	cup chopped spinach, cooked and drained	¼	teaspoon pepper
6	eggs	1	tablespoon butter or margarine

Heat oil and 2 tablespoons butter in a medium skillet. Add mushrooms and onion and cook until mushrooms are lightly browned. Stir in spinach. Set aside.

Beat eggs in a bowl. Mix in Parmesan cheese, parsley, salt, oregano and pepper. Blend well.

Heat 1 tablespoon butter in a large skillet over high heat. Pour egg mixture into hot skillet and cook until egg begins to set. Top with mushroom mixture and cook until almost firm. Transfer skillet to hot broiler and cook until top of omelet is browned. Slide onto a large serving plate. Cut into wedges and serve immediately.

Serves 6.

Need to clean up a broken egg? Cover generously with salt and allow to set 5 minutes, then scrape up with a spatula (or call your dog!).

Greek Scrambled Eggs

Scrambled eggs take on a Middle Eastern flair when topped with feta cheese and Greek olives.

12	eggs	6-8	ounces feta cheese
¼	cup water	1	medium tomato, diced
¾	teaspoon dried oregano	¼	cup chopped fresh parsley
⅛	teaspoon black pepper	10-12	whole Greek or pitted black olives
2	tablespoons butter or margarine		

Beat together eggs, water, oregano and pepper in a large bowl. Melt butter in a 12- to 14-inch skillet over low heat. Pour in egg mixture. As mixture sets, push aside cooked egg with a wide spatula allowing the uncooked portion to flow to bottom of pan. Cook until eggs are just softly set.

Break cheese into about ½-inch chunks and sprinkle evenly over eggs. Place skillet 4 to 6 inches under broiler and cook 1 to 2 minutes or just until cheese gets hot. Sprinkle evenly with tomato and parsley. Garnish with olives. Cut into wedges and serve.

Serves 6.

Huevos Rancheros (Mexican Eggs) Ⓓ

A terrific dish to serve for brunch. The key is to have all the ingredients ready before frying the eggs and to heat the tortillas at the last minute.

Do not freeze cheese, as it becomes mealy.

12	corn tortillas (7 to 8 inches)
2	tablespoons olive oil
6	eggs
3	cups finely shredded iceberg lettuce
	Black Beans (recipe follows)
	Canned chunky tomato salsa, heated
	Canned green tomatillo salsa, heated

1½	cups shredded mild Cheddar cheese (6 ounces)
6	tablespoons packed crumbled cotija or feta cheese
	Sliced avocado (optional)
	Thinly sliced fresh jalapeños (optional)
	Sour cream (optional)
2	limes, cut into wedges
	Salt to taste

Preheat oven to 375 degrees.

Stack tortillas, seal in foil and heat in oven 10 minutes or until hot. (Do this near end of the following preparation.)

Heat oil over medium heat in a 12-inch nonstick skillet. Break eggs into pan, slightly apart. Cover and cook 3 minutes or just until whites are almost firm and yolks are still soft.

Meanwhile, spread ½ cup lettuce on each of 6 serving plates. Lay a tortilla on lettuce on each plate. Spoon Black Beans over tortillas. With a wide spatula, transfer an egg onto each serving. Spoon tomato salsa around one side of the egg and green salsa around the other side. Sprinkle with cheeses. Garnish with avocado, jalapeños, sour cream and lime wedges and season with salt. Enclose remaining tortillas in a linen napkin to keep warm and serve along side.

Black Beans

3	tablespoons olive oil
2	cloves garlic, minced or pressed
1	onion, chopped

2	cans (15 ounces each) black beans, rinsed and drained
1	cup vegetable broth

Heat oil over medium-high heat in a 10- to 12-inch skillet. Add garlic and onion and sauté 3 minutes or until onion is limp. Add beans and broth. Cook, stirring often, for 5 to 7 minutes or until most of liquid evaporates; do not allow to dry out.

Serves 6.

Canned diced green chiles can be added to the green salsa.

Cranberry/Apple French Toast Ⓓ

Refrigerate overnight and bake in the morning.

¾ cup brown sugar
⅓ cup butter, melted
1 teaspoon cinnamon
3-4 tart Granny Smith or Pippin
    apples, peeled and thinly
    sliced
½ cup dried cranberries

¾-1 loaf French or Italian bread,
    cut into 1-inch slices
7-8 eggs, or equivalent egg
    substitute (enough to
    completely cover bread)
1¾ cups whole milk
1 tablespoon vanilla
2 teaspoons cinnamon

*For a change of pace,
use raisin bread for
French Toast.*

Preheat oven to 375 degrees.

Combine brown sugar, butter and 1 teaspoon cinnamon in a greased 13 x 9-inch baking dish. Add apple slices and cranberries and toss well. Spread apple mixture evenly over the bottom of the dish. Arrange bread snugly on top.

Mix together eggs, milk, vanilla and 2 teaspoons cinnamon until well blended. Pour mixture over bread, soaking bread completely. Cover with foil and refrigerate overnight.

Bake, covered, for 40 minutes. Uncover and bake 5 minutes longer. Remove from oven and let stand 5 minutes. Loosen edges and invert onto a large serving platter.

Serves 12.

Cottage Cheese Pancakes Ⓓ

1 cup cottage cheese
3 eggs
1 tablespoon oil

2 tablespoons flour
½ teaspoon salt

Place all ingredients in a blender or food processor and process until well blended. Grease a griddle and preheat to high heat (400 degrees). Drop batter, about 1 tablespoon at a time, onto hot griddle. Flip and remove when fully cooked, repeating until all batter is used. Serve with sour cream and strawberry preserves.

Makes 10 pancakes.

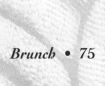

Puffed Pancake with Strawberries or Apples ⒟

It is so beautiful that you will want to serve it for a company brunch.

Batter

6	eggs	½	cup sugar
1	cup milk	1	cup all-purpose flour
¼	cup orange-flavored liqueur or orange juice	⅓	teaspoon salt
		½	cup butter or margarine

Strawberry Sauce

2	packages (10 ounces each) frozen strawberries in light syrup	2	tablespoons orange-flavored liqueur or orange juice
			Confectioners' sugar (optional)
			Sour cream (optional)

Preheat oven to 425 degrees.

In a blender or a large bowl, mix eggs, milk, liqueur, sugar, flour and salt until blended. If using a mixer, batter will be lumpy. Melt butter in a 13 x 9-inch baking dish in oven until it sizzles. Do not let the butter brown. Remove from oven and immediately pour batter into sizzling butter. Bake in center of oven for 20 minutes or until puffed and brown.

While pancake bakes, prepare strawberry sauce. Heat strawberries in a small saucepan until hot. Stir in liqueur. Serve warm.

When done baking, remove pancake from oven. Sprinkle with confectioners' sugar. Pancake falls quickly, so serve immediately with warm strawberry sauce and sour cream.

Serves 6 to 8.

For an apple variation, omit the strawberry sauce. Sauté 2 peeled and thinly sliced apples in 2 tablespoons butter or margarine with 2 to 3 tablespoons brown sugar. Omit confectioners' sugar. Serve apples over pancake while hot.

Blintz Soufflé in 3 Layers Ⓓ

The taste of fresh blintzes made easy.

Batter

4	eggs (no substitutions)	1⅓	cups flour
1¼	cups milk	1-2	tablespoons sugar
2	tablespoons sour cream	1¼	teaspoons baking powder
4	tablespoons butter, melted	1-1½	teaspoons lemon zest
¾	teaspoon vanilla		

Cheese Filling

2	packages (8 ounces each) farmer cheese	2-3	tablespoons sugar
1	pound ricotta cheese	2	tablespoons fresh lemon juice
2	eggs or ½ cup egg substitute		Fresh strawberries or blueberries (optional)

Preheat oven to 350 degrees.

Combine all batter ingredients in a food processor or blender and blend until smooth. Pour 1½ cups batter into a greased 13 x 9-inch baking dish; set remaining batter aside. Bake 10 minutes or until set. Remove from oven.

Meanwhile, combine all filling ingredients. Spread filling over baked batter. Stir remaining batter and spread carefully over filling so filling is completely covered. Carefully return to oven and bake 35 to 40 minutes or until puffed. Remove from oven and let stand 10 minutes before serving. Serve plain or with berries.

Serves 8 to 10.

Frozen Blintz Soufflé Ⓓ

Using frozen blintzes makes this delicious brunch dish so easy to prepare.

1	cup butter or margarine	2	teaspoons vanilla
12	cheese or fruit blintzes	¼	cup sugar
1-1½	cups sour cream	¼	cup orange juice
4-6	eggs		Cinnamon

Preheat oven to 350 degrees.

Melt butter in a 13 x 9-inch baking dish. Lay blintzes over butter in dish. Bake until browned.

Mix sour cream, eggs, vanilla, sugar and orange juice with an electric mixer. Pour mixture over blintzes and sprinkle with cinnamon. Bake 45 to 60 minutes or until set.

Serves 6 to 8.

Breakfast Burritos

2	tablespoons butter	6	medium flour tortillas
4	cups sliced mushrooms	2	cups Green Chile Sauce
3	bunches fresh spinach,		(recipe below)
	washed, dried, stemmed	2	cups shredded Monterey
	and chopped		Jack cheese

Preheat oven to 450 degrees.

Melt butter over medium heat in a large skillet. Add mushrooms and sauté 2 to 3 minutes or until tender. Add spinach and sauté until leaves are hot. Divide spinach mixture into 6 equal parts and spread over each tortilla. Roll tortillas up tightly and place, seam side down, in a greased baking dish. Cover burritos with Green Chile Sauce and sprinkle cheese on top.

Bake 5 minutes or until cheese is melted.

Green Chile Sauce

5	cans (7 ounces each) diced	1	clove garlic, minced
	mild green chiles,	3	cups water
	undrained		Salt to taste
2	cans (7 ounces each) diced	½	cup vegetable oil
	hot green chiles, undrained	½	cup flour

Combine all chiles, garlic, water and salt in a medium saucepan. Bring to a boil and remove from heat. Heat oil in a small saucepan over medium heat. Gradually blend in flour, stirring constantly, to form a paste. Reheat chile mixture to a simmer. Slowly blend flour paste into chile mixture, stirring constantly. Add more water, if necessary.

Serves 6, makes 4 cups sauce.

Artichoke Enchiladas

Since the artichoke capital of the world is in Castroville, California, and so many of our cooks have been influenced by Mexican cooking, here is an absolute winner that you will love.

1	can (14 ounces) artichoke bottoms, chopped	2-3	cloves garlic minced
3	cloves garlic, minced	½	pound Monterey Jack cheese, shredded
1	tablespoon olive oil	1	red bell pepper, finely diced
1½	tablespoons olive oil		
1	bunch or bag fresh spinach, washed, dried, and chopped, 3 tablespoons reserved for garnish	1	bunch scallions, chopped
		1	can (32 ounces) green enchilada sauce
3	portobello mushrooms, sliced, then cut into 1-inch pieces	10-12	flour tortillas (fajita size)

Preheat oven to 350 degrees.

Sauté artichokes and 3 cloves minced garlic in 1 tablespoon olive oil in a skillet until almost tender. Drain, remove and set aside. Add 1½ tablespoons olive oil to skillet. Add spinach, mushrooms and 2 to 3 cloves minced garlic and sauté.

In a small bowl, combine cheese, bell pepper and scallions. Set aside one-third of cheese mixture and 3 tablespoons cooked spinach mixture. Mix remaining cheese mixture with sautéed artichokes and spinach mixtures. Set aside.

Heat each tortilla over a flame on both sides until it puffs and has charred spots. Dip tortillas, one at a time, in enchilada sauce and stack on a plate. Spoon about 2 heaping tablespoons of cheese/vegetable mixture onto each tortilla. Sprinkle reserved cheese mixture on top and add 1½ tablespoons green enchilada sauce to each. Roll filled tortillas and place, seam side down, in a greased 13 x 9-inch baking dish. Pour remaining sauce over enchiladas. Scatter remaining cheese and reserved cooked spinach on top.

Bake 25 to 35 minutes or until sauce bubbles and cheese is completely melted. Near end of baking time, garnish with small dollops of raw chopped spinach.

Makes 10 to 12 enchiladas.

Chili Rellenos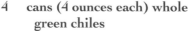

4	cans (4 ounces each) whole green chiles	¼	cup flour
		2	cups evaporated milk
¾-1	pound Monterey Jack cheese, shredded	4	eggs
		1	cup tomato sauce
¾-1	pound Cheddar cheese, shredded		

Preheat oven to 350 degrees.

Use about half of chiles to layer the bottom of a greased 13 x 9-inch baking dish. Evenly sprinkle cheeses over chiles. Lattice remaining chiles over cheese.

Mix flour, milk and eggs with a blender until smooth. Pour mixture over chiles and cheese.

Bake, uncovered, for 30 minutes. Pour tomato sauce over top and bake 15 minutes longer.

Serves 6.

Garden Zucchini Pie

1	egg, beaten	1	tablespoon margarine or butter
¼	cup finely chopped onion		
¼	cup Parmesan cheese	3	eggs, beaten
3	cups refrigerated loose-pack hash browns	¾	cup shredded Swiss cheese
		½	cup milk
2	medium zucchini, thinly sliced	½	teaspoon dried oregano, crushed
1	clove garlic, minced	¼	teaspoon salt
		¼	teaspoon pepper

Preheat oven to 400 degrees.

Combine 1 egg, onion, and Parmesan cheese in a large bowl. Stir in hash browns. Pat mixture into the bottom and up the sides of a greased 9-inch pie plate or 10-inch quiche dish. Bake, uncovered, for 35 to 40 minutes or until golden. Cool on a wire rack.

In a large skillet, sauté zucchini and garlic in margarine until zucchini is crisp-tender. Cool slightly. Arrange zucchini mixture over hash brown crust.

In a small mixing bowl, combine 3 eggs, Swiss cheese, milk, oregano, salt and pepper. Pour mixture over zucchini. Bake at 350 degrees for 25 to 30 minutes or until filling appears set when gently shaken. Let stand 10 minutes before serving.

Serves 8.

Kasha Breakfast Pudding Ⓓ

Surprise your family with a healthy fruity kasha pudding.

4½	cups milk	2	Granny Smith apples, peeled and cut into ½-inch dice
¾	cup kasha, whole or medium	¾	cup raisins
2	tablespoons brown sugar	3	tablespoons unsalted butter
1½	teaspoons cinnamon	3	eggs, beaten
½	teaspoon ground ginger	2	cups chopped walnuts
¾	teaspoon ground nutmeg	¼	cup brown sugar
¼	teaspoon salt		Yogurt

Preheat oven to 375 degrees.

Combine milk, kasha, 2 tablespoons brown sugar, cinnamon, ginger, nutmeg and salt in a medium saucepan. Bring slowly to a boil over medium heat, stirring occasionally. Simmer 1 minute. Remove from heat. Add apples, raisins and butter. Temper eggs by whisking about 1 cup of hot pudding into beaten eggs, then slowly whisk warmed eggs into pudding.

Pour pudding into a greased 2-quart casserole dish. Combine walnuts and ¼ cup brown sugar and sprinkle over pudding. Bake 45 minutes or until top is firm. If nuts begin to darken before the pudding is done, cover lightly with foil. Serve warm, either plain or with a dollop of yogurt.

Serves 6.

Kasha pudding can also be baked in individual portions. Fill 5 or 6 greased 8-ounce ramekins three-fourths full and sprinkle with walnuts and brown sugar. Place ramekins in a pan with enough water to reach halfway up the sides. Baking time may be slightly less; the tops should be firm.

Spring Vegetable Quiche Ⓓ

4	eggs	1	package spring vegetable or vegetable soup mix
1½	cups milk	1	frozen deep-dish pie crust (9 inches), unbaked
1	cup (4 ounces) shredded Swiss/Pepper Jack cheese		
1	package (10 ounces) frozen chopped spinach, thawed and squeezed dry		

Preheat oven to 350 degrees.

Place a baking sheet in oven while oven heats.

In a large bowl, lightly beat eggs with a wire whisk. Blend in milk, cheese, spinach and soup mix. Pour mixture into pie crust. Bake on baking sheet 50 minutes or until done.

Serves 6.

Artichoke Pie Ⓓ

1 tablespoon olive oil
1 clove garlic, minced
2 cans (6 ounces each) artichoke hearts, drained
½ cup Italian seasoned bread crumbs
¼ cup freshly grated Parmesan cheese
1 pie crust (9 inch), unbaked
3 eggs, beaten
¼ cup freshly grated Parmesan cheese
1 package (8 ounces) shredded mozzarella cheese

Preheat oven to 350 degrees.

Heat oil in a large skillet over medium heat. Add garlic and sauté until it starts to brown. Stir in artichoke hearts and cook 10 minutes. Stir in bread crumbs and ¼ cup Parmesan cheese. Cook until heated through.

Spread half of artichoke mixture to pie crust. Pour eggs over top and sprinkle with ¼ cup Parmesan cheese. Spoon remaining artichoke mixture into pie and top with mozzarella cheese. Bake 45 minutes or until crust begins to brown.

Makes 6 to 8 main course servings, 16 appetizers.

Spinach Pie (Spanakopita) Ⓓ

This is a classic Greek side dish served for holidays and special occasions.

3 scallions, chopped
2 tablespoons butter
5 eggs, beaten
3 packages (10 ounces each) frozen chopped spinach, thawed and pressed dry
1½ cups feta cheese, crumbled
½ cup cottage cheese
16 sheets phyllo dough
14 tablespoons butter, melted

Preheat oven to 350 degrees.

Sauté scallions in 2 tablespoons butter. Mix sautéed scallions with eggs, spinach, feta and cottage cheese.

Brush 8 sheets phyllo dough with melted butter and stack in a greased 13 x 9-inch baking dish. Spoon spinach mixture over phyllo sheets. Brush remaining phyllo dough with melted butter and layer sheets over spinach mixture. Brush top of dough sheets well with melted butter. Tuck top layer of dough sheets attractively into dish.

Bake 1 hour, 15 minutes or until crust is crisp and golden brown. Cut into squares or diamond shapes. Serve hot or at room temperature. Freezes well.

Makes 24 pieces.

Squash "Strudel" Squares ⓓ

Great for "break-the-fast meal".

5	cups (1½ pounds) coarsely shredded zucchini	1	tablespoon finely chopped onion, or ½ teaspoon dried flakes
5	cups (1½ pounds) coarsely shredded yellow squash	1	tablespoon snipped fresh dill, or ½ teaspoon dried
½	teaspoon salt	¼	teaspoon pepper
8	eggs, beaten	8	ounces crumbled feta cheese
2	tablespoons snipped fresh parsley, or 2 teaspoons dried	5	sheets frozen phyllo dough, thawed
2	cloves garlic, minced	4	tablespoons margarine or butter, melted

Preheat oven to 350 degrees.

Combine zucchini, summer squash and salt in a large mixing bowl. Let stand 15 minutes. Transfer mixture to a colander and squeeze to drain. In the same bowl, combine eggs, parsley, garlic, onion, dill and pepper. Stir in drained squash mixture and feta cheese. Spoon batter into an ungreased 13 x 9-inch baking pan.

Cut phyllo dough sheets in half crosswise. Lightly brush a sheet of phyllo with some of margarine and place over squash mixture. Top with another sheet of phyllo. Brush this sheet with margarine. Add remaining phyllo sheets, brushing each with margarine. With a sharp knife, score through phyllo, making 16 squares.

Bake 50 to 55 minutes or until a knife inserted near the center comes out clean. To prevent overbrowning, cover strudel with foil for the last 10 minutes of baking. Let strudel stand 10 minutes before serving.

Serves 16.

Zucchini Lasagna Ⓓ

A unique lasagna – NO NOODLES!

4 large zucchini	8 ounces mozzarella cheese, thinly sliced
½ cup chopped onion	8 ounces ricotta cheese, crumbled
2 cloves garlic, minced	1 jar (32-ounces) marinara sauce
2 tablespoons olive oil	½ cup Parmesan cheese
4 ounces fresh mushrooms, thinly sliced	

Preheat oven to 350 degrees.

Sauté zucchini, onion and garlic in olive oil until tender. Add mushrooms and cook another 1 to 2 minutes. Layer half the zucchini mixture in an 11 x 7-inch baking dish. Top with layers using half of mozzarella and ricotta cheeses. Repeat zucchini and cheese layers. Pour marinara on top and sprinkle with Parmesan cheese. Bake 30 minutes.

Makes 5 to 6 servings.

Macaroni and Cheese Ⓓ

6 slices crustless French bread, torn into ¼-inch pieces	¼ teaspoon cayenne pepper, or to taste
1 stick unsalted butter, divided	4½ cups shredded sharp white Cheddar cheese (about 18 ounces), divided
5½ cups milk	
½ cup flour	
1½ teaspoons salt	2 cups shredded Gruyère cheese (about 8 ounces), or 1¼ cups Pecornio Romano cheese (5 ounces), divided
¼ teaspoon nutmeg	
¼ teaspoon freshly ground white pepper	
	1 pound dry elbow macaroni

Preheat oven to 375 degrees.

Place bread in a medium bowl. In a small saucepan over medium heat, melt 2 tablespoons butter. Pour butter over bread and toss; set bread crumbs aside.

Heat milk in a medium saucepan over medium heat. Melt remaining 6 tablespoons butter in a deep skillet over medium heat. When butter bubbles, add flour and cook, whisking, for 1 minute. While whisking, slowly pour in hot milk. Continue to cook, whisking constantly, until mixture bubbles and becomes thick. Remove pan from heat. Stir in salt, nutmeg, white and cayenne peppers, 3 cups Cheddar cheese and 1½ cups Gruyère or 1 cup Pecorino Romano cheese. Set cheese sauce aside.

Cook macaroni in a large saucepan of boiling water until barely al dente. Drain and rinse in a colander under cold water, drain again. Stir macaroni into cheese sauce. Pour macaroni mixture into a greased 3-quart casserole dish. Sprinkle with remaining Cheddar and Gruyère or Pecorino Romano cheese. Top with bread crumbs. Bake 30 minutes or until browned on top.

Makes 12 servings.

Poultry

Poultry

Barbecued Pacific Rim Chicken

2	tablespoons minced garlic		1	teaspoon fresh ground pepper
2	tablespoons soy sauce			
2	tablespoons maple syrup		6	boneless, skinless chicken
2	tablespoons rice vinegar			breast halves (about 5
1	tablespoon salad oil			ounces each)
1	tablespoon Asian sesame oil			Mango Sauce (recipe below)
1	tablespoon minced fresh			Mint springs
	ginger			Salt to taste

In a 1-gallon plastic food bag, mix garlic, soy sauce, maple syrup, vinegar, salad oil, sesame oil, ginger, pepper and chicken. Seal bag and turn to coat meat. Chill at least 30 minutes, or up to 2 hours, turning bag occasionally.

Preheat barbecue grill to medium-hot. Grease hot grill with oil.

Place chicken on grill, reserving marinade. Cook chicken, turning occasionally to evenly brown, for 10 to 12 minutes or until no longer pink in center of thickest part. Baste chicken often during first 5 minutes of cooking with marinade. Discard remaining marinade.

Spoon Mango Sauce equally onto serving plates. Set a chicken breast half in sauce on each plate. Garnish with mint and season with salt.

Mango Sauce

1	firm, ripe mango (1 pound), pitted, peeled and chopped		1	tablespoon tamarind paste (available at large supermarkets or Asian grocery stores)
¾	cup water			
½	cup ketchup			
⅓	cup soy sauce		2	teaspoons chili powder
¼	cup rice vinegar		2	teaspoons minced garlic
2	tablespoons packed brown sugar		1	teaspoon minced fresh ginger
			½	teaspoon cayenne pepper
			½	teaspoon fresh ground pepper

In a 2- or 3-quart saucepan, combine all sauce ingredients. Bring to a boil over medium-high heat. Reduce heat and simmer, stirring occasionally, for 25 minutes or until reduced to 2 cups. Pour mixture into a blender or food processor and whirl until smooth. Serve warm. If making up to 2 days ahead, cool, then chill in an airtight container; reheat until steaming.

Serves 6, makes 2 cups sauce.

Serve chicken and sauce with steamed rice and stir-fried vegetables.

Stir-fry Chinese pea pods and baby peas together for a novel presentation.

Cut branches of rosemary about 6 inches long. Strip leaves and soak twigs in water for about 30 minutes. Skewer lamb, beef or chicken pieces on the bare twig. The rosemary flavor will permeate the meat while barbecuing.

A hint from a world-renowned chef about poultry: for a richer flavored chicken, season and refrigerate 24 hours before roasting.

Sautéed Chicken Breasts with Apricots

½	pound dried apricots	½	cup chicken broth
⅓	cup bourbon	1	shallot, finely chopped
¼	cup chicken broth	1	teaspoon tomato paste
2	teaspoons safflower oil	2	teaspoons grainy mustard
2	whole chicken breasts (1 pound each), boned, skinned and halved	¼	cup pecans, toasted and crushed with a rolling pin
¼	teaspoon salt Freshly ground black pepper	1	scallion, cut into 2-inch pieces and thinly sliced lengthwise

Marinate apricots in bourbon and ¼ cup broth for 8 hours or overnight; or, bring bourbon and ¼ cup broth to a boil, turn off heat and steep apricots in liquid 10 minutes or until softened.

Heat oil in a heavy 10- to 12-inch skillet over medium-high heat. Sauté chicken breasts on 1 side for 4 minutes or until lightly colored. Turn and sprinkle with salt and pepper. Sauté on second side for 4 minutes.

Drain apricots and pour marinade over chicken in skillet. Add ½ cup broth to skillet, reduce heat to low and cook 5 minutes or until chicken feels firm but springy to the touch. Transfer chicken to a plate and cover with foil to keep warm.

Add apricots and shallot to the skillet. Simmer 2 minutes. Stir in tomato paste and mustard and simmer 3 minutes, stirring occasionally. Return chicken to skillet and cook 1 minute or until heated through.

Arrange chicken and apricots on a warmed serving platter. Spoon sauce over the chicken and sprinkle with pecans and scallion.

Serves 4.

To toast pecans, bake in 350 degree oven for 5 minutes.

Chicken with Balsamic Vinegar Ⓜ

Served at room temperature.

4	whole chicken breasts, skinned, boned, halved and trimmed of fat
	Coarse salt and freshly ground black pepper to taste
½	cup fruity white wine or water
¼	cup, plus 3 tablespoons balsamic vinegar

⅔	cup fruity olive oil
4	sprigs fresh tarragon, or 1 teaspoon dried, crumbled
	Zest of 1 small lemon
¼	cup raisins, plumped in hot water for 15 minutes and drained
	Arugula or baby spinach leaves for garnish

Preheat oven to 375 degrees.

Slightly flatten chicken breasts with palm of hand. Place in a lightly greased shallow roasting pan. Lightly season with salt and pepper. Add wine to pan and cover lightly with greased parchment paper or wax paper, cut to just fit in pan. Bake 20 minutes or until cooked though. Cool chicken in pan.

Whisk together vinegar and olive oil in a bowl. Add tarragon, lemon zest and drained raisins. Arrange chicken breasts in a single layer in a shallow dish just large enough to hold them. Pour vinegar dressing over chicken. Cover with plastic wrap and marinate in refrigerator at least 12 hours, turning chicken occasionally.

Before serving, return to room temperature. Garnish individual plates or a serving platter with arugula and arrange chicken on arugula. Sprinkle raisins and lemon zest over chicken and drizzle with some of marinade.

Serves 4 to 6.

Balsamic vinegar is made in Modena, Italy, according to ancient, secret recipes. Because of its full-bodied taste, it is often used with meats in place of meat stock. Here it is paired with the delicate flavor of the chicken. Serve on arugula leaves; their pungency adds to the intriguing blend of flavors. If arugula is not available, baby spinach leaves will work very well.

Flavorful Roast Chicken Ⓜ

1	roasting chicken (7- to 8-pounds), washed and patted dry
⅓	cup olive oil

⅓	cup whole grain Dijon mustard
2	tablespoons chopped fresh rosemary
	Salt and pepper to taste

Preheat oven to 375 degrees.

Place chicken in a roasting pan. Combine olive oil, mustard, rosemary and salt and pepper in a bowl and whisk well. Brush mixture over entire chicken. Roast 1½ to 1¾ hours or until golden brown. Carve and serve.

Makes 6 to 8 servings.

To get a crisp, golden skin on roasted chicken, rub the bird all over with mayonnaise before roasting.

Super Bowl White Chicken Chili Ⓜ

This is a lighter, healthier version of chili.

¼ cup all-purpose flour	2 cans (15 to 16 ounces each) white kidney beans, drained and rinsed
½ teaspoon salt	
1½ pounds boneless, skinless chicken breasts, cut into 1-inch cubes	1 can (14½ ounces) chicken broth
2½ tablespoons olive oil	1 bottle (12 ounces) beer
1½ cups chopped onion	2½ teaspoons chili powder
1½ cups diced yellow bell pepper	1½ teaspoons ground cumin
3 jalapeño chiles, seeded and minced	¾ pound fresh plum tomatoes, diced
1 tablespoon minced garlic	1 tablespoon peanut butter
	1 tablespoon fresh lime juice
	½ cup chopped fresh cilantro

Combine flour, ½ teaspoon salt and chicken in a 1-gallon size plastic storage bag. Transfer chicken to a large sieve and shake to remove excess flour.

In a 6-quart nonstick Dutch oven, heat 1½ teaspoons oil. Add chicken in 3 batches and sauté 3 minutes per batch or until cooked through. Add 1½ teaspoons oil to Dutch oven for each batch. Set aside cooked batches in a bowl until all chicken is cooked.

Add remaining oil to same pot. Add onion, bell pepper, jalapeño and garlic and sauté 5 minutes or until tender, but not browned. Reduce heat to low. Add beans, broth, beer, chili powder, cumin, tomatoes, peanut butter and lime juice. Cook 20 to 30 minutes or until flavors are blended. Garnish individual servings with cilantro.

Can be easily doubled or tripled.

Serves 4.

Bake potatoes and spoon chili over the top.

Southwest Chicken with Chipotles and Lime Ⓜ

9   large boneless, skinless chicken thighs, fat trimmed, meat cut into ½-inch pieces

1½ tablespoons fresh lime juice

1½ teaspoons crushed chipotle chiles (available in spice section of supermarkets)

    Salt and pepper to taste

4   teaspoons olive oil

9   scallions, white and pale green parts only, thinly sliced

1   cup chicken broth

1½ tablespoons fresh lime juice

2   teaspoons olive oil

6   radishes, thinly sliced

1   tablespoon fresh lime juice

2   tablespoons chopped fresh cilantro

    Lime wedges

12 corn tortillas, heated

Combine chicken, 1½ tablespoons lime juice and crushed chipotles in a large bowl. Sprinkle with salt and pepper and toss to blend. Let stand 10 minutes.

Heat 4 teaspoons oil in a large nonstick skillet over high heat. Add chicken mixture and sauté 3 minutes. Stir in scallions and broth. Cover and cook 3 minutes. Uncover and cook and stir 2 minutes longer or until chicken is cooked through and most of liquid evaporates. Stir in 1½ tablespoons lime juice and season with salt and pepper. Transfer to a bowl and cover to keep warm.

Heat 2 teaspoons oil in same skillet over high heat. Add radishes and sauté 1 minute. Stir in 1 tablespoon lime juice and season with salt and pepper. Add radishes and cilantro to bowl with chicken and toss to blend.

Divide chicken mixture among 6 plates. Garnish with lime wedges and serve hot tortillas alongside.

Serves 6.

Sticky Coconut Chicken

This recipe uses Southeast Asian ingredients with boneless chicken thighs. Marinate the meat for at least 1 hour and make the chili glaze well ahead of time.

6-8	boneless, skinless chicken thighs (1¼ to 1½ pounds total)	1	teaspoon fresh ground pepper
¾	cup canned coconut milk, stir before measuring	1	teaspoon hot chile flakes Chili Glaze (recipe below)
1	tablespoon minced fresh ginger	4-5	scallions, ends trimmed and cut lengthwise into thin slivers (including tops)

Rinse chicken and pat dry. In a large bowl, combine coconut milk, ginger, pepper and chile flakes. Add chicken and mix. Cover and chill at least 1 hour, or up to 1 day.

Preheat barbecue grill. Lightly oil grill.

Remove chicken from bowl, reserving marinade. Open chicken thighs and lay flat on grill. Close lid and cook, turning thighs as needed to brown on both sides, for 10 to 12 minutes or until meat is no longer pink in the center of thickest part. Baste frequently while cooking with reserved marinade, using all of it.

Transfer chicken to a warm platter. Pour Chili Glaze evenly over meat and garnish with scallions.

Chili Glaze

¾	cup rice vinegar	3	tablespoons soy sauce
½	cup sugar	1	teaspoon hot chile flakes

In a 2- to 3-quart saucepan, combine all glaze ingredients. Bring to a boil over high heat. Cook 8 to 10 minutes or until mixture is reduced to ½ cup. Use hot. If making glaze up to 1 week ahead, cover and chill; reheat before serving.

Serves 6 to 8, makes ½ cup sauce.

Cornish Game Hens with
Mustard Crust and Wild Rice Dressing

4	tablespoons margarine, melted	4	Cornish game hens (1¼ to 1½ pounds each), thawed if frozen
¼	cup Dijon mustard		Fresh rosemary sprigs (optional)
1	tablespoon minced fresh or crumbled dried rosemary		Salt and pepper to taste
2	cloves garlic, pressed or minced		

Wines that go with white meats, like veal or white meat poultry, chicken or game hens, are lighter style Pinot Noirs or red Burgundies, and rich and buttery Sauvignon Blancs from California.

Preheat oven to 450 degrees.

Combine margarine, mustard, rosemary and garlic; set aside.

Remove necks and giblets from game hens and discard or reserve for a different use. With a poultry shears or knife, split hens lengthwise along 1 side of backbone. Pull hens open and place skin-side up on a flat surface. Press firmly, cracking bones slightly until hens lie reasonably flat. Rinse hens and pat dry. Coat both sides with mustard mixture and set slightly apart in two 15 x 10-inch baking pans.

Bake 25 to 30 minutes or until meat is no longer pink at the thigh bone. Transfer to a platter or dinner plates. Garnish with rosemary sprigs and season with salt and pepper. Serve with Wild Rice Dressing.

Wild Rice Dressing

½	cup dry rice	4	ounces mushrooms, diced
1½	cups chicken broth	2	tablespoons chopped fresh parsley
¼	cup dry wild rice		
¾	cup chicken broth	½	teaspoon dried thyme
2	tablespoons margarine	1	egg, beaten
¼	cup diced onion		Salt and pepper to taste

Preheat oven to 350 degrees.

Place 1½ cups broth in a saucepan. Add plain rice and bring to a boil. Reduce heat and cover. Cook 20 minutes or until tender. To a separate saucepan, add ¾ cup broth and wild rice and cook until tender and until grains begin to burst.

Melt margarine in a skillet. Add onion and mushrooms and cook until just soft. Combine vegetables with both rices, parsley, thyme and egg. Season with salt and pepper. Toss to combine and transfer to a baking dish. Bake 30 minutes.

Serves 4.

Chicken Fajitas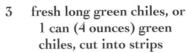

3	fresh long green chiles, or 1 can (4 ounces) green chiles, cut into strips	1	yellow or red bell pepper, thinly sliced
¼	teaspoon ground cumin	1	tablespoon fresh lime juice
¼	teaspoon dried oregano	½	teaspoon salt, or to taste
¼	teaspoon paprika	1	clove garlic, minced
¼	teaspoon chili powder	1	tablespoon minced fresh cilantro
¼	teaspoon sugar	1½	pounds boneless, skinless chicken, cut into strips
2	tablespoons vegetable oil		
1	onion, sliced		

Condiments

Guacamole, store bought or home made (recipe below)

Pico de Gallo, store bought or home made (recipe below)

Shredded lettuce

California black beans

Steamed tortillas, without lard

If using fresh chiles, roast by charring chiles over an open flame, holding with a long-handed fork and turning frequently, for 2 to 3 minutes or until skins are blackened. Or place fresh chiles on a broiling pan and broil 2 inches from the heat source, turning frequently, for 15 minutes or until skins blackens. Transfer chiles to a plastic bag. Seal tightly and allow to steam until cool enough to handle. Wash, peel, seed and cut chiles into thin strips.

Combine cumin, oregano, paprika, chili powder and sugar in a small bowl; set aside. Heat oil in a 12-inch skillet over low heat. Add onion, bell pepper, lime juice, salt and chiles. Sauté 10 minutes or until vegetables are tender. Add garlic and cilantro and continue to sauté 2 minutes. Increase to high heat. Add chicken to vegetable mixture and sauté until chicken is lightly browned. Season to taste with salt. Serve with assorted condiments.

Serves 4.

Guacamole

2	medium-size ripe avocados, peeled and pitted (1 pit reserved)	⅓	cup thinly sliced scallions (use white and 3 inches of green parts)
2	tablespoons fresh lime juice	⅛	teaspoon ground cumin
1	clove garlic, minced	⅛	teaspoon sugar
		1	ripe plum tomato, chopped Salt and pepper to taste

Mash avocado with lime juice and garlic in a small bowl using a fork until creamy. Add scallions, cumin, sugar and tomato. Season with salt and pepper and mix well. Place reserved avocado pit in the center of the guacamole and cover tightly to prevent darkening. Remove pit before serving. Guacamole is best served within 2 hours.

Pico de Gallo

6	ripe plum tomatoes, chopped	1	serrano chile, minced with seeds (remove seeds for a milder taste)
1	small onion, chopped		
1	tablespoon minced fresh cilantro	1	teaspoon fresh lime juice or vinegar
			Salt to taste

Combine tomatoes, onion, cilantro, chile and lime juice in a small bowl. Season with salt. Allow to stand 1 hour at room temperature for flavors to blend.

Lemon Chicken

This chicken has a crisp golden crust and the zing of fresh California lemons. You can serve this either hot or cold.

2	chickens (2½ pounds each), cut into quarters	1	teaspoon freshly ground black pepper
2	cups freshly squeezed lemon juice	½	cup corn or olive oil
2	cups flour	2	tablespoons lemon zest
2	teaspoons salt	¼	cup brown sugar
2	teaspoons paprika	¼	cup chicken broth
		1	teaspoon lemon extract
		2	lemons, sliced paper-thin

Preheat oven to 350 degrees.

Combine chicken pieces and lemon juice in a bowl just large enough to hold them comfortably. Cover and marinate in refrigerator overnight, turning occasionally. Drain chicken thoroughly and pat dry. Place flour, salt, paprika and pepper in a plastic bag. Shake to mix well. Add chicken, 2 pieces at a time, to bag and shake to coat chicken completely.

Heat oil in a skillet or cast iron Dutch oven until hot. Add chicken, a few pieces at a time, and fry 10 minutes or until well browned and crisp. Arrange browned chicken in a single layer in a shallow, large baking pan. Sprinkle evenly with lemon zest and sugar. Mix broth and lemon extract and pour around chicken pieces. Place a lemon slice on top of each piece of chicken. Bake 35 to 40 minutes or until tender.

Serves 6 to 8.

Add fresh lemon juice and capers to mayonnaise for a zesty sauce for grilled fish or poached chicken. You can also put a little prepared wasabi into the mayonnaise. It's great!

Greek Garlic Chicken

8	chicken leg/thigh quarters (about 5 pounds), or chicken breasts	2½	tablespoons dried oregano
⅔	cup minced garlic (about 3 heads)	2	tablespoons coarsely ground pepper
½	cup lemon juice	1-2	teaspoons salt
¼	cup olive oil	½	cup boiling water
		¼	cup chopped fresh parsley
			Parsley sprigs for garnish

Preheat oven to 375 degrees.

Rinse chicken, pat dry and discard lumps of fat. Place chicken in a 17-x 12-inch pan. In a bowl, mix garlic, lemon juice, oil, oregano, pepper and salt. Smear garlic mixture evenly over chicken. Arrange chicken, cut-side down, in a single layer.

Bake 1½ hours or until chicken skin is well browned. After baking 45 minutes, baste chicken every 10 to 15 minutes with pan juices. Transfer chicken to a warm serving platter. Skim off fat from pan drippings. Add ½ cup boiling water to pan and stir to loosen browned bits. Pour sauce into a bowl. Sprinkle chopped parsley over chicken and garnish with parsley sprigs. Add sauce to taste.

Serves 8.

To skin a tomato, dip tomato in boiling water for 30 seconds, then plunge in cold water.

Curried Peanut Chicken

4	pounds chicken, cut into serving pieces	1	green bell pepper, cut into strips
¼	cup oil	1	large tomato, skinned and sliced
2	teaspoons salt, or to taste		
1	tablespoon curry powder, or to taste	¼	cup crunchy peanut butter
1	large onion, sliced	¼	cup water

Brown chicken in oil in a skillet. Set chicken aside, reserving pan drippings. Stir salt and curry into pan drippings and cook and stir 1 minute. Add onion, bell pepper and tomato. Cover and simmer 5 minutes. Add chicken and simmer 30 minutes or until tender.

Remove skillet contents to a serving dish. Add peanut butter and water to skillet and stir until blended. Heat to a boil while stirring and pour over chicken.

Serves 6.

To prepare chicken in oven, pour the sauce over the chicken and bake 1 hour at 350 degrees, turning chicken halfway through.

Ginger Chicken

Cooking Sauce

3	tablespoons soy sauce	1	tablespoon brown sugar, firmly packed
3	tablespoons dry sherry		
3	tablespoons water	1½	teaspoons cornstarch

Stir-Fry

1	tablespoon olive or salad oil	1	pound boneless, skinless chicken breast, cut into bite-size pieces
1	pound yams, peeled and julienned		
1	small red onion, cut into 8 wedges and layers separated	2	tablespoons minced fresh gingerroot
1	tablespoon olive or salad oil	⅓	cup minced scallions

Combine all cooking sauce ingredients and stir until dissolved and smooth.

Heat a 10- to 12-inch skillet or a wok over medium heat. Add 1 tablespoon oil, yams and onion and stir-fry 5 minutes or until vegetables are just tender to bite. Spoon vegetables onto a platter and cover loosely to keep warm. Turn heat to high and add 1 tablespoon oil to skillet. When hot, add chicken and ginger and stir-fry 4 minutes or until chicken is no longer pink in the center. Add cooked vegetables and cooking sauce. Stir until sauce boils. Add scallions and return mixture to platter to serve.

Serves 4.

Chicken Scaloppine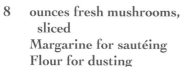

8	ounces fresh mushrooms, sliced	1	tablespoon flour
		¼	teaspoon dry mustard
	Margarine for sautéing	⅛	teaspoon black pepper (optional)
	Flour for dusting		
6	chicken breast halves	⅛	teaspoon onion powder
	Oil	1	cup chicken broth
1	tablespoon margarine	½	cup Chardonnay

Preheat oven to 350 degrees.

Sauté mushrooms in margarine; set aside. Lightly dust chicken breasts with flour and sauté in oil. Transfer sautéed chicken to a baking pan and set aside.

Melt 1 tablespoon margarine in a saucepan. Add 1 tablespoon flour and heat until bubbly. Add mustard, pepper and onion powder. Slowly add chicken broth and cook and stir until thickened. Add mushrooms. Pour sauce over chicken in pan. Drizzle wine over chicken and sauce. Cover and bake about 30 minutes. Uncover and bake until chicken is tender.

Serves 6.

For wonderfully
crisp breading,
refrigerate coated
food for 20 minutes
before cooking.

Chicken with
Green Beans, Sephardic Style 🌳

The aroma of the cinnamon and nutmeg cooking will attract people to your kitchen long before this delicious meal is ready to serve. Arrange over a bed of rice. This tastes better the next day.

2	pounds green beans		Juice of 1 lemon
2	onions, finely chopped	¾-1	teaspoon cinnamon
2	tablespoons oil	¼	teaspoon nutmeg
4	pounds chicken, cut into pieces, or 6 to 8 breasts or thighs		Salt and pepper to taste
		6	tablespoons tomato paste

Trim away ends of beans and cut beans into halves or thirds. Rinse, pat dry and set aside.

Sauté onions in oil in a large skillet until transparent. Add chicken and brown on all sides. Transfer chicken and onions to a Dutch oven, reserving pan drippings.

Add beans to skillet and cook lightly until softened. Add lemon juice, cinnamon and nutmeg. Season with salt and pepper. Stir in tomato paste. If too thick, add 1 to 2 tablespoons water to prevent burning. Spread mixture over chicken. Cover and simmer over low heat for 1 hour or until tender.

Serves 6.

Grilled or Barbecued
Tequila-Lime Chicken 🌳

Great for a "Hollywood Bowl picnic".

1	cup fresh lime juice	1½	tablespoons chili powder
½	cup tequila	1	teaspoon salt
½	cup orange juice	¾	teaspoon black pepper
¼	cup chopped fresh cilantro	8	boneless chicken breast halves with skin on
2	tablespoons seeded and minced jalapeño chiles		

Combine lime juice, tequila, orange juice, cilantro, jalapeño, chili powder, salt and pepper in a bowl. Add chicken and turn to coat. Cover and refrigerate overnight.

Heat a barbecue to medium heat. Brush grill rack with oil. Add chicken and grill 18 minutes or until cooked through, turning occasionally.

Serves 8.

Moroccan Chicken

4	pounds chicken, cut up and skin removed, or 4 pounds skinless breasts
½-¾	cup matzo meal
	Vegetable oil
2-3	cups chopped onion
1	cup chicken broth, plus more if needed
2	tablespoons lemon juice
1	tablespoon freshly ground ginger
1-2	teaspoons cinnamon
1½-2	cups pitted prunes
2	tablespoons lemon zest
2	tablespoons orange zest
	Red, green and yellow bell peppers cut into long strips for garnish
¾	cup slivered almonds for garnish

Preheat oven to 350 degrees.

Wash chicken pieces in ice water and pat dry with paper towel. Put matzo meal in a large plastic bag or plastic storage container. Add chicken, 1 piece at a time, and shake until chicken is well coated.

Heat oil in a skillet. Brown chicken on all sides in oil and remove. Add onion to pan drippings and sauté until tender. Arrange chicken and onion in a roasting pan. Combine chicken broth, lemon juice, ginger and cinnamon. Pour mixture over chicken. Bake 25 to 30 minutes.

Add prunes, lemon zest and orange zest. Bake 30 minutes longer. If necessary, add more chicken broth or water to pan. Five minutes before cooking time is complete, lay pepper strips over chicken. Sprinkle almonds on top. Serve on a bed of seasoned couscous.

Serves 8.

Chicken with Walnut and Pomegranate Sauce

2-3	pounds chicken, cut into small pieces
	Salt and pepper to taste
¼	cup oil, olive oil preferred
1	medium onion, diced
2	cups chopped walnuts
2	cups chicken broth
2	tablespoons pomegranate molasses (available in Middle Eastern markets)
2-3	tablespoons lemon juice

Dry chicken and season with salt and pepper. Heat oil in a large skillet. Add chicken and brown; set aside. Add onion to same skillet and sauté until golden. Add walnuts, broth, molasses and lemon juice. Simmer 10 minutes. Add chicken back to skillet and baste with sauce. Cover skillet and simmer 30 minutes. Serve with a savory rice dish of your choice.

Serves 4.

Chianti goes well with dishes made with a red sauce, such as Chicken Cacciatore.

CRANBERRY-APPLE RELISH

1 pound fresh cranberries,

2 Granny Smith or Pippin apples, peeled and cored

1 large orange, cut into small segments

1 cup sugar

1 teaspoon lemon juice, or to taste

¼ cup chopped pecans or walnuts (optional)

Chop cranberries and apples in a food processor, making sure the small chunks still remain. Add orange, sugar and lemon juice and mix well. Add nuts. Refrigerate until needed.

Serves 12.

Paella

1	frying chicken, cut into serving pieces	¼	teaspoon freshly ground black pepper
1	package (8 ounces) beef or Italian sausage	2	cups long-grain white rice
¼	cup olive oil	4	cups water
1	clove garlic, minced	1	package (10 ounces) frozen peas
1	onion, finely chopped	1	red bell pepper, chopped
2	teaspoons salt, or 2 bouillon cubes	1	package (10 ounces) frozen artichokes
1	pound fresh tomatoes, chopped	1	clove garlic
		1	teaspoon saffron

In a deep, extra large heavy skillet, brown chicken and sausage in oil. Add minced garlic and onion and cook until translucent. Drain excess oil, leaving some for flavor. Add salt, tomatoes and black pepper. Cover and simmer 10 minutes. Stir in rice, water, peas, peppers and artichokes. Cover and cook over low heat for 20 minutes. Mash 1 clove garlic and mix with saffron. Stir garlic mixture into skillet. Cover and simmer 10 to 15 minutes longer over very low heat.

Serves 6.

To make beef sausage taste like Italian sausage, brown sausage with cayenne pepper and anise seeds.

Ground Turkey and Black-Bean Chili

1	tablespoon olive oil	1	pound ground turkey breast
2	cups finely chopped red bell pepper	2	cans (15 to 16 ounces each) black beans, rinsed and drained
1	cup chopped onion		
½	cup finely chopped carrot	3	cups canned chicken broth, fat skimmed from surface
2	large garlic cloves, minced		
4	teaspoons chili powder	1	tablespoon tomato paste
2	teaspoons ground cumin		Salt and pepper to taste

Heat oil in a large heavy saucepan or Dutch oven over medium-low heat. Add bell pepper, onion, carrot and garlic and sauté 12 minutes or until tender. Add chili powder and cumin and stir to blend. Increase heat to medium-high and add turkey. Cook, breaking up meat with a spoon, for 3 minutes or until turkey is no longer pink. Add beans, broth and tomato paste and bring to a boil. Reduce heat and simmer 1 hour or until chili thickens, stirring occasionally. Season with salt and pepper.

Chili can be prepared a day ahead, covered and chilled. Reheat over medium heat before serving.

Serves 6.

Apple-Juniper Berry Turkey Breast

Instead of the usual Friday night chicken, try this deliciously seasoned alternative.

1	turkey breast with bone (7 pounds)	1	medium onion, quartered
1	lemon, halved	1	stalk celery, cut into 4 equal pieces
	Salt and freshly ground pepper to taste	1	bunch Italian parsley or cilantro, tied together with kitchen twine
5	shallots		
½	cup apple or red currant jelly	1	cup chicken broth
¼	cup apple cider	¼	cup apple cider
½	teaspoon ground ginger	2	tablespoons crushed juniper berries*
1	teaspoon dried thyme		
1	teaspoon vegetable oil	1	bay leaf

Preheat oven to 425 degrees.

Place turkey breast in a large roasting pan. Squeeze lemon juice over all sides of breast and season with salt and pepper. Chop shallot in a food processor. Add jelly, ¼ cup apple cider, ginger and thyme and pulse to blend. Brush underside of breast with jelly glaze. Place breast skin-side up and rub with oil. Tuck half of onion under the breast and remaining half in neck cavity. Tuck celery and parsley under breast cavity.

Bake 20 minutes. Remove from oven and brush with some of glaze. Add remaining ¼ cup cider, broth, juniper berries and bay leaf to pan. Cover with foil and bake 1 hour longer, basting twice.

Reduce heat to 375 degrees. Roast, uncovered, for 20 to 30 minutes or until meat is a lovely caramel color, juices run clear when pierced with a fork and internal temperature in thickest part of breast registers 160 degrees. Remove from oven and allow to rest 20 minutes before carving. Discard bay leaf. Serve with pan juices passed separately.

Serves 8.

*Can be found at a gourmet market.

With turkey, a bigger Pinot Noir, or red Burgundy works well. Also, certain Merlots with lots of fruit and soft tannins go well. A great California Zinfandel from Amador County is a great turkey wine.

Turkey Cutlets a L'Orange

2	teaspoons olive oil	2	tablespoons red wine vinegar
1	pound turkey cutlets	1	tablespoon grated fresh
½	teaspoon salt		gingerroot
¼	teaspoon coarsely ground black pepper	1	small navel orange, cut into wedges for garnish
⅓	cup orange marmalade		Parsley sprigs for garnish

Heat oil in a 12-inch nonstick skillet over medium-high heat. Add turkey cutlets and season with salt and pepper. Cook turkey, turning once, for 2 minutes per side or until lightly browned on the outside and just ready to lose pink color on the inside.

In a small bowl, combine marmalade, vinegar and ginger. Add mixture to cooked cutlets in skillet. Bring to a boil. Garnish individual servings with orange wedges and parsley and serve.

Serves 4.

Cran-Apple Chutney

1	Granny Smith apple (about 8 ounces), cored and chopped	1	tablespoon minced fresh gingerroot
1	cup dried cranberries	6	whole cloves
½	cup golden raisins	1	cinnamon stick (3 inches)
½	cup finely chopped onion	½	teaspoon black peppercorns
¾	cup brown sugar	¼	teaspoon dried red pepper flakes
⅓	cup cider vinegar	2	cups water
1	tablespoon mustard seed		

Combine all ingredients in a 3- to 4-quart saucepan. Bring to a boil over high heat, stirring often. Reduce heat and simmer, stirring often, for 20 minutes or until apple mashes easily when pressed and most of liquid has evaporated. If desired, discard cloves and cinnamon stick. Serve warm, at room temperature or chilled. Can be stored up to 1 week in an airtight container in refrigerator.

Makes about 2 cups.

Meats

Meats

Orange and Mustard Glazed Beef Ribs

1	cup fresh orange juice	2	teaspoons minced fresh thyme
3	tablespoons Dijon mustard	2	cloves garlic, minced
2	tablespoons honey		Salt and pepper to taste
2	teaspoons horseradish	4	pounds beef ribs

Cook orange juice over medium heat for 6 to 8 minutes or until reduced by half. While the juice reduces, whisk together mustard, honey, horseradish, thyme, garlic and salt and pepper. Stir in reduced orange juice.

Grill ribs over a medium-hot fire, basting frequently with orange juice glaze, for 15 minutes or until medium-rare and slightly charred.

Serves 4.

Barbecued Chuck Roast

This marinade does wonders in tenderizing this flavorful cut of meat.

1	large onion, chopped	½	teaspoon dried thyme
2	tablespoons canola or olive oil	1	teaspoon ground ginger
3	tablespoons red wine vinegar	2	tablespoons dark brown sugar, packed
5	cloves garlic, crushed	1	boneless chuck roast (3 pounds), sliced to 1½-inch thickness
¼	cup chopped fresh parsley		
⅓	cup soy sauce		
1½	cups beef broth		
1	teaspoon dried rosemary		

Sauté onion in oil in a medium saucepan until soft and golden. Add vinegar, garlic, parsley, soy sauce, broth, rosemary, thyme, ginger and sugar. Whisk well and bring to a boil. Remove from heat and cool.

Place roast in a glass or plastic container. Pour cooled marinade over meat and cover. Marinate in refrigerator 6 hours or overnight, turning meat several times.

Remove meat from marinade an hour before cooking. Grill meat about 10 minutes per side. Cut into thin slices when ready to serve.

Serves 10 to 12.

California entertaining is casual. We love to dine "al fresco". Since it rarely rains in the summer, we can enjoy the outdoors any time of day or night. Gather flowers from the garden and put into a bowl, or use luscious summer fruit for a centerpiece.

With more rustic meats like stew, skirt steak or burgers, serve Syrah from California, the south of France or Australia, Petite Syrah from California, Chianti from Italy, Rioja from Spain or hearty red blends.

Forty Cloves of Garlic Brisket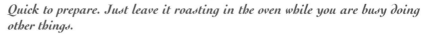

Once the meat is done, mash the roasted garlic cloves, discarding skins, into pan sauce and serve with meat and mashed potatoes.

1	beef brisket (6 to 7 pounds) Salt and pepper to taste	½	cup red wine, plus more if needed
2	teaspoons paprika	1	cup beef bouillon, plus more if needed
1	teaspoon bouquet garni or salad herbs	2-3	heads garlic, separated into cloves, unpeeled
2	teaspoons garlic powder		
2	tablespoons Dijon mustard		

Preheat oven to 350 degrees.

Dust brisket with salt and pepper, paprika, herbs and garlic powder. Place in a large roasting pan. Smear mustard over meat and pour wine and bouillon on top. Surround roast with garlic cloves. Cover tightly with foil. Roast 3 to 4 hours.

Reduce heat to 325 degrees. Remove brisket from oven and cool until able to handle, reserving contents of pan. Cut into ¼-inch or slightly thinner slices, removing fat. Return slices to pan and spoon juices over meat. Add more wine and bouillon if needed to barely cover meat. Roast 1½ to 2 hours longer or until very tender. Mash garlic cloves, remove skins and stir into sauce.

Serves 8 to 10.

Never-Fail Brisket

Quick to prepare. Just leave it roasting in the oven while you are busy doing other things.

1	beef brisket (4 to 5 pounds) Olive oil Garlic powder to taste Black pepper to taste	1	package (1 ounce) dried onion soup mix
		¼	cup kosher dill pickle juice

Preheat oven to 325 degrees.

Wash brisket and pat dry. Lay out 2 long sheets of aluminum foil to wrap the meat (one on top of the other for double thickness). Place brisket, fat-side down, on foil. Rub meat with olive oil, garlic powder and pepper until surface is covered. Sprinkle half the package of soup on top. Spoon pickle juice over meat. Turn brisket and repeat. Wrap meat loosely in foil and crimp tightly around the edges. Place on a baking sheet. Roast 4 to 5 hours or until tender. Slice and serve.

Serves 6 to 8.

Barbecued Brisket Sandwiches

This prize-winning brisket, which can be made a day or two ahead, makes a great Super Bowl meal.

1 beef brisket (4 to 5 pounds)	Barbecue Sauce
Salt and pepper to taste	(recipe below)
	Assorted sandwich rolls

Preheat oven to 325 degrees.

Sprinkle brisket with salt and pepper. Roast in a covered roasting pan for 3 to 4 hours or until tender when pierced with a fork. Cool and refrigerate.

Cut excess fat from beef and cut meat into thin slices across the grain. Place a layer of meat in the bottom of a large casserole dish. Spread a layer of barbecue sauce over meat. Continue layering meat and sauce until all is used. Cover with aluminum foil. Meat can be refrigerated up to 48 hours at this point.

When ready to serve sandwiches, bring meat and sauce mixture to room temperature. Bake at 350 degrees for 1 hour or until heated through. Serve with sandwich rolls.

Barbecue Sauce

3	cans (8 ounces each) tomato sauce	⅓	cup brown sugar, firmly packed
½	cup water	2	tablespoons honey
½	cup chopped onion	2	teaspoons dry mustard
1	clove garlic, minced	1	teaspoon chili powder
¼	cup red wine vinegar	1	teaspoon salt
3	tablespoons Worcestershire sauce	1	small lemon, thinly sliced

Combine all sauce ingredients in a medium saucepan. Bring to a boil. Reduce heat and simmer, uncovered, for 30 minutes, stirring occasionally. May be frozen.

Serves 10 to 12, makes 4 cups sauce.

Beef Brisket Braised with Dried Fruit, Yams and Carrots

3 tablespoons vegetable oil	4 pounds lean beef brisket, first cut
3 medium onions, chopped	Paprika to taste
4 large cloves garlic, chopped	6 ounces dried apricots
1 teaspoon paprika	1½ cups pitted prunes
½ teaspoon ground allspice	3 pounds yams, peeled and cut into 1½-inch pieces
¼ teaspoon dried red pepper flakes, crushed	6 large carrots, peeled and cut into 1½-inch pieces
3½ cups chicken broth	Minced fresh parsley for garnish
1½ cups dry red wine	
3 bay leaves	

Preheat oven to 325 degrees.

Heat oil in a large heavy pot or Dutch oven over medium-high heat. Add onions and garlic and cook 15 minutes or until beginning to brown, stirring frequently. Add 1 teaspoon paprika, allspice and pepper flakes and stir 20 seconds. Add broth, wine and bay leaves. Boil 10 minutes to allow flavors to blend.

Sprinkle brisket with paprika and rub in. Add brisket to pot, fat-side up. Add apricots and prunes. Cover and bake 90 minutes. (If you want to display fruit, add to brisket during the last 1½ hours of baking.) Add yams and carrots to pot. Cover and bake 2½ hours longer or until brisket is very tender. Remove from oven and let stand 20 minutes. Remove brisket from pot and slice thinly across the grain. Arrange slices on a serving platter. Skim fat from pan juices and spoon juices over meat. Arrange fruit and vegetables around meat. Garnish with parsley.

Serves 8.

Brisket can be prepared 2 days ahead, covered and refrigerated before slicing. To serve, remove meat from pot and slice across the grain. Remove any solid fat from sauce. Return sliced meat to pot and bake at 325 degrees for about 30 minutes or until heated through. Wonderful for Passover.

Sweet and Sour Brisket

1	bottle (12 ounces) beer
1	cup whole berry cranberry sauce
½	cup ketchup
2	tablespoons olive oil

1	flat-cut brisket (4 to 5 pounds)
	Salt and pepper to taste
1	large onion, sliced

Preheat oven to 350 degrees.

Combine beer, cranberry sauce and ketchup in a medium bowl; set aside.

Heat oil in a heavy Dutch oven over high heat. Season brisket with salt and pepper. Add brisket to oil and sear 5 minutes on each side or until browned. Transfer brisket to a plate. Add onion to same Dutch oven and sauté 8 minutes or until softened and browned, stirring and scraping bottom of pot frequently. Place brisket on onion and pour beer mixture over brisket. Bring to a boil.

Cover tightly and transfer to oven. Bake 3 hours or until brisket is tender. Cool 30 minutes before slicing. Skim fat off top of gravy and transfer brisket to a cutting board. Thinly slice brisket across the grain. Return brisket to gravy and cover. Rewarm in 350 degree oven for 30 minutes.

Brisket can be prepared 2 days ahead. Cover and refrigerate. Rewarm for 45 minutes.

Serves 6 to 8.

Unstuffed Cabbage with Meatballs

This method is so much easier than rolling leaves of cabbage.

Sauce

1	can (15 ounces) whole cranberry sauce
1	cranberry sauce can water (15 ounces)
1	jar (15 ounces) spaghetti sauce

1	can (8 ounces) tomato sauce
2	teaspoons salt, or less if desired
3-5	pounds cabbage, shredded

Meatballs

2	pounds lean ground beef
1	onion, chopped
¼	cup dry rice

1	teaspoon black pepper
1-2	teaspoons salt
1	egg

Combine all sauce ingredients in a large saucepan. Cover and cook over medium heat for 1 hour. To make meatballs, mix all ingredients and shape into 1 to 2 tablespoon-size balls. Place meatballs under a layer of sauce. Cover and simmer 1 hour.

Serves 8 to 10.

To decorate a main dish with brightly-colored parsley, simply place chopped parsley in cheesecloth and wring under running water until the water is clear. Unwrap and the parsley is ready to sprinkle on a plate before placing the entrée.

BRISKET SAUCE VARIATION

1 cup dry red wine

1 cup beef or chicken broth

½ cup frozen cranberry juice concentrate, thawed

¼ cup flour

1 large onion, sliced

4 cloves garlic, chopped

12 ounces medium portobello mushrooms, dark gills scraped away, thinly sliced

1 cup dried cranberries (about 4 ounces)

Whisk together wine, broth, concentrate and flour until blended in a medium bowl. Add mixture to baked and sliced brisket in pan with onion and garlic. Place mushrooms and cranberries around brisket and cover with foil. Bake 30 additional minutes at 350 degrees, or 40 minutes if meat has been refrigerated.

Hungarian Stuffed Cabbage

1	pound lean ground beef	1	onion, halved and sliced lengthwise
1	medium onion, chopped		
½	cup dry white or brown rice	1	can (15 ounces) sauerkraut, drained
2	tablespoons oil		
	Salt and pepper to taste	1	can (15 ounces) tomato sauce
	Paprika to taste	1	can (28 ounces) tomato juice, or more if needed
	Garlic powder to taste		
1	head cabbage (3 pounds)	1	teaspoon salt
		1	tablespoon sugar

Preheat oven to 350 degrees.

Combine ground beef, onion, rice, oil, salt and pepper, paprika and garlic powder.

Remove core of cabbage, leaving head intact. Cook whole cabbage in boiling water for about 10 minutes. Drain and cool. Peel off leaves, trimming off the hard center. Place a heaping tablespoon of meat mixture in each cabbage leaf and roll up like an envelope. To keep rolls from opening while cooking, rolls can be secured with a toothpick.

Place some of onion slices in bottom of a roasting pan along with some sauerkraut. Arrange a layer of cabbage rolls on top. Continue to layer until rolls are used up. Pour tomato sauce on top, followed by tomato juice. Top with 1 teaspoon salt and 1 tablespoon sugar and finish with sauerkraut on top.

Cover and bake for 1½ hours, adding more juice if needed. Bake, uncovered, 1 hour longer or until brown on top.

Serves 12.

This freezes well.

To make sure your cabbage leaves are softened enough to use in making stuffed cabbage, freeze the cored cabbage overnight, then defrost. It will take several hours to defrost but the leaves peel off very easily.

ALTERNATE SAUCE FOR STUFFED CABBAGE

2 cans (12 ounces each) ginger ale

1 bottle (28 ounces) ketchup

Juice of 1 lemon

½ cup dried cranberries

Combine ginger ale, ketchup and lemon juice and pour over cabbage rolls. Sprinkle cranberries on top. Bake at 350 degrees for 2 to 2½ hours.

Stuffed Eggplant
with Meat, Pine Nuts and Almonds Ⓜ

In Israel, eggplant, zucchini and peppers are the most frequently chosen vegetables for stuffing.

2-2½	pounds small eggplants, or 2 medium eggplants	1	medium onion, finely chopped
	Salt	½	pound lean ground beef
½	cup dry long-grain white rice, rinsed and drained	2	tablespoons chopped fresh parsley
3	cups boiling salted water	½	teaspoon salt
2	teaspoons vegetable oil	½	teaspoon black pepper
3	tablespoons pine nuts	2	tablespoons olive oil
3	tablespoons slivered almonds	1-2	tablespoons tomato paste
1	tablespoon olive or vegetable oil	¼	cup water
		4	medium cloves garlic, halved
		1	tablespoon olive oil

Preheat oven to 425 degrees.

Cut stem end from eggplants and halve lengthwise. Use a spoon to scoop out centers, leaving boat-shaped shells. Set aside centers to use in stuffing. Sprinkle eggplant shells with salt. Place upside-down in a colander and leave to drain 30 minutes.

Cook rice in 3 cups boiling salted water for 10 minutes. Rinse with cold water and drain well. Transfer to a large bowl. Heat 2 teaspoons vegetable oil in a medium skillet. Add pine nuts and almonds and sauté over medium heat for 3 minutes or until lightly browned. Remove with a slotted spoon. Add 1 tablespoon olive oil to skillet and heat. Add onion and cook over low heat until softened, but not browned. Cool. Mix sautéed onion, cooked rice, sautéed nuts, beef, parsley, salt and pepper. Chop flesh removed from eggplant. Heat 2 tablespoons olive oil in a skillet and add chopped eggplant. Season with salt and sauté over medium-low heat for 10 minutes, stirring often. Cool and mix with meat stuffing. Adjust seasoning as needed.

Rinse eggplant shells, pat dry, and arrange in a baking dish. Fill shells with stuffing. Mix tomato paste with ¼ cup water and spoon mixture over eggplant. Add enough water to dish to cover eggplant by one-third. Add garlic and drizzle 1 tablespoon olive oil over eggplant. Cover and bake 15 minutes. Reduce oven temperature to 350 degrees and bake 15 minutes longer. Uncover and bake, basting occasionally, for 30 minutes or until eggplant is very tender. Serve hot or warm.

Serves 4 to 6.

Israeli Kabob (Small Hamburgers)

There is hardly a restaurant in Israel that does not feature Kabob at the top of its menu.

2 pounds ground beef or lamb	Salt and pepper to taste
Ground cumin to taste	1 large onion, chopped
½ cup water	½ cup chopped fresh parsley

Combine ground meat, cumin, ½ cup water and salt and pepper. Knead well for 5 minutes. Mix in onion and parsley. Form mixture into a ball and refrigerate 12 hours.

Wet fingers and shape mixture into stick-like 3 x 1-inch hamburgers. Grill 5 to 8 minutes over hot coals, turning from side to side to brown.

Serves 6 to 8.

Lamb Chops Mongolian Style

SERVING LAMB CHOPS

Stand chops on their rib ends or place against a mound of potatoes, rice or vegetables. You can do this with poultry as well as firm fish.

1 tablespoon hoisin sauce	4 lamb chops
1 tablespoon dark soy sauce	(6 to 8 ounces each)
2 cloves garlic, finely chopped	2 tablespoons peanut oil
1 teaspoon sea salt	2 medium onions, sliced
¼ teaspoon white pepper	¼ cup vegetable broth

Sauce

1 fresh hot red chile, seeded and sliced	½ teaspoon sea salt
	1 tablespoon lemon juice
1 fresh hot green chile, seeded and sliced	1 teaspoon brown sugar
	2 tablespoons peanut oil

Mix hoisin sauce, soy sauce, garlic, salt and pepper in a bowl. Coat chops in mixture and let stand 1 hour.

Heat oil in a wok until smoking. Add onions and stir-fry 2 minutes or until transparent. Reduce heat. Add chops and cook about 5 minutes on each side. Add broth, cover and simmer 5 minutes.

Meanwhile, in a bowl, combine all sauce ingredients and pour into a small saucepan. Heat gently. Transfer cooked chops to a warmed serving platter and top with sauce.

Serves 4.

Barbecued Lamb Chops Shish Kebab

Precooking and marinating some ingredients insure that everything on the skewer is at the right degree of doneness when the chops are grilled to your taste.

12	single-rib lamb chops (each 1 inch thick), long ends cut off	2	small zucchini, ends trimmed, cut into ½-inch slices
	Herb Marinade (recipe below)	2	green bell peppers, cut into sixths
12	white onions (each 1- to 1½-inch diameter)	12	cherry tomatoes, stemmed
		12	thick lemon slices
12	mushroom caps, wiped clean	2	tablespoons margarine

Arrange lamb chops in a single layer in a shallow glass baking pan. Pour Herb Marinade over chops.

Drop onions into a pan of boiling water and parboil 5 minutes. Drain onions in a colander and rinse under cold running water, then slip off skins. Add onions, mushrooms, zucchini and bell pepper to baking pan with chops and coat with marinade. Cover pan and marinate 2 hours at room temperature, or at least 4 hours in the refrigerator. Turn lamb and vegetables once or twice while marinating.

Heat barbecue and grease rack.

To assemble each skewer, thread 2 chops lengthwise onto a skewer, alternating with 2 each of the onions, mushroom caps, zucchini slices, pepper pieces, cherry tomatoes and lemon slices. Press foods firmly together as threading them onto skewer. Brush mushroom caps with margarine. Lay the skewers over the baking pan or on a tray lined with foil, so excess marinade can drip off for a few minutes.

Grill kebabs directly on rack, or use a broiler. Cook 7 to 8 minutes for rare, 10 to 12 minutes for medium-rare. To serve, slide vegetables and lamb chops off each skewer onto heated individual plates. Remove only a few pieces at a time to avoid breaking the vegetables.

Serves 6.

Herb Marinade

1½	cups vegetable oil	½	teaspoon dried thyme, crumbled
1	cup fresh lemon juice	¼	teaspoon dried rosemary, crushed
1	tablespoon finely chopped onion		
1	clove garlic, finely chopped	1	teaspoon salt
1	tablespoon dried oregano, crumbled		Freshly ground black pepper

Combine all marinade ingredients in a bowl and stir well.

Ground Lamb with Peas

6	tablespoons oil	1	teaspoon finely chopped
1	medium onion, sliced		fresh ginger
3	fresh red chiles	1	teaspoon crushed garlic
	Fresh cilantro to taste	1	teaspoon chili powder
2	tomatoes, chopped	1	pound lean ground lamb
1	teaspoon salt	1	cup peas

Heat oil in a medium saucepan. Add onion and sauté until golden brown. Add 2 of the chiles, half of cilantro and all the tomatoes and reduce heat to a simmer. Add salt, ginger, garlic and chili powder. Stir until well combined. Add lamb and stir-fry 7 to 10 minutes. Add peas and cook 3 to 4 minutes longer, stirring occasionally.

Transfer mixture to a warm serving platter. Garnish with remaining chile and cilantro.

Serves 4.

Japanese Lamb (M)

A meal in a crockpot.

2	pounds lamb shoulder	2	tablespoons sherry
¼	cup soy sauce	2	cloves garlic, crushed
1	tablespoon honey	1½	cups chicken broth
2	tablespoons vinegar		

Combine all ingredients in a crockpot. Cook on low for at least 8 hours. Serve with rice.

Makes 6 servings.

Lamb Shanks with Artichoke Caponata (For electric slow cooker)

Serve with soft polenta or hot cooked orzo pasta.

4	lamb shanks (3¾ to 4¼ pounds total), bones cracked
	Fresh ground pepper
1	onion (8 ounces), chopped
1	red bell pepper (8 ounces), thinly sliced
1	cup thinly sliced celery
1	package (8 ounces) frozen artichoke hearts
1	cup pitted kalamata olives, drained
1	tablespoon capers, drained
1	teaspoon dried basil
1	can (14½ ounces) diced tomatoes, undrained
1½	tablespoons red wine vinegar
1½	tablespoons cornstarch
1½	tablespoons water
2	tablespoons chopped parsley or toasted pine nuts

Preheat oven to 450 degrees.

Rinse shanks, pat dry and arrange slightly apart in a 15 x 10-inch baking pan. Sprinkle all over with pepper. Bake 20 to 30 minutes or until well browned.

Meanwhile, in a 4½-quart electric slow cooker, combine onion, bell pepper, celery, artichoke hearts, olives, capers and basil. Set shanks on vegetables in cooker. Add tomatoes with juice, vinegar and any lamb juices from baking pan. Cover and cook 6 to 6½ hours on low or 4 to 4½ hours on high or until lamb is very tender when pierced with a fork.

With a slotted spoon, transfer each shank to a wide, shallow bowl and keep warm. Skim off and discard fat from cooking liquid. Turn cooker to high. In a small bowl, mix cornstarch and 1½ tablespoons water and pour into cooking liquid. Stir often for 10 minutes or until sauce is bubbling. Spoon sauce and vegetables over lamb. Sprinkle with parsley or pine nuts.

Serves 4.

LAMB RUB FOR BONELESS LAMB

Fresh herbs are a must!

1 boneless lamb roast (4 to 4¾ pounds)

8 cloves garlic

3 tablespoons chopped fresh thyme

2 tablespoons chopped fresh rosemary

2 tablespoons chopped fresh parsley

½ teaspoon black pepper

1 tablespoon kosher salt

3 tablespoons olive oil

1 lemon, halved

Cut 1-inch slits over lamb. Macerate herbs and seasonings with oil and rub over lamb. Let stand at room temperature for 1 hour. Pat lamb dry. Roast at 425 degrees on top oven rack, 5-inches from top of oven, for 25 minutes. Squeeze lemon over lamb when cooked. Let stand 15 minutes before slicing.

Serves 12.

Lamb Shanks with Portobello Mushrooms and Dried Cranberries

Shanks should be prepared 1 to 2 days ahead.

Lamb Shanks

½	cup flour	1½	cups dry red wine
1	teaspoon salt	1½	cups beef broth
½	teaspoon black pepper	1½	cups cranberry juice cocktail
6	lamb shanks (1 pound each), trimmed of fat	6	cloves garlic, minced
2-3	tablespoons vegetable oil	2	tablespoons chopped fresh rosemary

Sauce/Serving

3	tablespoons flour	¾	cup dried cranberries
5	tablespoons red wine	12	ounces extra-wide egg noodles, cooked, or mashed potatoes
2	tablespoons chopped fresh rosemary		Fresh rosemary sprigs for garnish
12	ounces frozen pearl onions, not thawed (optional)		
12-16	ounces portobello mushrooms, cut into 1½-inch strips		

Preheat oven to 350 degrees.

In a large plastic bag, mix flour, salt and pepper. Add lamb, 1 to 2 pieces at a time, shaking to coat and patting off excess. In a large, wide, non-aluminum saucepan or Dutch oven, heat 2 tablespoons oil over high heat. Brown lamb in batches, turning to brown all sides. If drippings begin to burn, reduce heat. If needed, add more oil. Remove lamb to a plate and pour off fat. Stir wine, broth and juice into pan. Bring to a boil, scraping up any brown bits. Stir in garlic and rosemary. Return lamb to pan and bring to a boil.

Cover and bake 1 hour. Rearrange shanks, putting top ones on the bottom. Bake 1½ hours longer or until tender when pierced with a fork. Remove lamb and immediately cover with wax paper and foil. Refrigerate sauce separately until fat rises to the top and solidifies. Refrigerate lamb and sauce up to 2 days.

To reheat, scrape hardened fat from top of sauce and discard. Simmer sauce for 10 minutes. Remove from heat and, stirring briskly, whisk in flour dissolved in wine. Add rosemary and bring to a boil, stirring constantly. Place shanks in a roasting pan and pour sauce over top. Sprinkle with pearl onions, mushrooms and cranberries, pushing them into the sauce. Bake at 350 degrees, covered, for 1 hour or until sauce is bubbling and meat is heated through. Serve over cooked noodles and garnish with rosemary.

Serves 6.

Sweet and Sour Meatballs

By popular demand.

Meatballs

2	pounds ground meat	½	cup water	
2	eggs		Salt and pepper to taste	
2	handfuls crushed corn flakes		Oil for frying	

Sauce

3   large onions, chopped
3   cans (8 ounces each) tomato
       sauce
2   tomato sauce cans water

1   cup pineapple chunks,
       drained (optional)
¾   cup white raisins
    Juice of ½ lemon
3   tablespoons brown sugar

Preheat oven to 275 degrees.

Combine all meatball ingredients except oil and roll into balls. Fry in oil until brown on all sides; set aside.

For sauce, sauté onions in a Dutch oven until golden brown. Add tomato sauce, water, pineapple, raisins, lemon juice and sugar. Add browned meatballs to sauce. Bake, uncovered, for 2½ hours. (Does not need basting.)

Makes 16 meatballs.

Square plates make for a beautiful modern food presentation. Mound the food in the center of the plate for an eye appealing look.

Asian Short Ribs

1   bunch scallions, sliced
¼   cup soy sauce
¼   cup sesame oil
½   cup water
3   tablespoons brown sugar
2   tablespoons sesame seeds,
        toasted

2   tablespoons finely chopped
        garlic
1   inch fresh gingerroot,
        peeled and finely chopped
½   teaspoon dried red pepper
        flakes
4   pounds beef short ribs, with
        or without bones

Preheat oven to 400 degrees.

Combine all ingredients except ribs and mix well. Add ribs and marinate in refrigerator for 6 to 8 hours, turning occasionally.

Remove ribs, reserving marinade. Bake 1 hour or until well browned and done, turning and basting with reserved marinade every 15 minutes.

Serves 3 or 4.

*Refrigerate onions
30 minutes before cutting
to avoid tears.*

*Another way to
stop tears is to dampen
the cutting board with
white vinegar.*

Middle Eastern Spiced Meatloaf with Sesame Topping (Siniyeh) Ⓜ

A popular Yemenite meatloaf served in Israel.

Meatloaf

2	pounds lean ground beef or ground lamb	¼	cup finely chopped fresh parsley
1	medium onion, finely chopped or grated	½	teaspoon ground cumin
2	cloves garlic, finely minced or pressed	¼	teaspoon cinnamon
		¼	teaspoon allspice
		1	teaspoon salt
		¼	teaspoon black pepper

Topping

½	cup tahini, stirred very well (available in Middle Eastern food stores)	1	clove garlic, finely minced or pressed (optional)
⅓	cup water	¼	teaspoon paprika (optional)
2	tablespoons lemon juice	⅛	teaspoon salt
2	tablespoons finely chopped fresh parsley	⅛	teaspoon freshly ground black pepper
		3	tablespoons pine nuts for garnish

Preheat oven to 400 degrees.

In a large bowl, combine all meatloaf ingredients and mix by squeezing through your fingers until well combined and smooth. Press mixture into a greased 13 x 9-inch baking dish. Bake 20 minutes or until top is browned.

Meanwhile, prepare topping. Place tahini in a small bowl. Slowly add water, stirring vigorously. At first, mixture will become very stiff, but will eventually thin out and become lighter in color. Stir in lemon juice, parsley, garlic, paprika, salt and pepper. Adjust seasonings as desired.

When meatloaf is browned, remove dish from oven and carefully drain off any excess fat. Spread topping over meatloaf. Sprinkle pine nuts on top. Return to oven and bake 10 minutes longer or until topping is puffed and lightly browned and meat is completely cooked through in the center.

Serves 6 to 8.

Barbecued Rib-Eye Steaks with Mediterranean Rub ⓜ

This spice rub is also great with chicken.

¼	teaspoon cayenne pepper	2	tablespoons olive oil
2	tablespoons ground cumin	4	boneless rib-eye steaks
1	tablespoon ground paprika		(each about 1 pound,
1½	teaspoons ground ginger		1¼ inches thick), trimmed
1¼	teaspoons ground coriander		Salt to taste
1	teaspoon black pepper	8	lemon wedges

Blend cayenne, cumin, paprika, ginger, coriander and pepper in a small bowl. Mix in oil to form a smooth paste. Rub mixture over steaks and transfer to a baking pan. Cover and refrigerate at least 3 hours or overnight.

Prepare a barbecue to medium-high heat. Sprinkle steaks with salt. Grill 5 minutes per side for medium-rare, or to desired degree of doneness. Place on a cutting board and let stand 4 minutes. Cut steaks into ½-inch thick diagonal slices. Transfer to a serving platter and sprinkle with salt. Serve with lemon wedges.

Serves 8.

Use a 4 pound rib roast, butterflied. Rub 2 to 3 tablespoons tapenade (recipe below, or use purchased to save time) on all sides of meat. Barbecue 8 to 10 minutes on each side for rare, 12 to 14 minutes for medium to well done.

Tapenade (May also be purchased in jars to save time.)

1¼	cups kalamata olives, pitted	1½	teaspoons freshly ground
	(or replace up to half of		black pepper
	kalamata olives with oil-	¾	teaspoon lemon zest
	cured olives)	1	tablespoon fresh lemon juice
2	cloves garlic, minced	2	canned anchovy fillets,
			drained

Combine all ingredients in a food processor and purée coarsely. Tapenade can be prepared up to a week ahead of time and kept, covered, in the refrigerator.

Makes 1 cup tapenade.

Wines that go with red meats, like steak, prime rib or rack of lamb are elegant, well-balanced Cabernets, Bordeaux, Claret-style Zinfandels, Merlot or big-bodied Pinot Noirs or red Burgundies.

MUSTARD SHALLOT SAUCE

Wonderful flavors on grilled, boneless rib-eye steak.

Over medium heat, combine 2 tablespoons olive oil and ⅓ cup chopped shallots in a 6- to 8-inch skillet. Sauté 3 minutes or until limp. Add 1 tablespoon Dijon mustard, 3 tablespoons dry vermouth and 1 teaspoon balsamic vinegar. Stir 30 seconds or until hot.

Makes ¼ cup sauce, enough for ¾ to 1 pound cooked rib-eye steak.

Adjust sauce ingredient amounts according to amount of steak being served.

Osso Buco ⓜ

Italian comfort food at its finest.

1	tablespoon olive oil	½	teaspoon dried basil leaves
2	veal cross-cut shanks (1½ pounds)	½	can (7¼ to 8 ounces) Italian style diced tomatoes, undrained
½	teaspoon salt		
½	cup chopped onion	½	cup dry white wine
2	cloves garlic, crushed		Gremolata (recipe below)
¼	cup finely chopped carrot		

Heat oil in a Dutch oven over medium heat. Add veal shanks and brown evenly. Remove veal and season with salt.

In same pan, add onion, garlic and carrot and cook 6 to 8 minutes or until tender, stirring occasionally. Add basil, tomatoes with juice and wine. Return veal to pan and bring to a boil. Reduce heat to low and cover. Simmer 1½ hours or until veal is tender.

Remove veal to a warm platter and skim fat off cooking liquid. Bring cooking liquid to a boil and cook, stirring occasionally, until slightly reduced. Spoon about ½ cup sauce over shanks. Sprinkle with Gremolata. Serve remaining sauce on the side, or over orzo.

Serves 4.

Gremolata

1	tablespoon chopped fresh parsley	½	teaspoon finely chopped garlic
2	teaspoons lemon zest		

Combine all ingredients.

Veal Stew

An old European recipe, handed down through generations.

1	medium onion, chopped	1	cup water
2	tablespoons solid vegetable		Salt and pepper to taste
	shortening or vegetable oil	3-4	whole cloves (not garlic)
2	pounds cubed veal	2	bay leaves
⅓	cup lemon juice		Paprika to taste
2	tablespoons flour	½	cup ketchup

Sauté onion in shortening. Add veal and immediately pour lemon juice over meat and let it steam. Sprinkle with flour. Mix in 1 cup water. Add salt and pepper, cloves, bay leaves, paprika and ketchup. Cover and simmer 1 hour or until meat is tender. Serve with noodles.

Serves 4 to 6.

One-half cup each mushrooms and wine may be added.

Veal Scaloppine alla Marsala

This is an elegant, but easy standby for special occasions.

1¼	pounds boneless veal	3	tablespoons olive oil
	scallops, cut ⅜-inch thick	8	ounces mushrooms, sliced
½	cup all-purpose flour	¾	cup Marsala wine
	Coarse salt and freshly	2	tablespoons freshly
	ground black pepper		squeezed lemon juice
2	tablespoons unsalted		Lemon slices for garnish
	margarine		(optional)

Using a sharp knife, cut slashes ½-inch deep across the edges all around each scallop to prevent veal from curling as it cooks. Place veal between 2 sheets of plastic wrap. Using a meat pounder, pound veal to a thickness of ¼ inch. Season flour with salt and pepper in a shallow dish. Very lightly coat each scallop with seasoned flour, tapping off excess.

In a large skillet, heat margarine and oil until very hot but not smoking. Quickly brown scallops, 30 to 60 seconds per side. Transfer to a serving platter and keep warm. Sauté mushrooms in same skillet over medium-high heat and quickly remove from pan.

Add wine and lemon juice to skillet. Cook over high heat, scraping with a wooden spoon to loosen browned bits from bottom of skillet. Add lemon slices and continue to cook 4 minutes or until sauce thickens. Add mushrooms to wine sauce and cook 1 minute longer. Remove lemon slices from sauce and use to garnish platter. Pour sauce over meat and serve immediately with noodles or rice.

Serves 4.

COOKING WITH ONIONS

Before chopping onions in your food processor, peel and quarter them and freeze 30 minutes. This will prevent the onions from becoming mushy and will lessen your tears.

Veal Shoulder with Porcini Mushrooms, Garlic and Rosemary ⓜ

Start making this at least one day ahead.

The flavor of garlic can be changed according to how it is prepared. For instance, a whole garlic clove added to a dish will give it the flavor but not the "bite" of garlic; a halved clove will add a little bite, a finely chopped clove will release most of the flavor, and a crushed clove will release all of the flavor.

1	package (¾ ounce) dried porcini mushrooms	¼	cup olive oil
8	large cloves garlic	2	pounds meaty veal bones
1	tablespoon chopped fresh rosemary	4	cups canned low salt chicken broth
1	tablespoon fresh thyme leaves	½	cup dry red wine
1	teaspoon kosher salt	½	cup drained and chopped canned tomatoes
½	teaspoon black pepper	3	tablespoons tomato paste
1	veal shoulder clod roast (5 pounds), tied to hold shape	1	tablespoon balsamic vinegar

Preheat oven to 350 degrees.

Grind dried mushrooms to a powder using a coffee or spice mill. Coarsely chop garlic, rosemary, thyme, salt and pepper in a food processor. Set aside 1 tablespoon garlic mixture and press remainder, ½ teaspoon at a time, into center of veal through openings of string, or poke holes in veal and push garlic mixture into holes. Coat outside of veal with mushroom powder.

Heat oil in a large, heavy pot over medium-high heat. Add bones and brown well for about 8 minutes. Transfer bones to a bowl. Add veal to pot and cook 5 minutes or until brown on all sides. Add reserved tablespoon garlic mixture and any remaining mushroom powder around veal and cook and stir 1 minute. Arrange bones around veal. Add broth, wine, tomatoes, tomato paste and vinegar. Bring to a boil. Cover and place in oven. Bake 2 hours or until veal is tender, turning veal every 30 minutes.

Cool veal, uncovered, for 1 hour. Discard bones. Refrigerate until cold, then cover and leave refrigerated 1 day.

Scrape off fat from surface of sauce. Transfer veal to a work surface, scraping any sauce back in pot. Remove strings. Cut veal crosswise into ½-inch thick slices. Overlap slices in a large baking dish. Boil sauce 20 minutes or until reduced to 3½ cups. Season to taste with salt and pepper. Spoon sauce over veal. (Veal can be prepared to this point 2 days ahead.) Bake at 350 degrees for 35 minutes or until warm.

Serves 8.

Fish

Fish

Ceviche (P)

Fresh fish cured in lime juice – influenced by our Latin neighbors.

2	pounds white fish or red snapper, diced	½	cup fresh lime juice, or enough to cover fish
1	large onion, finely chopped	3	cans (7 ounces each) mild green chili sauce
1	large green bell pepper, chopped		Black pepper to taste
4	stalks celery, chopped		

Combine fish, onion, bell pepper and celery in a glass dish. Add lime juice to cover. Refrigerate, covered, for at least 4 hours or overnight.

Drain fish in a colander and wash with cold water. Transfer fish mixture to a bowl. Add chili sauce and black pepper and let stand 1 hour or more, allowing seasonings to infuse into fish. Serve with toast rounds.

Serves 6.

Palos Verdes Cioppino (P)

A hearty fish stew for a cold night.

⅔	cup olive oil	2	cans (28 ounces each) diced tomatoes, with juice, or 6 cups chopped fresh
4	medium onions, thinly sliced		
5	leeks, white and pale green portions only, halved lengthwise, rinsed and sliced diagonally ½-inch thick	2	cans (16 ounces each) tomato sauce
		2	tablespoons fresh lemon juice
		1	bottle (750 ml) dry red or white wine
5	cloves garlic, minced or pressed		Hot pepper sauce
⅓	cup chopped fresh parsley		Salt to taste
4	bay leaves	5	pounds firm, light-flesh fish, such as orange roughy, cod or sea bass, cut into 1½-inch chunks
¾	teaspoon dried thyme		
¾	teaspoon dried oregano		
1	teaspoon black pepper		

Combine oil, onions, leeks, garlic, parsley, bay leaves, thyme, oregano and pepper in a 12- to 14-quart saucepan. Cook over medium-high heat, stirring occasionally, until onions are limp. Add tomatoes with juice, tomato sauce, lemon juice and wine. Cover and boil gently to blend flavors for 15 minutes for canned tomatoes, 45 minutes for fresh. Add pepper sauce and salt. If making ahead, cool, cover and refrigerate at this point. Heat to a simmer to continue.

Add fish and cook 8 to 10 minutes longer or until fish is set and opaque. Ladle into large, wide bowls. Enjoy with plenty of crusty bread.

Serves 10 to 12.

The specialty of Acapulco is ceviche de pescado; it's made on the beach with freshly caught fish. Ceviche cannot be claimed as a Mexican creation; Peru and Colombia also insist on having invented it. But there's no dispute that the coast of America was where Europeans first learned of the Indian method of "cooking" fresh fish with the acidity of a citrus fruit. The "ceviche style" is currently used in many countries, especially those along the Pacific Rim. A well-prepared ceviche includes just the right amount of lime juice; the freshness of the tomato, onion and chile provides a delicious, refreshing contrast to the soft smoothness of the fish.

Chardonnay seems called for here, but look for one that is balanced and not too much oak, or try the Australian blend of Sauvignon Blanc and Semillon.

Tahini Baked Cod

This fish dish is a favorite in many Middle Eastern countries.

6	cod filets	1	clove garlic, crushed
	Juice of 2 lemons, divided	3	tablespoons water, or more
1	tablespoon olive oil		if needed
3	tablespoons olive oil		Salt and freshly ground
2	large onions, chopped		pepper to taste
1	cup tahini		

Preheat oven to 350 degrees.

Arrange filets in a large shallow casserole or baking dish. Pour 1 tablespoon lemon juice and 1 tablespoon olive oil over fish. Bake 20 minutes or until cooked.

Meanwhile, heat 3 tablespoons oil in a large skillet. Add onions and cook 6 to 8 minutes or until well-browned and almost crisp.

Combine tahini and garlic in a small bowl. Beat in remaining lemon juice and water, a little at a time, until sauce is light and creamy. Season to taste with salt and pepper.

Sprinkle onions over fish and pour tahini sauce on top. Bake 15 minute longer or until flesh is cooked through and sauce is bubbling. Serve immediately with cooked rice and a salad.

Serves 6.

Nut-Crusted Fish Filets ⓟ

1	tablespoon Dijon mustard	1	pound orange roughy,
1	tablespoon mayonnaise		tilapia or other firm white
⅛	teaspoon garlic powder		fish filets
⅛	teaspoon black pepper	⅓	cup chopped macadamia
			nuts, hazelnuts or peanuts

Preheat oven to 400 degrees.

Mix mustard, mayonnaise, garlic powder and pepper until well blended. Place fish in a single layer on a lightly greased baking sheet. Spread mustard mixture evenly over fish. Sprinkle with nuts. Bake 10 to 12 minutes or until fish flakes easily with a fork.

Makes 4 servings.

Mediterranean Halibut

A fish dish for olive and garlic lovers.

4	halibut filets (8 ounces each), sliced 1-inch thick	1	red bell pepper, chopped
1	lemon, halved	12	garlic-stuffed green olives, sliced
	Salt and pepper to taste	12	cloves pickled garlic, sliced, or 6 cloves fresh garlic, sliced
3	tablespoons olive oil		
1	large onion, chopped		
3	cups carrots, sliced ¼-inch thick	1½	teaspoons Hungarian hot paprika, or less if desired

Preheat oven to 375 degrees.

Place halibut in a 10-inch baking dish. Squeeze juice of ½ lemon over halibut and season with salt and pepper.

Heat oil in a nonstick medium skillet over medium-high heat. Add onion, carrot and bell pepper and sauté 6 minutes or until crisp-tender. While sautéing, squeeze juice of remaining lemon half over vegetables. Add olives, garlic and paprika and continue to sauté 1 minute or until fragrant. Season to taste with salt and pepper.

Spread vegetable mixture over halibut. Bake, uncovered, for 20 minutes or until halibut is cooked through. Serve with a side dish of rice.

Serves 4.

A medium-bodied Chardonnay would be good with this, or try a California Sauvignon Blanc from Santa Barbara. For those who like a little sweetness in their wines, an off-dry Riesling or French Vouvray would be suitable.

Halibut with Sake and Scallions

If you like halibut, you will love this Japanese-inspired barbecued dish.

6	tablespoons coarsely chopped scallions	1	tablespoon sesame oil
3	tablespoons soy sauce, regular or light	4	halibut steaks, ¾-inch thick (about 2 pounds)
3	tablespoons finely chopped fresh gingerroot		Vegetable oil
2	tablespoons sake or dry sherry	1½	tablespoons minced fresh cilantro

Purée scallions, soy sauce, ginger, sake and sesame oil in a blender or food processor, stopping occasionally to scrape down sides of container. Arrange halibut on a large dish. Spread half of purée over fish. Turn fish and spread with remaining purée. Marinate in refrigerator 2 hours.

Prepare a barbecue or broiler over high heat. Remove fish from marinade, reserving marinade. Grill fish on a lightly greased rack or broiler pan. Grill over ash-white coals, or 3 to 3½ inches from broiler heat source, for 4 minutes or just until opaque, brushing occasionally with reserved marinade. Transfer to a serving plate and sprinkle with cilantro.

Serves 4.

When cooking fish, you can remove the fish odor from your hands by rinsing with a few drops of lemon juice before you wash with your usual soap.

**ROASTED
FENNEL SALSA**

*This salsa complements
a full-flavored fish such
as grilled tuna and can
be made the day before.*

1 whole head garlic

2 medium fennel bulbs,
thinly sliced

1 tablespoon olive oil

¼ teaspoon salt

¼ teaspoon freshly
ground black pepper

¼ teaspoon lemon zest

3 tablespoons
fresh lemon juice

¼ teaspoon minced
fresh rosemary

Preheat oven to 400 degrees.

Remove white paper
skin from garlic head,
but do not peel or
separate cloves. Cut off
top of garlic head and
discard. Wrap in foil.
Place garlic and fennel
on a greased baking
sheet. Brush fennel with
olive oil and sprinkle
with salt and pepper.

Bake 25 minutes or
until lightly browned.
Remove from oven
and cool 10 minutes.
Separate cloves and
squeeze to extract garlic
pulp; discard skins.
Chop fennel. Combine
fennel, garlic, lemon
zest, lemon juice and
rosemary in a bowl.
Serve warm or chilled.

Makes 2 cups.

California Corn-Crusted Baked Orange Roughy

The kids will love this.

2	cups chopped tomato, Roma preferred	1	pound fresh, white fish filets, such as orange roughy or sole, halved if large
½	cup sliced ripe olives		
2	tablespoons minced fresh garlic	½	cup yellow cornmeal
¼	cup olive oil	½	teaspoon salt
1	tablespoon dried oregano or thyme, crumbled	½	teaspoon black pepper
			Freshly grated Parmesan cheese

Preheat oven to 450 degrees.

Mix tomato, olives, garlic, oil and oregano in the bottom of a 1½-quart casserole dish. Rinse fish and pat dry. Dip filets into cornmeal mixed with salt and pepper. Place coated filets in baking dish. Bake 20 to 25 minutes or until coating is crusty. Sprinkle with Parmesan cheese and serve.

Serves 4.

Mustard-Crusted Salmon

A quick and elegant meal for the family for that special night.

2	pounds salmon filets, divided into 4 (½-pound) pieces	¾	cup whole-grain Dijon mustard
¼	cup finely minced garlic	½	cup dry white wine
3	tablespoons butter or margarine		Salt and pepper to taste
			Lemon wedges for garnish

Rinse fish and pat dry. Place fish, skin-side down, on a greased broiler pan. In a 6- to 8-inch skillet, stir garlic in butter over medium heat for 3 minutes or until softened. Spoon butter from garlic and drizzle over salmon, reserving garlic in pan. Broil salmon 2 to 3 inches from the heat source for 2 minutes.

Meanwhile, mix mustard and wine with sautéed garlic. Remove pan from oven. Spoon mustard mixture evenly over filets. Season with salt and pepper. Return to oven and broil 4 to 6 minutes or until crust is golden brown and fish is barely opaque in thickest part. Transfer to a serving platter and serve with lemon wedges.

Serves 4.

Poached Salmon and 2 Wonderful Sauces Ⓟ

This fish dish is an absolute favorite for a Southern California summer dinner, or for a special luncheon. Here is an alternate poaching method if you do not own a fish poacher.

2-3 pounds salmon filet
  (as much as will fit in a
  large skillet)
White wine, mixed with
  water (see directions)
Salt and pepper to taste

Chopped dill to taste
1-2 scallions, chopped (optional)
  Yogurt Sauce (recipe below)
  Mustard Dill Sauce
    (recipe below)

Fit a cake rack or a flat round steamer insert into a large skillet. Cut salmon into 2 pieces as needed to fit in skillet. Pour a mixture of half white wine and half water into skillet about ½-inch deep. Place fish on rack. Season salmon with salt and pepper and dill. Cover pan tightly and steam salmon over medium heat for 10 to 12 minutes. If fish is thick, steaming 2 to 3 minutes longer may be needed. Check doneness by using a sharp knife down the center to determine opaqueness of the fish. Remove from heat and cool in liquid. Remove cooled fish from liquid, cover and refrigerate until chilled. Serve with sauces.

Serves 5 to 6.

Yogurt Sauce Ⓓ

¾ cup plain yogurt
3 tablespoons fresh lemon juice
3 tablespoons extra virgin
  olive oil

3 tablespoons chopped fresh
  dill
¾ teaspoon sugar
  Salt and pepper to taste

Blend all ingredients and refrigerate until ready to use.

Makes 1 cup.

Mustard Dill Sauce Ⓟ

1½ tablespoons white wine
  vinegar
1½ tablespoons sugar
½ cup extra virgin olive oil

⅓ cup Dijon mustard
1 tablespoon white pepper
1 tablespoon chopped fresh
  dill

Whisk together vinegar and sugar in a small bowl until sugar dissolves. Gradually whisk in oil, blending well. Stir in mustard, pepper and dill. Cover and refrigerate until ready to serve.

**CREATIVE
CONDIMENT
CONTAINERS FOR
A SUMMER
COOKOUT:**

*Remove the tops from
3 perfectly plump-shaped
bell peppers, 1 green, 1 red
and 1 yellow. Remove pith
and seeds and rinse out.
Fill peppers with ketchup,
mustard and relish,
coordinating colors of
peppers and fillings.
Save the pepper tops to use
as a covering to keep
the insects out.*

*To freshen the air in
your kitchen, simmer
lemon slices and cloves
in a saucepan for
10 minutes.*

Barbecued Sugar-Spice Salmon

Salmon's Secret Spice: it's cocoa.

¼	cup sugar	1	tablespoon ground cumin
1	teaspoon dry mustard	2	teaspoons fresh ground
	Dash of cinnamon		pepper
1	tablespoon paprika	1½	tablespoons coarse salt
1	teaspoon cocoa	4	salmon filets (6 ounces each)
¼	cup chili powder	3	tablespoons oil

Preheat barbecue grill over medium-high heat.

Combine sugar, mustard, cinnamon, paprika, cocoa, chili powder, cumin, pepper and salt. Dip salmon in oil and tap off any excess, then dip filets in spice mixture to coat both sides and around edges. Pat spice mixture onto surface. Some spice mixture will be left over.

Grill salmon about 4 minutes on each side for 1-inch filets, or until salmon just begins to flake.

Chinese Mustard Sauce

¼	cup dry mustard	2	tablespoons hot water
¼	cup sugar		

Mix all sauce ingredients together well. Pass the sauce at the table.

Serves 4.

Spicy Italian Red Snapper

A favorite created by an Italian chef.

¼	cup olive oil	4	cups cherry tomatoes, halved
2	pounds red snapper or	1	cup marinara sauce, or more
	orange roughy filets		if needed
	Salt and pepper to taste	¾-1	cup kalamata olives, chopped
½	cup chopped fresh parsley	6	cloves garlic, minced
½	teaspoon dried red pepper		
	flakes		

Heat oil in a large heavy skillet over medium-high heat. Season fish with salt and pepper. Add half of fish to skillet and sauté 4 minutes per side or just until opaque in the center. Transfer fish to a platter and repeat with remaining fish. Add parsley and pepper flakes to same skillet and sauté 1 minute. Add tomatoes, marinara sauce, olives and garlic and continue to sauté 2 minutes or until tomatoes are soft. Add salt and pepper as desired. Spoon sauce over fish. Serve with freshly cooked pasta.

Serves 4.

Asian Fusion Baked Red Snapper ⓟ

A taste of the Pacific Rim.

1	whole red snapper (2 pounds), ready to cook
1	teaspoon ground ginger
1	teaspoon sea salt
1	teaspoon black pepper
1	onion, sliced into rings
1	inch piece gingerroot, peeled and finely chopped
1½	teaspoons salted fermented black beans, soaked 20 minutes and drained
1	tablespoon rice wine or dry sherry
1	tablespoon soy sauce
1	teaspoon brown sugar
2	tablespoons peanut oil

Preheat oven to 350 degrees.

Using a sharp knife, cut both sides diagonally in one direction on the fish, and then in the opposite direction to give a diamond pattern on the skin of the fish. In a small bowl, mix together ground ginger, salt and pepper. Rub mixture into both sides of fish and sprinkle some of mixture on inside. Cut a piece of foil large enough to completely enclose fish and lay foil on a baking sheet. Arrange onion and gingerroot on half of the foil. Top with fish.

Mash black beans with wine, soy sauce and sugar. Spread mixture over fish. Heat oil until smoking and drizzle over fish. Fold foil over fish and seal seams tightly. Bake 20 minutes until the fish turns opaque. Serve topped with cooking juices.

Serves 4.

Broiled or Baked
Sea Bass Dijon with Capers ⓟ

4	sea bass filets or other white fish (6 to 8 ounces each), ¾- to 1-inch thick
4	teaspoons lemon juice
3	tablespoons Dijon mustard
1	clove garlic, pressed or minced
⅛	teaspoon paprika
2	tablespoons drained capers

Arrange fish in a single layer in a 15 x 10-inch baking or boiler pan. Drizzle lemon juice evenly over each filet. Stir together mustard and garlic. Cover top of each filet completely with mixture. Broil fish 6 to 8 inches from heat source for 10 to 14 minutes or until fish is opaque in center. Rotate pan as needed to cook fish evenly. Or, bake fish at 375 degrees for 10 to 15 minutes.

Sprinkle fish lightly with paprika. Scatter capers over filets. Transfer filets to a platter using a wide spatula. Serve hot with rice and a green vegetable. To serve cold, let filets cool, cover and chill in refrigerator for at least 30 minutes or up to 2 hours.

Serves 4.

Baked Petrale Sole in Packets

This version of a French classic is baked in foil. An easy do-ahead preparation.

1	large carrot, peeled and shredded on a large grater	6	small fresh shiitake or large cremini mushrooms, thinly sliced
1	large turnip, peeled and shredded on a large grater	2	tablespoons plus 2 teaspoons butter
	Salt to taste	½	cup white wine
4	petrale sole filets (4 to 5 ounces each)	4	teaspoons finely chopped fresh chives

Preheat oven to 400 degrees.

Combine carrot, turnip and salt in a bowl. Drain any liquid that accumulates. Season fish with salt. Spread some of butter over 1 side of four 12-inch squares of aluminum foil. Divide carrot mixture and mushrooms evenly among center of each square of foil. Place a fish filet on each mound of vegetables. Drizzle wine over top and dot with remaining butter. Sprinkle chopped chives over each filet. Bring sides of foil toward middle, then fold over the other 2 sides, crimping tightly to seal. Place on a baking sheet. If refrigerated in advance, bring to room temperature before proceeding.

Bake 15 to 20 minutes. When ready to serve, place a packet in center of each serving plate. Slit the top and spread open slightly. Wait a couple of minutes to allow steaming to stop before eating.

Serves 4.

Stir-Fry Tilapia with Fresh Ginger

½	cup cornstarch	4	scallions, thinly sliced
½	teaspoon ground ginger	1	tablespoon red wine vinegar
1	inch piece fresh gingerroot, peeled and finely chopped	2	tablespoons rice wine or dry sherry
1	teaspoon sea salt	3	tablespoons dark soy sauce
1½	pounds tilapia filets, or other firm white fish, skinned and cubed	1	teaspoon sugar
3	tablespoons peanut oil	3	tablespoons fresh orange juice

Combine cornstarch, ground ginger, chopped gingerroot and salt in a bowl. Add fish in batches, mixing to coat evenly.

In a wok or skillet, heat oil over medium-high heat. Add fish and stir-fry, turning gently, 4 minutes or until evenly browned.

In a separate bowl, mix together scallions, vinegar, wine, soy sauce, sugar and orange juice. Stir mixture into wok. Reduce heat to a simmer. Cover and cook 4 minutes. Serve on steamed rice.

Serves 4.

Baked Chilean Sea Bass
with Tomatillo Sauce

A South-of-the-Border treat, this dish is enhanced by the wonderfully tart tomatillos which resemble small, hard green tomatoes with a husk.

1	pound tomatillos, husks removed and rinsed	1	teaspoon salt
2	cups water	2	teaspoons lime juice
1	large clove garlic, minced	4	sea bass steaks (4 ounces each), about 1-inch thick
¼	medium onion, chopped	¼	cup low-fat sour cream
1	serrano chile pepper, seeded and minced		Chopped fresh cilantro for garnish
2	teaspoons oil		

Preheat oven to 375 degrees.

Combine tomatillos and 2 cups water in a saucepan. Bring to a boil. Reduce heat to a simmer and cook 10 minutes or until tomatillos are tender. Purée tomatillos with liquid and set aside.

Sauté garlic, onion and chile pepper in oil in a skillet coated with nonstick cooking spray for 1 to 2 minutes or until tender. Stir in tomatillo purée. Bring to a simmer and cook 5 minutes or until purée thickens slightly. Season with salt and lime juice.

Place fish in 4 individual baking dishes. Pour tomatillo sauce over fish. Bake 30 minutes or until fish flakes easily when tested with a fork. Just before serving, spoon sour cream over fish and sprinkle with cilantro. Serve with rice and squash dishes.

Serves 4.

With this dish, the tomatillos make a red wine more desirable. Try a Pinot Noir, either California or New Zealand would be good, or a French Beaujolais.

Green Chile Sole

This delicate, but lively tasting dish originated in Baja California.

1	pound fresh white or brown mushrooms, stems trimmed, thinly sliced	2	tablespoons all-purpose flour
2	tablespoons butter or olive oil, divided	⅔	cup vegetable broth
½	cup chopped onion	½	cup sour cream
1	can (7 ounces) diced green chiles	1	tablespoon lime juice
		2	pounds filet of sole
			Salt to taste
			Watercress sprigs for garnish

Preheat oven to 400 degrees.

Sauté mushrooms in 1 tablespoon butter or olive oil in a 10- to 12-inch skillet over high heat for 12 to 15 minutes or until lightly browned. Spoon mushrooms into a shallow 1½-quart casserole dish, or divide equally among 4 shallow 1½-cup ramekins.

Return skillet to heat. Add 1 tablespoon butter or olive oil, onion and chiles to skillet. Cook, stirring often, for 5 minutes or until onion is limp. Blend in flour. Stir in broth. Purée mixture in a blender or food processor and return to skillet. Add sour cream and cook and stir over medium heat until almost boiling. Remove from heat and stir in lime juice.

Rinse fish and arrange in an even layer over mushrooms in casserole dish or ramekins. Cover with sauce. Bake 12 to 15 minutes or until fish flakes. Season with salt. Garnish with watercress sprigs and serve with rice or colored pasta.

Serves 4.

Grilled Tuna Fajitas Ⓓ

An authentic taste of California.

1	tablespoon olive oil	2	tablespoons butter, melted
1	large yellow onion, thinly sliced	1	tablespoon vegetable oil
1	large green bell pepper, thinly sliced	8	flour tortillas, heated, without lard
2½	teaspoons finely minced garlic	¾	cup shredded longhorn cheese
1	teaspoon black pepper	1	cup shredded lettuce
	Salt to taste	1	cup diced tomatoes
2	pounds fresh yellowfin tuna, cut into ¼-inch thick steaks		Salsa, medium or hot
			Sour cream
			Guacamole (recipe below)

Heat oil in a large skillet over high heat. Add onion and bell pepper and sauté 2 minutes. Add garlic, black pepper and salt. Sauté 3 minutes or until onion is golden.

Preheat broiler. Brush tuna with melted butter. Brush a broiler pan with oil. Broil tuna 3 to 4 minutes or until done. Cut broiled tuna into long, thin strips.

Divide tuna among warm tortillas, arranging strips on one side of each tortilla. Sprinkle with cheese. Place sautéed vegetables on other half of each tortilla. Broil tortillas, open faced, until cheese melts. Fold tortillas over and serve with lettuce, tomatoes, salsa, sour cream and guacamole.

Guacamole
This classic Mexican avocado recipe can be served as an appetizer with chips, or served as a topping for many Mexican dishes.

3	small avocados	1	medium tomato, or 2 small tomatillos with husks removed, finely chopped
1	small onion, minced		
4	cloves garlic, minced or pressed	3	tablespoons lemon juice
		1	small jalapeño pepper, seeded
			Salt and pepper to taste

Place all ingredients in a food processor and coarsely chop; or mash avocado, finely mince onion and garlic and finely chop tomato and jalapeño, then mix all ingredients thoroughly.

Serves 8.

To heat tortillas, place a short stack between paper towels and place in microwave for 20 to 30 seconds.

California avocados have a buttery flavor and ultra-rich creamy flesh. These are best for guacamole and other spreads, and in blended dressings and cold soups. Most of the fat in avocado is the health-friendly monounsaturated kind. To keep guacamole from discoloring, place plastic wrap directly onto surface to seal out the air.

With Asian or curry dishes, the wine of choice is Gewürztraminer. It is a white wine with a spicy taste that stands up to the heat of Szechwan or other spicy cuisine. Favorites are the ones from Alsace in France, as they are bone dry and elegant.

Pan-Seared Tuna with Ginger, Soy and Cilantro Sauce Ⓟ

2	tablespoons fresh lemon juice	6	tuna steaks (5 ounces each, about 1 to 1¼-inches thick)
2	tablespoons sesame oil		Ginger, Soy and Cilantro Sauce (recipe below)
2	tablespoons soy sauce		Fresh cilantro sprigs for garnish
1	teaspoon black pepper		

Whisk lemon juice, sesame oil, soy sauce and pepper in a small bowl to blend. Place tuna steaks in a 13 x 9-inch glass baking dish. Pour lemon juice marinade over tuna, turning to coat. Cover and refrigerate 3 hours, turning occasionally.

Remove tuna from marinade. Spray a large nonstick skillet with cooking spray and place over high heat. Add 3 steaks to skillet and cook about 3 minutes per side for medium-rare. Transfer steaks to a plate and tent with foil to keep warm. Repeat with remaining 3 steaks. Place steaks on individual serving plates. Spoon Ginger, Soy and Cilantro Sauce over steaks and garnish with cilantro.

Ginger, Soy and Cilantro Sauce

1½	teaspoons sesame oil	3	tablespoons rice vinegar
½	cup minced shallots	2	tablespoons soy sauce
1	tablespoon minced fresh gingerroot	2	tablespoons chopped fresh cilantro
1	cup canned vegetable broth		Salt and pepper to taste
¼	cup frozen orange juice concentrate, thawed		

Heat oil in a small saucepan over medium-high heat. Add shallots and ginger and sauté 2 minutes. Add broth, orange juice concentrate and vinegar. Boil mixture until reduced to ¾ cup. This can be made a day ahead, covered and refrigerated; bring to a boil before continuing. Stir in soy sauce and cilantro. Simmer 1 minute. Season with salt and pepper.

Serves 6, makes ¾ cup sauce.

Kugels
& Pasta

Kugels & Pasta

Buttermilk Noodle Kugel

1	pound medium egg noodles, cooked and drained	4	eggs, well beaten
½	cup margarine, melted	½	cup sugar
		1	quart buttermilk

Topping

1	cup corn flake crumbs	2	tablespoons margarine, melted
1	cup brown sugar		

Preheat oven to 350 degrees.

Place cooked noodles in a large bowl. Add melted margarine, eggs, sugar and buttermilk in order listed. Mix well and pour into a greased 13 x 9-inch pan. Bake 45 minutes.

Meanwhile, combine all topping ingredients.

After kugel has baked initial 45 minutes, sprinkle on topping. Bake 30 minutes longer.

Serves 12 to 15.

Fruit-Filled Noodle Kugel Ⓓ

1	package (8 ounces) medium-size flat noodles	½	cup sugar
1	can (16 ounces) pitted dark cherries in syrup, drained	2	teaspoons vanilla
		4	eggs, or 1 cup egg substitute
1	can (10 ounces) Mandarin oranges in syrup, drained	1	can (8 ounces) crushed pineapple, with juice
1	cup low-fat sour cream	2	tablespoons sugar
1	package (8 ounces) cream cheese, softened and cut into small pieces	1	teaspoon cinnamon

Preheat oven to 350 degrees.

Cook noodles until al dente. While they are cooking, drain cherries and oranges in a colander and rinse lightly with water; set aside. When noodles have cooked, drain and return to pot; set aside.

In a food processor or blender, combine sour cream, cream cheese, ½ cup sugar, vanilla and eggs. Process 1 minute or until mixture is smooth. Pour mixture over noodles and mix well. Add drained cherries and oranges and pineapple with juice and mix gently until fruit is evenly distributed.

Transfer to a greased 13 x 9-inch baking dish. Push down any cherries that float to the top. Combine 2 tablespoons sugar and cinnamon and sprinkle over top of noodles. Bake 1 hour.

Serves 12.

Kugel may be made ahead and reheated, or frozen. To freeze, cover with plastic wrap, defrost in refrigerator and reheat in microwave oven.

Noodle Kugel with Mushrooms and Sour Cream Ⓓ

This would be a good savory kugel for Shavout.

*Cook a quantity
of pasta. Package pasta
in portion sizes in plastic
bags and freeze. When
ready to use, run
cold water over bag
to defrost.*

6 tablespoons butter	Dash of cayenne pepper
2 large onions, chopped	(optional)
1½ pounds mushrooms, halved	12 ounces medium egg noodles
and cut into thick slices	2 cups creamed cottage cheese
Salt and freshly ground	1⅓ cups sour cream
pepper to taste	4 eggs, beaten
2 teaspoons sweet paprika,	2 tablespoons butter
plus extra for sprinkling	

Preheat oven to 350 degrees.

Melt 6 tablespoons butter in a large skillet over medium-low heat. Add onions and cook 10 minutes or until very tender. Add mushrooms and season with salt and pepper, paprika and cayenne. Cook 10 minutes or until onions are browned and mushrooms are tender. If there is liquid remaining in the pan, cook and stir over high heat until liquid evaporates.

Cook noodles, uncovered, in a large pot of boiling salted water over high heat for 5 minutes or until nearly tender, but still firm. Drain, rinse with cold water and drain again well. Transfer noodles to a large bowl. Add mushroom mixture, cottage cheese and sour cream. Stir in eggs.

Transfer mixture to a greased 3-quart baking dish. Dot top with 2 tablespoons butter and sprinkle lightly with paprika. Bake, uncovered, for 1 hour or until set and lightly browned on top. Serve from baking dish.

Serves 12.

Orange Currant Noodle Kugel 🅓

¾	cup currants	1½	teaspoons vanilla
2	cups sour cream	½	teaspoon cinnamon
2	cups cottage cheese	¼	teaspoon salt
5	eggs	1	package (12 ounces) wide egg noodles
½	cup plus 1 tablespoon sugar		
5	tablespoons unsalted butter, melted	1½	large Granny Smith apples, peeled and grated
1½	tablespoons orange zest		

Topping

¼	cup sugar	2	tablespoons unsalted butter, melted
¼	teaspoon cinnamon		
⅓	cup sliced blanched almonds		

Preheat oven to 350 degrees.

In a small bowl, soak currants in enough hot water to cover for 5 minutes. Drain well.

In a blender, combine sour cream, cottage cheese, eggs, sugar, butter, zest, vanilla, cinnamon and salt. Blend until smooth.

Cook noodles in boiling salted water for 5 minutes or until tender. Drain well.

Combine cooked noodles, sour cream mixture, currants and apples. Transfer mixture to a greased 13 x 9-inch baking dish or other shallow baking dish.

To make topping, combine sugar, cinnamon and almonds together and sprinkle evenly over kugel. Drizzle melted butter on top.

Bake in center of oven for 55 to 60 minutes or until cooked through and golden.

Serves 12 to 15.

Pecan Noodle Ring Ⓓ

Adding ½ cup golden raisins makes a perfect Rosh Hashanah dish.

4	tablespoons butter	4	tablespoons butter, melted
½	cup dark brown sugar	½	teaspoon cinnamon
	Pecan halves	⅓	cup sugar
8	ounces broad noodles, cooked and drained	⅛	teaspoon salt
2	eggs, lightly beaten	1	cup applesauce

Preheat oven to 350 degrees.

Melt 4 tablespoons butter in the bottom of a greased Bundt pan. Add brown sugar and press into bottom of pan. Press pecan halves, flat-side up, into sugar to form a pattern.

Combine drained noodles, eggs, 4 tablespoons melted butter, cinnamon, sugar, salt and applesauce. Carefully spread mixture over pecans.

Bake 1 hour. Unmold onto a serving plate.

Serves 12.

Noodle Kugel Soufflé Ⓓ

1	package (8 ounces) medium noodles	2	cups sour cream
½	cup margarine, softened	½	teaspoon salt
½	cup sugar	2	teaspoons vanilla
1	cup cottage cheese	5	eggs
			Cinnamon

Preheat oven to 350 degrees.

Cook noodles in boiling salted water for about 8 minutes. Drain and set aside.

In a large bowl, beat margarine and sugar together. Add cottage cheese, sour cream, salt and vanilla. Mix in eggs, one at a time, beating after each addition. Stir in cooked noodles. Pour mixture into a greased 13 x 9-inch baking dish. Sprinkle with cinnamon. Bake 50 to 55 minutes. Let stand 5 minutes before cutting into squares.

Serves 12.

May be frozen and reheated.

Spinach Noodle Ring

2	packages (10 ounces each) frozen chopped spinach, thawed and drained	1	teaspoon salt
3	eggs, lightly beaten	1	package (8 ounces) broad noodles, cooked and drained
1	cup sour cream (regular or low fat)	1	onion, chopped
		½	cup butter

Preheat oven to 350 degrees.

Combine spinach, eggs, sour cream and salt in a bowl. Add drained noodles and mix well. Sauté onion in butter until tender. Fold sautéed onion into noodle mixture and blend well. Transfer into a greased 6-cup ring mold Bundt or a 3-quart glass baking dish.

Place pan in oven in a pan filled with ¾ cup water. Bake 45 minutes. (The water in the other pan keeps top of noodles from burning.)

Serves 12.

PESTO

For an authentic Italian taste, you can use homemade or store bought pesto for flavoring baked potatoes, rice, sliced tomatoes or pasta.

Moroccan Eggplant Lasagna

3	tablespoons olive oil	1	can (8 ounces) tomato sauce
1	large eggplant, diced	¼	cup red wine vinegar
1	green bell pepper, chopped	¼	cup cilantro leaves (optional)
2	cloves garlic, minced or mashed	⅓	pound lasagna noodles
1	tablespoon ground cumin	8	ounces mozzarella cheese, sliced
¼	teaspoon cayenne pepper	¼	cup freshly grated Parmesan cheese
2	teaspoons sugar		
1	teaspoon salt		

Preheat oven to 350 degrees.

Heat oil in a large saucepan over medium heat. Add eggplant, bell pepper, garlic, cumin, cayenne, sugar, salt, tomato sauce and vinegar. Cover and cook 20 minutes, stirring occasionally. Add cilantro just before assembling lasagna.

Cook noodles in boiling water for 15 minutes or until tender; drain. Cut drained lasagna noodles into 7 inch long strips. Place half of noodle strips in an 8-inch square baking dish. Cover with half of tomato sauce and half of cheeses. Repeat layers. Bake 20 to 30 minutes or until cheese is melted and lasagna is heated through.

Serves 4 to 6.

Fennel-Broccoli Lasagna Ⓓ

This dish is assembled with uncooked pasta. It really works!

1	large fennel bulb, chopped	1	large green bell pepper, chopped
1	large onion, chopped		
4	cloves garlic, chopped	1	quart ricotta cheese
2	tablespoons olive oil	¾	cup freshly grated Parmesan cheese
1	jar (30 ounces) mushroom spaghetti sauce		
		1	package (16 ounces) part-skim mozzarella cheese, sliced
1	pound dry lasagna noodles		
1	package (16 ounces) frozen broccoli pieces		

Preheat oven to 350 degrees.

Sauté fennel, onion and garlic in oil in a large skillet until they just start to brown. Add spaghetti sauce. Simmer, uncovered, for about 30 minutes. Add ½ cup or more of water after 15 minutes of simmering to keep the sauce liquid.

Cover the bottom of a greased 13 x 9-inch baking pan with some of the sauce. Layer half the uncooked lasagna noodles over the sauce. Scatter broccoli and bell pepper on top. Dot with ricotta cheese and sprinkle with half the Parmesan cheese. Cover with remaining noodles and sauce. Top with mozzarella cheese and remaining Parmesan cheese. At this point, lasagna can be refrigerated until ready to bake.

Cover pan with foil. Bake 30 minutes. Uncover pan and bake 15 minutes longer.

Serves 8 to 10.

Baked Ziti Ⓓ

1	package (10-ounces) dry ziti pasta	1	egg, beaten
		1	jar (32-ounces) spaghetti sauce, divided
24	ounces ricotta cheese		
1	pound mozzarella cheese, shredded	¼	cup Parmesan cheese

Preheat oven to 375 degrees.

Bring a large pot of lightly salted water to a boil. Add ziti and cook 8 to 10 minutes or until al dente; drain and rinse. Transfer drained pasta to a medium bowl. Add ricotta cheese, mozzarella cheese, egg and 1½ cups spaghetti sauce. Spoon ziti mixture into a lightly greased 9 x 13-inch baking dish. Top with remaining spaghetti sauce. Sprinkle Parmesan cheese on top. Bake 30 minutes. Let stand 15 minutes before serving.

Makes 6 to 8 servings.

Spinach Lasagna D

Once again, a lasagna recipe featuring uncooked noodles.

1	pound ricotta cheese	⅛	teaspoon black pepper
1	cup shredded mozzarella cheese	1	jar (32 ounces) marinara sauce
1	egg, beaten	12	lasagna noodles, uncooked
2	packages (10 ounces) frozen chopped spinach, thawed and well drained	1	cup water
		½	cup shredded mozzarella cheese
¾	teaspoon dried oregano		

Preheat oven to 350 degrees.

In a medium bowl, combine ricotta cheese, 1 cup mozzarella cheese, egg, spinach, oregano, and pepper. Cover bottom of a greased 13 x 9-inch glass baking pan with one-fourth of sauce. Top with 4 noodles, then half of ricotta mixture and another fourth of sauce. Repeat layers with 4 more noodles, remaining ricotta mixture and another one-fourth of sauce. Top with remaining 4 noodles and remainder of sauce. Pour 1 cup water around the edges and cover tightly with foil.

Bake 1 hour. Remove foil and sprinkle ½ cup mozzarella cheese over lasagna. Return to oven and bake 10 minutes longer or until cheese is melted.

Serves 6 to 8.

Low-Fat Pasta Frittata D

Instead of throwing out leftover pasta, use it to make a frittata.

4	green onions, sliced	½	cup low-fat ricotta cheese
2	teaspoons olive oil	1	teaspoon chopped fresh rosemary
2	cups cooked pasta (any small variety)	½	teaspoon salt
¾	cup sliced roasted red peppers (from a jar)	¼	teaspoon black pepper
4	eggs	¼	cup shredded Cheddar cheese (optional)
4	egg whites		

In a medium, nonstick, ovenproof skillet, sauté onions in olive oil for 2 minutes. Remove from heat and stir in pasta and red peppers. In a large bowl, whisk together eggs, egg whites, ricotta cheese, rosemary, salt and pepper. Return skillet to low heat and stir in egg mixture. Cover and cook 8 minutes or until eggs are almost set. Place under a preheated broiler, 5 inches from heat source, and cook 2 to 4 minutes or until top is set. Top with Cheddar cheese.

Makes 4 servings.

Fresh Artichoke Pasta D

Since California is the artichoke capital of the world, we wanted you to enjoy this flavorful dish. Serve with any of our green salads.

Toss pasta with prepared pesto sauce mixed with sun-dried tomatoes.

3	pounds fresh baby artichokes	2	tablespoons fresh lemon juice
1-2	cups water	1	packet vegetable bouillon
2	tablespoons lemon juice		Salt and pepper to taste
⅓-½	cup olive oil	½-1	cup white wine (optional)
1	large white or yellow onion, chopped	1	pound dry fettuccini, linguine or rigatoni pasta, cooked and drained
3	cloves garlic, minced		Freshly grated Parmesan cheese
2	teaspoons dry mixed Italian herbs		

Wash artichokes well, cutting off stems at base. Cut artichokes in half and peel back and snap off petals until the cone of yellow petals remain. Cut off top third of each artichoke and drop them into a bowl of 1 cup water with 2 tablespoons lemon juice to prevent browning. Drain.

In a skillet, cook artichokes in enough boiling water to cover for 4 to 5 minutes, depending on the size of artichokes. Drain well and set aside.

In same skillet, heat oil over medium-high heat. Add baby artichokes, onion, garlic and Italian herbs. Cook and stir 5 to 6 minutes or until lightly browned. Sprinkle with 2 tablespoons lemon juice, vegetable bouillon, salt and pepper. If more liquid sauce is desired over pasta, add ½ to 1 cup white wine to mixture at this time. Toss with drained noodles. Sprinkle with cheese.

Serves 6.

Substitute risotto for the pasta.

Cheese Ravioli with Salsa Verde

A South-of-the-Border Italian taste.

1	pound tomatillos	½	cup fresh cilantro
¾	pound fresh poblano or pasilla chiles, rinsed	2	packages (9 ounces each) cheese ravioli
1	onion (8 ounces)	¼	cup finely chopped tomato
3	cloves garlic, unpeeled		Salt to taste
1	cup vegetable broth		

Discard husks and rinse tomatillos well. Cut chiles in half lengthwise and remove and discard stems, seeds and veins. Cut onion crosswise into 1-inch slices. Arrange tomatillos, chiles, cut-side down, onion and garlic in a single layer in a 15 x 10-inch baking pan. Broil 4 to 6 inches from heat for 15 to 20 minutes or until vegetables are well-browned. Peel garlic when cool.

Transfer vegetables and any liquid to a blender or food processor. Add broth and cilantro and process until smooth. Pour mixture into a 3- to 4-quart pan. Cook over medium heat, stirring occasionally, until steaming.

Meanwhile, in a 5- to 6-quart saucepan over high heat, bring 2 quarts water to a boil. Add ravioli and cook, stirring occasionally, for 4 to 6 minutes or until pasta is tender to bite; drain. Add ravioli to chile mixture and stir gently. Spoon into wide individual serving bowls. Garnish with tomato and season with salt.

Serves 4.

Penne with Eggplant, Garlic and Cherry Tomatoes Ⓓ

For an easy pasta toss in some chopped fresh or roasted red bell peppers, olive oil and lemon zest. Add some crumbled feta cheese. Add chopped fresh thyme or oregano if you have it on hand.

¾-1 pound eggplant, grilled
1 large whole head garlic (about 2 ounces), grilled
1 teaspoon salt
3 tablespoons olive oil
¼ cup fresh lemon juice
¼ cup olive oil
⅓ cup packed thinly sliced fresh basil
¾ pound red, or yellow and red cherry tomatoes, grilled, in 1 tablespoon olive oil

¾ pound red, or yellow and red cherry tomatoes, halved
¼ cup pine nuts
1 pound penne or other tubular pasta
¼ cup finely grated pecorino or Parmesan cheese (about 1 ounce)
 Salt and freshly ground pepper to taste
4 fresh sprigs basil for garnish

Halve grilled eggplant, scrape out pulp with a knife and place in a food processor. Break grilled garlic into individual cloves, peel and add to food processor with salt. Process 5 minutes or until eggplant mixture is very smooth, pulsing on and off and stopping to scrape down sides of container. With machine running, slowly pour 3 tablespoons oil through feed tube. Transfer mixture to a small bowl if not using immediately.

Place lemon juice in a medium bowl. Gradually whisk ¼ cup oil into lemon juice. Add basil, grilled tomatoes and tomato halves. Mix gently and let marinate at least 1 hour.

Stir pine nuts in a small heavy skillet over medium heat until brown. Cool, then place in a covered container.

Cook pasta in a large pot of boiling water, stirring occasionally, for 12 minutes or until cooked al dente. Meanwhile, add ¼ cup pasta cooking water to eggplant mixture. Drain pasta and place in a large container. Add grated cheese and mix well. Add eggplant purée and mix again. Stir in tomato mixture. Season with salt and pepper.

To serve, stir pasta and divide among 4 individual plates. Sprinkle with toasted pine nuts and garnish with basil sprigs.

Serves 4 to 6.

Planning ahead: Dish can be completely prepared the day before and brought to room temperature (allow 2 hours). Another option is to toast the pine nuts, purée the eggplant and marinate the tomatoes a day in advance. Bring these preparations to room temperature, cook the pasta and mix everything together before heading off to your picnic.

Rotini with Roasted Peppers, Spinach and Pine Nuts Ⓓ

2	red bell peppers	¼	teaspoon dried red pepper flakes
1	tablespoon all-purpose flour		Salt and pepper to taste
1	tablespoon butter, softened	1	package (10 ounces) fresh spinach leaves, stems removed, leaves chopped
1	tablespoon olive oil		
1½	cups chopped onion		
2	teaspoons minced garlic	8	ounces dry rotini pasta
1¼	cups canned low-salt vegetable broth	¾	cup freshly grated Parmesan cheese (about 2½ ounces)
¾	cup dry white wine		
½	teaspoon dried thyme	½	cup pine nuts, toasted

Char bell peppers over a gas flame or in the broiler until blackened on all sides. Wrap in a paper bag and let stand 10 minutes. Peel and seed peppers and cut into ½-inch strips.

Mix flour and butter in a small bowl to form a paste. Heat oil in a large skillet over medium heat. Add onion and sauté 5 minutes or until tender. Add garlic and sauté 1 minute. Add broth, wine, thyme and pepper flakes. Simmer 6 minutes or until liquid is reduced by half. Whisk in flour paste and simmer 1 minute or until sauce thickens slightly. Season with salt and pepper. Add roasted pepper strips and spinach and simmer 2 minutes or until spinach wilts.

Meanwhile, cook pasta, stirring occasionally, in a large pot of boiling salted water until just tender but still firm to bite. Drain well. Add pasta, cheese and pine nuts to sauce and toss to coat.

Serves 4 appetizers or 2 main courses.

Baked Pasta with Spinach, Goat Cheese and Tomatoes Ⓓ

1 package (8 ounces) fusilli pasta, cooked and drained
1 tablespoon olive oil
1 can (28 ounces) diced tomatoes, drained with 3 tablespoons liquid reserved
2 tablespoons olive oil
¼ teaspoon dried red pepper flakes
2 cloves garlic
1 medium scallion
2 packages (10 ounces) frozen chopped spinach, thawed, drained and squeezed dry

1 egg
1 cup ricotta cheese
½ teaspoon salt
¼ teaspoon nutmeg
¼ teaspoon black pepper
1 tablespoon olive oil
¼ teaspoon dried rosemary
¼ teaspoon dried basil
¼ teaspoon dried oregano
7 ounces mild goat cheese, softened
1 tablespoon olive oil (for drizzling)
  Salt to taste

Preheat oven to 375 degrees.

Toss drained pasta with 1 tablespoon oil; set aside. Toss tomatoes with 2 tablespoons oil and pepper flakes in a small bowl; set aside.

Mince garlic and scallion in a food processor. Add spinach, egg, ricotta cheese, ½ teaspoon salt, nutmeg and pepper and process until just combined. Spread mixture evenly in a lightly greased 2-quart shallow baking dish.

Spread pasta evenly over spinach and press gently into place. Drizzle reserved tomato liquid over pasta. Scatter tomatoes and any juices from bowl over pasta, pressing lightly into place.

Combine 1 tablespoon oil, rosemary, basil and oregano in a small bowl. Cut goat cheese into small chunks and toss lightly in herb mixture. Arrange goat cheese pieces on top of casserole so pasta is completely covered with tomatoes and cheese. Drizzle with 1 tablespoon olive oil and sprinkle lightly with salt.

Loosely cover dish with tented foil and place on a baking sheet. Bake 1 hour, 10 minutes. Remove foil and bake 10 minutes longer. Serve hot.

Serves 4 to 6.

Baked Pasta with Tomatoes, Shiitake Mushrooms and Three Cheeses

2	cups finely chopped onion		2	cans (28 ounces each) Italian tomatoes, drained and chopped
2	large cloves garlic, minced			
¼	teaspoon dried red pepper flakes, or to taste		4	ounces Italian fontina cheese, shredded (about 1 cup)
1	teaspoon dried basil, crumbled		4	ounces Gorgonzola cheese, crumbled (about 1 cup)
1	teaspoon dried oregano, crumbled		1¼	cups freshly grated Italian Parmesan cheese
2	tablespoons olive oil		⅔	cup minced fresh parsley
1	pound fresh shiitake mushrooms, sliced		1	pound dry farfalle (large bow tie) or penne pasta
3	tablespoons unsalted butter			Salt and pepper to taste
3	tablespoons all-purpose flour		¼	cup freshly grated Italian Parmesan cheese
2	cups milk		1	tablespoon butter

Preheat oven to 450 degrees.

Cook and stir onion, garlic, pepper flakes, basil and oregano in oil in a large skillet over medium-low heat until onion is softened. Add mushrooms and cook and stir mixture over medium heat for 10 to 15 minutes. Transfer mixture to a large bowl.

Return skillet to medium-low heat and add 3 tablespoons butter until melted. Whisk in flour to make a roux. Blend in milk and cook and stir 2 minutes or until thickened. Pour sauce over mushroom mixture. Add tomatoes, fontina cheese, Gorgonzola cheese, 1¼ cups Parmesan cheese and parsley.

In a large pot of boiling salted water, cook pasta 5 minutes; drain well. Pasta will not be tender. Add drained pasta to mushroom mixture. Season with salt and pepper. Toss to combine well. Transfer to a greased 3- or 4-quart baking dish. At this point, dish can be covered and refrigerated overnight. Bring to room temperature before continuing.

Sprinkle with ¼ cup Parmesan cheese. Dot with 1 tablespoon butter. Bake 25 to 30 minutes or until top is golden and pasta is tender.

Serves 8 to 10.

Did you know that Italian parsley has more nutrients and a better flavor than curly parsley?

Keep fresh by sprinkling parsley with water, wrapping in paper towels and refrigerating in a plastic bag. You can freeze parsley by washing, drying and chopping the leaves, then freezing in a plastic container or bag. Remove just the amount you need for each recipe.

For a simple pasta dish, add chopped, cooked broccoli and finely chopped fresh garlic that have been briefly sautéed in olive oil, adding some vegetable broth to create sufficient sauce to coat your pasta. Sprinkle with freshly chopped basil and kalamata olives.

Fresh Tuna Pasta Puttanesca

Made with grilled fresh tuna, this quick-cooking pasta dish gains fresh summer flavor. If you prefer, this fish can be cooked on the barbecue rather than indoors.

¼ cup olive oil	1½ teaspoons fresh oregano leaves, or ½ teaspoon dried
1 medium onion, thinly sliced	
1 teaspoon dried red pepper flakes	8 ounces dry vermicelli pasta
2 cloves garlic, minced or pressed	8 ounces fresh tuna fillet, about ½-inch thick
2 cups chopped Roma tomatoes	1 tablespoon olive oil
	Salt and freshly ground pepper to taste
¾ cup dry white wine	
¼ cup sliced ripe olives	¼ cup chopped Italian or curly parsley
1 tablespoon drained capers	

Pour ¼ cup oil into a 10- or 12-inch skillet over medium heat. Add onion and pepper flakes and cook 5 minutes or until onion is softened. Stir in garlic, tomatoes, wine, olives, capers and oregano. Adjust heat so mixture boils gently. Continue to cook, uncovered and stirring occasionally, for 10 to 12 minutes or until tomatoes are soft and sauce is slightly thickened.

Meanwhile, in a 5- to 6-quart saucepan, cook pasta in 3 quarts boiling water for 8 to 10 minutes or until al dente.

While pasta cooks, brush tuna on all sides with 1 tablespoon oil. Preheat a ridged cooktop grill pan over medium-high heat until a drop of water dances on the surface. Place tuna on grill pan and cook, turning once, for 3 to 4 minutes total or until fish is slightly translucent or wet in the thickest part.

Season sauce with salt and pepper. If sauce becomes too thick, add a spoonful of water from pasta. Stir in parsley. Slice tuna across the grain into thin, bite-size strips.

Drain pasta and place in a serving bowl. Top with sauce and tuna.

Serves 4.

Side Dishes

Side Dishes

Roasted Asparagus Ⓓ

1	tablespoon olive oil	3	tablespoons balsamic vinegar
1½	pounds asparagus, very slender stalks (¼-inch), tough ends removed		Salt and pepper to taste
		¼	cup Parmesan cheese curls (½ ounce)

Preheat oven to 500 degrees.

Place a 10-inch ovenproof skillet in oven 5 minutes. Remove hot skillet from oven. Add oil to skillet and swirl. Roll asparagus in oil with a tongs. Bake 5 to 7 minutes or until tender-crisp. Drizzle with vinegar and season with salt and pepper. Scatter cheese curls on top.

Serves 4.

Poached Asparagus with Wasabi Butter Ⓓ

3	tablespoons unsalted butter, softened		Pinch of salt
2	teaspoons wasabi powder (available in Asian food stores)	2	pounds medium asparagus, tough ends removed
1	teaspoon water	½	tablespoon salt
			Salt and pepper to taste

Cut butter into small pieces and place in the bowl of an electric mixer. Mix wasabi powder with water until a paste forms. Add paste to butter. Add a pinch of salt and beat until thoroughly blended. Scoop out wasabi butter and place in a small bowl. Refrigerate until cold.

With a vegetable peeler, carefully peel the bottom of the asparagus stalks. Fill a 10- or 12-inch skillet with several inches of water. Add ½ tablespoon salt and bring to a boil. Add asparagus and cook 10 minutes or until stalks are easily pierced with the tip of a sharp knife. They should still be bright green; do not overcook. Drain thoroughly.

Divide the asparagus into 6 equal portions and arrange on individual plates. Top each portion with wasabi butter. Sprinkle to taste with salt and pepper. Serve immediately.

Serves 6.

PARSLEY AND LEMON GREMOLATA

This refreshing seasoning mixture can be added to freshly cooked broccoli, asparagus, green beans or fresh peas. Just place in a covered container and chill until ready to mix with vegetables.

In a food processor, whirl 1 cup coarsely chopped Italian or regular parsley, 3 tablespoons olive oil, 2 teaspoons lemon zest, 1 peeled garlic clove and ¼ teaspoon black pepper until finely chopped. Salt to taste. This makes about ¼ cup and can season between 1½ to 2 pounds of vegetables.

Sprinkle balsamic vinegar on baked new potatoes in place of butter or sour cream, or drizzle over stir-fried vegetables.

Black Bean and Mixed Rice Casserole

Cut fresh mushrooms
easily and quickly by
using an egg slicer.

1	package (6 ounces) white and wild rice mix	1	can (15 ounces) black beans, drained and rinsed
1	cup chopped onion	1	cup whole kernel corn
1	cup chopped green bell pepper	½	cup peas
1	cup chopped red bell pepper	1½	cups sour cream
2	cups sliced mushrooms	1	cup shredded Cheddar cheese
2	teaspoons Italian seasoning		Salt and pepper to taste
		¼	cup shredded Cheddar cheese

Preheat oven to 350 degrees.

Cook rice mix according to package directions, discarding seasoning packet.

Spray a skillet with nonstick cooking spray and place over medium heat until hot. Add onion, bell peppers, mushrooms and Italian seasoning. Cover and cook 5 minutes or until vegetables are tender and excess moisture evaporates.

In a large bowl, combine cooked rice, vegetable mixture, beans, corn, peas, sour cream and 1 cup Cheddar cheese. Season with salt and pepper. Spoon mixture into a 2-quart casserole dish. Sprinkle ¼ cup Cheddar cheese on top. Bake, uncovered, for 30 minutes or until heated through.

Serves 6 to 8.

Black Beans with Onions and Balsamic Vinegar

Microwaving vegetables
offers you the best
nutritional value next to
steaming them. You lose
vitamins in the water
if you cook them in a
pot on the stove.

1	tablespoon olive oil	2	cans (16 ounces each) black beans, rinsed and drained
1	medium-size red onion, chopped	1	tablespoon plus 2 teaspoons balsamic vinegar
2	cloves garlic, minced	¼	teaspoon salt, or to taste
1½	teaspoons ground cumin		
1½	teaspoons hot chile powder		

Heat oil in saucepan over medium heat until hot. Add onion and cook 8 minutes or until translucent. Add garlic, cumin and chile powder. Cook and stir 30 seconds or until mixed. Add beans, vinegar, and salt. Cook, stirring often, until heated through. Beans can be refrigerated up to 2 days, or frozen.

Serves 12.

To make in microwave, combine oil, onion and garlic in a 6- or 8-cup microwave-safe bowl. Cover with plastic and microwave on high for 2 minutes. Stir and microwave 2 to 3 minutes longer or until translucent. Stir in cumin, chile powder, beans, vinegar and salt. Cover and microwave 5 minutes or until heated through.

Sautéed Broccoli and Sugar Snap Peas with Mushrooms and Garlic Ⓟ

A wonderful side dish for fish or poultry. May be served hot, at room temperature, or chilled.

1½	pounds broccoli	4	large mushrooms, thinly sliced
8	ounces sugar snap peas, strings removed	¼	teaspoon salt, or more to taste
3	tablespoons olive oil		Freshly ground pepper
2-3	large cloves garlic, minced		

Cut off broccoli florets. Peel stems and cut into ⅓-inch slices. Bring a large pot of salted water to a boil. Add broccoli stems and cook 3 minutes. Add florets and cook 1 minute. Add peas and cook 20 seconds. Drain vegetables immediately into a colander. Rinse with cold running water until vegetables are cool. This can be done ahead of time and refrigerated in a covered container overnight.

Heat oil in 10-inch nonstick skillet over medium-high heat. Add garlic and mushrooms and cook, stirring often, for 3 minutes or just until mushrooms are heated through. Add cooked vegetables and cook, stirring gently, for 2 to 3 minutes over high heat or until hot. Season with salt and pepper. Refrigerate at least 2 to 3 hours to serve chilled.

Serves 4.

Mushrooms, whether white button or brown cremini, are freshest when the caps are closed and the gills are not showing.

Sweet and Sour Red Cabbage Ⓓ Ⓟ

This dish can be prepared up to 2 days ahead, covered and refrigerated. When reheating, warm until excess liquid is evaporated, then serve. This is a great accompaniment to chicken or fish.

1	head (3 pounds) red cabbage, core removed, shredded (about 14 cups)	⅓	cup red currant jelly
		2	tablespoons margarine or butter
1	red onion, thinly sliced	1	teaspoon salt, or to taste
2	cups peeled, shredded apple	3¼-3½	cups water
½	cup red wine vinegar		

Combine all ingredients in a 6- to 8-quart saucepan. Cover and cook over medium heat, stirring occasionally, for 75 to 90 minutes or until cabbage is very limp. If mixture begins to stick, add more water as needed, ½ cup at a time.

Serves 10 to 12.

Fresh tomatoes keep longer when placed with the stem side down.

Cabbage Kugel

Serve this kugel for a deliciously different meat accompaniment whose flavor no one can determine.

1 head (1½ to 2 pounds) cabbage	½ cup oil
3-4 eggs	1 teaspoon salt
2 large onions, chopped and sautéed	½ teaspoon pepper
	½ cup matzo meal

Preheat oven to 350 degrees.

Grate cabbage as for coleslaw and place in a colander. Pour boiling water over cabbage 2 or 3 times. (This completely removes cabbage odor.) Drain thoroughly, then transfer cabbage to a large bowl. Add eggs, sautéed onions, oil, salt, pepper and matzo meal. Spoon mixture into a greased 13 x 9-inch glass baking dish. Bake 1 hour or until browned.

Serves 12.

Chiles Stuffed with Tzimmes

A unique tzimmes with a Southwestern flair.

¾ pound pitted prunes	½ teaspoon cinnamon
6 medium carrots, cut into chunks	½ teaspoon salt
3 medium sweet potatoes, peeled and diced (about 2 pounds)	1 tablespoon lemon juice
	¼ cup orange juice
6 tablespoons honey	2 tablespoons chopped fresh coriander
½ teaspoon nutmeg	12 green or red Anaheim chiles

Preheat oven to 250 degrees.

Combine prunes, carrots, sweet potatoes, honey, nutmeg, cinnamon, salt, lemon juice and orange juice and place in a 3-quart baking dish. Cover and bake, stirring occasionally, for 2 hours or until vegetables are soft but not mushy. Cool. Using a potato masher or fork, coarsely mash mixture with the coriander. This tzimmes stuffing mixture can be made a day ahead.

Place chiles on a baking sheet. Roast, turning occasionally, at 450 degrees for 20 minutes or until skin is black. Remove to a plastic or paper bag and leave until cool. Peel off skin.

With a sharp knife, make a slit from the bottom of the stem to the point of each chile. Gently scrape out seeds and rinse the inside of the chiles. Pat each dry and stuff with tzimmes until slightly overstuffed.

Bake at 350 degrees for 10 to 15 minutes.

Serves 10.

Tzimmes stuffing can be placed in a 9 x 13-inch casserole dish and baked at 350 degrees for 20 minutes or until warm.

Carrot Torte Ⓓ Ⓟ

This is a signature dish from one of our members who was the recipient of this "secret" recipe over 50 years ago. It has been featured in several recipe books since that time. She had prepared this for special occasions with rave reviews.

1	cup shortening, margarine or butter	½	teaspoon baking soda
½	cup brown sugar	1	teaspoon baking powder
1	egg	½	teaspoon nutmeg
2	cups grated carrots	½	teaspoon salt
1½	cups flour	½	teaspoon cinnamon

Preheat oven to 350 degrees.

Cream shortening and brown sugar. Add egg, carrots, flour, baking soda, baking powder, nutmeg, salt and cinnamon. Mix well and place in a greased 8 x 8-inch or 7 x 10-inch baking dish.

Refrigerate at least 5 hours or overnight. Remove from refrigerator 1 hour before baking. Bake 1 hour.

Serves 6 to 8.

Leftover baked potatoes can be rebaked if you dip them in water and bake at 350 degrees for 20 minutes.

Plum Ratatouille Ⓟ

2	cups sliced zucchini	¼	teaspoon black pepper
2½	cups sliced eggplant	1½	teaspoons dried basil, crumbled
1	onion, cut into wedges		
1	tablespoon vegetable oil	1	teaspoon dried oregano, crumbled
2	cups diced tomatoes		
4	fresh plums, cut into wedges	1	lemon, cut into wedges
2	teaspoons minced garlic		

In a large nonstick skillet, sauté zucchini, eggplant and onion in oil for 15 minutes or until tender. Add tomatoes, plums, garlic, pepper, basil and oregano. Cover and cook over low heat, stirring occasionally, for 4 minutes or until plums are tender. Squirt fresh lemon juice over top just before serving.

Serves 6.

Avoid wilted vegetables by removing the band on asparagus spears, broccoli or lettuce before storing in refrigerator. Wrap in paper towels, place in a plastic bag and seal. The paper will absorb excess moisture and the vegetables will last longer.

Corn Dressing

A good side dish for poultry.

1	cup butter or margarine	2	cans (14 ounces each) creamed-style corn
4	large onions, diced	1⅓	cups matzo meal
6	eggs		Salt and pepper to taste

Preheat oven to 350 degrees.

Melt butter or margarine in a saucepan. Add onions and sauté. Cool mixture slightly. Gently beat eggs and add to cooled onions. Add corn, matzo meal and salt and pepper. Mix well; mixture will be somewhat loose. Pour mixture into a greased 13 x 9-inch pan. Bake 45 to 60 minutes or until golden brown. Cut into squares.

Serves 12 to 16.

Wild Mushroom Risotto

This risotto is creamy, rich and flavorful if prepared carefully. Italians also like to top the rice with the mushrooms instead of incorporating them into the dish. Try it both ways.

¼	cup dried wild mushrooms Boiling water	½	pound fresh white or cremini mushrooms, chopped
4-5	cups vegetable broth		Salt and pepper to taste
1	tablespoon olive oil	½-¾	cup freshly grated
½	cup finely chopped onion		Parmesan cheese to taste
1	cup Arborio rice		
½	cup white wine		

Place dried mushrooms in a small bowl and cover with boiling water. Soak 10 minutes. Drain and reserve soaking liquid. Dice mushrooms.

Heat broth in a large saucepan and keep warm.

Heat oil in a separate saucepan. Sauté onion in oil until lightly browned. Add rice to onion and stir to coat. Add wine and stir until absorbed. Add all mushrooms and soaking liquid and cook until all is absorbed. Add about a cup of simmering broth to rice and cook over high heat, stirring often with a wooden spoon, until absorbed. Continue to add broth, 1 cup at a time, until rice appears creamy, but firm. Cooking time is about 45 minutes. Season with salt and pepper and stir in cheese. Serve immediately.

Serves 4 side dishes or 2 main courses.

Recipe can easily be doubled.

COOKING FRESH CORN

To keep sweet corn yellow, add 1 teaspoon lemon juice to the cooking water a minute before you remove it from the stove. Salted cooking water only toughens fresh corn.

Keep mushrooms cool and dry. Refrigerate them in a basket or an open paper bag and avoid cleaning them until ready to use. They should stay fresh for 4 to 5 days. Because mushrooms absorb water like a sponge, use a damp cloth to wipe them clean instead of washing them with water.

Maui Onion Tart

Maui onion tarts flavored with a wonderfully complex blend of herbs. The whole wheat crust is a nice contrast to the filling.

2 shallots, thinly sliced	½ teaspoon salt
5 cups thinly sliced Maui onions	½ teaspoon black pepper
1 teaspoon minced fresh thyme	Pie crust (recipe below), or buy frozen pie crust
2 tablespoons olive oil	3 tablespoons bread crumbs
1 can (16 ounces) unsalted Italian plum tomatoes, well drained	¼ cup freshly grated Parmesan cheese
2 tablespoons chopped fresh basil	1 each red and yellow bell peppers, cut into strips
	Niçoise olives

Preheat oven to 425 degrees.

Sauté shallots, onion and thyme in oil in a heavy skillet. Cover and cook over low heat 30 minutes. Break up drained tomatoes and add to skillet with basil, salt and pepper. Cook 45 minutes or until onions are tender, clear and caramelized. Remove from heat. Sprinkle bottom of pie crust with bread crumbs. Spoon onion mixture on top. Sprinkle with cheese.

Bake 25 minutes. Garnish with pepper strips and olives. Serve warm or at room temperature.

Pie Crust

½ cup unbleached flour	⅓ cup unsalted butter
½ cup whole wheat flour	2 tablespoons ice water, or as needed

Combine flours in a bowl. Cut butter into flour in thin slices. Rub butter into flour until mixture resembles coarse meal. Add ice water and mix lightly until just blended and smooth. Use additional water, as needed. Roll out crust and fit into an 8- or 9-inch round tart pan. Refrigerate until ready to use.

Serves 6.

Jalapeño peppers need special handling. To chop and seed, cut a narrow strip along the length of the pepper from stem to tip. Roll pepper, cut-side down and cut off another strip. Repeat twice, resulting in 4 strips to chop or mince. The core and seeds can be discarded. This prevents the juices from spraying.

Mushroom and Goat Cheese Strudel with Balsamic Syrup Ⓓ

If phyllo dough is frozen, thaw in refrigerator at least 8 hours or overnight. For a crisp crust, fill the phyllo dough, cover airtight and chill. When ready to use, uncover and bake according to directions.

2	tablespoons olive oil	3	sheets fresh or frozen phyllo pastry dough, thawed if frozen
½	cup thinly sliced shallots		
4	cloves garlic, minced		
1	pound mushrooms, chopped	6	teaspoons olive oil
¼	cup sherry wine vinegar	½	cup crumbled soft fresh goat cheese (such as Montrachet)
⅓	cup dry sherry		
	Salt and pepper to taste	½	cup balsamic vinegar
2	tablespoons finely chopped fresh parsley	1	tablespoon light molasses

Preheat oven to 375 degrees.

Heat 2 tablespoons oil in a large heavy skillet over medium heat. Add shallots and garlic and sauté 4 minutes. Increase heat to high and add mushrooms. Sauté 15 minutes or until mushrooms are tender and golden. Add sherry wine vinegar, then sherry. Boil 6 minutes or until almost all liquid evaporates. Season with salt and pepper. Cool. Mix in parsley.

Place a sheet of phyllo on a work surface. Brush with 2 teaspoons oil. Top with a second phyllo sheet and brush with 2 teaspoons oil. Add third sheet of phyllo. Sprinkle cheese along one side of phyllo, 1 inch in from edge. Spoon mushroom mixture over cheese. Fold short ends over. Starting at long filled side, roll phyllo up tightly. Place seam-side down on a baking sheet. Brush with remaining 2 teaspoons oil. Using a long sharp knife, score top of strudel through phyllo, making 8 evenly spaced cuts. This can be done covered and chilled, up to 4 hours before baking.

Bake strudel 50 minutes or until golden brown.

Meanwhile, boil balsamic vinegar and molasses in a small heavy saucepan over medium heat for 10 minutes or until reduced to 2½ tablespoons. Cool.

Using a serrated knife, cut hot strudel at score marks into 8 rounds. Drizzle balsamic syrup onto each of 8 plates. Place 2 slices of strudel over syrup on each plate.

Serves 8.

Potato, Spinach and Onion Gratin

1¾ pounds medium Yukon Gold potatoes, unpeeled
2 large onions, halved and thinly sliced
¼ cup water
2 tablespoons extra-virgin olive oil
8 ounces mushrooms, thinly sliced
1 package (10 ounces) frozen chopped spinach, thawed and drained
4 cloves garlic, minced
4 teaspoons chopped fresh thyme
¼ teaspoon nutmeg
1 cup non-fat sour cream
½ cup low-fat milk
Salt and pepper to taste
2 ounces Gruyère cheese, thinly sliced

Preheat oven to 350 degrees.

Cook potatoes in a large saucepan of boiling salted water for 30 minutes or until just tender. Drain and cool. Cut potatoes into ⅓-inch thick slices, removing any loose peel. Set aside.

Combine onions and ¼ cup water in a large nonstick skillet. Cover and simmer over medium heat about 12 minutes or until onions are tender. Stir occasionally while cooking and add water, a tablespoon at a time, if mixture is dry. Increase heat to medium-high and add oil. Add mushrooms and sauté, uncovered, for 10 minutes or until onions are deep golden. Add spinach, garlic, thyme and nutmeg and cook and stir 3 minutes. Remove from heat. Stir in sour cream and milk. Season with salt and pepper.

Layer half of potato slices in a lightly greased 11 x 7 x 2-inch glass baking dish, overlapping slightly. Season with salt and pepper. Spread half on onion mixture over potatoes. Repeat potato and onion layers. Top with cheese. Bake 30 minutes or until hot. Remove from oven and let stand 5 minutes before serving.

Serves 8.

Peel and cut a medium red onion into chrysanthemum flowers by cutting the onion into fourths and then into eighths. Do not cut through core. Drizzle with olive oil and kosher salt. Bake at 400 degrees on a baking sheet for 45 minutes. Onion will spread out like petals. Serve one-half onion per person.

When you purchase a bag of potatoes, put an apple in the bag so the potatoes will last without sprouting and wrinkling for about 2 months. Storing potatoes in a cool, dry place will also minimize sprouting.

Spinach and Artichoke-Stuffed Portobellos Ⓓ

To cook an artichoke fast, microwave it upside down in a glass dish with a little water in the bottom (add lemon juice and olive oil if you like). For 1 artichoke, microwave 7 to 8 minutes on high; for 4 artichokes, about twice as long.

Portobellos

1	tablespoon extra-virgin olive oil			Salt and fresh ground black pepper to taste
5	medium portobello mushroom caps		2	tablespoons balsamic vinegar

Stuffing

1	tablespoon extra-virgin olive oil			Salt and fresh ground black pepper to taste
3	cloves garlic, chopped		4-6	sprigs fresh thyme, chopped (about 2 tablespoons)
1	small yellow onion, chopped			
1	pound fresh spinach, coarsely chopped		3	slices Italian bread, toasted and cut into small cubes
1	can (15 ounces) artichoke hearts in water, drained well on paper towel		½	cup vegetable broth
			¼	cup grated Parmigiano-Reggiano cheese

Preheat oven to 375 degrees.

Heat a large nonstick skillet over medium-high heat. Add oil and mushroom caps. Season caps with salt and pepper and cook 3 minutes on each side. Add vinegar to skillet and allow vinegar to cook away as it coats the caps. Transfer balsamic glazed caps to a baking sheet.

To make stuffing, return skillet to stove and add oil, garlic and onion. Sauté 3 minutes. Add spinach and cook until wilted. Coarsely chop artichoke hearts in a food processor and add to spinach mixture. Season with salt and pepper and thyme. Add bread cubes. Dampen stuffing with broth. Mix to combine. Sprinkle with cheese. Divide stuffing among the top of the mushroom caps. Bake 5 minutes to set filling. Cut each mushroom cap into 4 pieces and transfer to a serving dish.

Serves 10 side dishes or 5 main courses.

Roasted Vegetables

Add any one of the compound butters listed below.

1	eggplant (1 pound)	1	teaspoon dried rosemary or basil
1	red onion	⅓	cup olive oil
2	pounds pattypan or crookneck squash	½	teaspoon salt, or to taste
3	red bell peppers (8 ounces each)	¼	teaspoon black pepper, or to taste
2	pounds small red potatoes, unpeeled	3-4	tablespoons balsamic vinegar

Preheat oven to 400 degrees.

Trim and discard ends of eggplant, onion and squash. Stem and seed bell peppers. Cut eggplant, onion, squash and bell peppers into 1½-inch chunks. Cut potatoes into quarters. Combine vegetables with rosemary, oil, salt and pepper in an 11 x 7-inch roasting pan. Mix well.

Bake, stirring occasionally, 1 hour or until potatoes are browned and tender. Sprinkle balsamic vinegar on top.

Serves 6 to 8.

Sweet Potato Surprise

4	pounds sweet potatoes or yams, peeled	2	tablespoons minced fresh ginger
4	bananas, chopped	½	teaspoon cinnamon
2	large green apples or ripe pears (any kind but Bosc), chopped	½	teaspoon allspice
		1	teaspoon salt
2	tablespoons butter or margarine	1½	cups apple juice
		½	cup fresh lemon or lime juice
		½	cup chopped dried apricots
		2	cups chopped nuts (optional)

Preheat oven to 350 degrees.

Cook potatoes in boiling water until soft; drain.

Meanwhile, sauté bananas and apples in butter with ginger, cinnamon, allspice and salt. Reduce heat and cover. Cook slowly, stirring occasionally, for 10 to 15 minutes.

Purée cooked potatoes with apple and lemon juices. A food processor fitted with a steel blade attachment works well. Mix sautéed fruit into potato purée. (For a smoother texture, fruit can be puréed before adding to potatoes.) Stir in apricots. Heap mixture into a greased 13 x 9-inch baking dish or deep casserole. Sprinkle with nuts. (If pan is too full, place extra in a greased pie pan.) Bake, uncovered, for 45 minutes.

Serves 8.

COMPOUND BUTTERS

Although these are called butters, you can substitute margarine when serving a non-dairy meal. These are terrific when serving fresh cooked corn as well as steamed vegetables.

Soften butter or margarine, then add fresh herbs such as minced dill, chives, basil, rosemary or cilantro. You can also use aromatics such as chopped green onions, shallots or fresh ginger. Adding spices such as dried crushed chipotle chiles, cayenne pepper or nutmeg are also a hit.

CORN ON THE COB MADE EASY IN THE MICROWAVE

Lay 4 large, unhusked ears of corn spoke-style on a double thickness of paper toweling in the microwave. Microwave on high for 10 minutes. Let stand 1 minute before removing husk. The silks come off with ease.

Tofu Vegetable Stir-Fry 🅟

This flavorful Asian dish will certainly change the minds of non-tofu lovers.

¼ cup soy sauce
¼ cup rice wine vinegar
1 teaspoon brown sugar
1 teaspoon cornstarch, or
    more as desired (adding
    more produces a glaze)
1 package (12 ounces) firm
    tofu, drained, patted dry
    and cut into 1-inch cubes
    Vegetable oil
    (peanut or canola)
1 teaspoon sesame oil
    (optional)
2 inches gingerroot, peeled
    and cut into fine strips

6 cloves garlic, coarsely
    chopped
4 green onions, sliced
    diagonally into sticks
1 chile pepper (preferably
    serrano), finely chopped
4 carrots, julienne
8 ounces green beans, ends
    trimmed, or broccoli or
    asparagus
1 can (8 ounces) bamboo
    shoots, rinsed and drained
1 can (6 ounces) peeled whole
    straw mushrooms
2 ounces slivered almonds,
    toasted

Combine soy sauce, vinegar, brown sugar and cornstarch. Set aside.

Deep fry tofu in a wok in 365 degree oil for 5 minutes or until golden on all sides; watch carefully to not burn. Remove tofu with a slotted spoon to paper towel to drain; set aside.

Pour out all but a few tablespoons oil from wok. Add sesame oil, if desired, for flavor. Add ginger, garlic, onions, and chile pepper and stir-fry 1 minute. Add carrots and stir-fry 2 to 3 minutes or until carrots just start to soften. Add green beans and stir-fry 1 minute longer. Add bamboo shoots, mushrooms, almonds and fried tofu. Stir until mixed.

Pour sauce over top and mix well until evenly coated. Cook 1 minute or until vegetables glisten. Cover and reduce heat. Cook a few minutes longer or until vegetables reach desired tenderness. Serve immediately over steamed rice.

Serves 4.

Desserts

Desserts

Classic Cheesecake Ⓓ

A comfort dessert.

Crust

16	graham crackers, crushed into crumbs	1	tablespoon honey, or 2 tablespoons sugar
4	tablespoons butter, softened	1	tablespoon flour

Filling

2	packages (8 ounces each) cream cheese, softened	4	eggs
⅓	cup sugar	1	teaspoon vanilla
			Juice and zest of 1 lemon

Topping

2	cups sour cream	1	teaspoon vanilla
½	cup sugar		

Preheat oven to 375 degrees.

Mix all crust ingredients with fingers and press firmly into the bottom of an 8- or 9-inch springform pan.

To make filling, beat all ingredients well until smooth and creamy. Pour filling over crust. Bake 25 minutes or until set. Center should be soft, but not wobbly. Cool.

For topping, blend sour cream with sugar and vanilla. Spread topping over cooled filling. Bake at 375 degrees for 5 to 8 minutes.

Cool in refrigerator at least 12 hours.

Serves 10 to 12.

HOW TO MAKE A SUCCESSFUL CHEESECAKE

There is something irresistible about cheesecake. Rich, creamy and satin smooth, it is one of the best-loved desserts of all time.

These techniques will help you master the art of making a successful cheesecake.

Before using, make sure all the ingredients are at room temperature as they mix more easily and finish with a much smoother texture. The paddle attachment of an electric mixer is ideal as regular whipping beaters incorporate too much air into the batter, which can lead to cracks in the finished cake. If you must use regular whipping beaters, set the mixer on low or medium-low speed so only a minimum amount of air is whipped into the batter.

To avoid cracks, do not cool the baked cakes in a cold or drafty place. You can even turn off the oven 5 minutes earlier, then leave cake in the turned-off oven to begin its cooling process. Of course, covering the cakes with sour cream or fruit toppings will mask any problems you might have experienced.

Ginger Brandy Cheesecake Ⓓ

Make sure to tightly
wrap foil around the
springform pan so that
water doesn't seep in while
the cheesecake bakes.

Crust

5	tablespoons butter	2	cups finely crushed ginger snaps
2	tablespoons honey		

Filling

1½	packages (12 ounces total) cream cheese, softened	1-2	tablespoons brandy
1½	cups sour cream	1	teaspoon grated peeled fresh gingerroot
4	eggs		Dash of salt
5	tablespoons honey		

Glaze

¾	cup orange juice	¼	teaspoon orange zest
2	tablespoons cornstarch		Crystallized strips of ginger for garnish (optional)
2	tablespoons honey		
2	teaspoons brandy		

Preheat oven to 350 degrees.

Melt butter with honey in a microwave. Add ginger snap crumbs and mix well. Press firmly into the bottom of a greased springform pan.

For filling, combine all ingredients in a bowl. Beat with an electric mixer on medium-low to medium speed until fluffy. Pour filling into an 8- or 9-inch springform pan. Bake in a pan of 1 inch deep water for 40 to 50 minutes or until a pick in the center comes out clean. Cool completely before adding glaze.

To make glaze, whisk orange juice into cornstarch in a small saucepan. Cook over low heat, whisking constantly, for 8 minutes or until thick and glossy. Remove from heat. Whisk in honey, brandy and orange zest. Pour glaze over cooled cheesecake. Garnish with strips of crystallized ginger. Chill thoroughly for several hours.

Serves 8 to 10.

When preparing to bake,
take out all your
ingredients and put them
on a baking sheet. Put
each ingredient away after
you use it, so that you
won't forget anything, or
put it in twice.

Chocolate Cheesecake

Chocolate Crumb Crust

1⅓ cups Oreo cookie crumbs	4 tablespoons butter, softened
1 tablespoon sugar	

Filling

¼ cup Kahlúa*	¼ teaspoon salt
1½ cups semisweet chocolate chips	1 cup sour cream
2 tablespoons butter	2 packages (8 ounces each) cream cheese, softened and cut into small pieces
2 eggs	
⅓ cup sugar	½ cup sour cream for topping

Kahlúa Chocolate Sauce

1 cup semisweet chocolate chips	⅓ cup Kahlúa
	⅓ cup light corn syrup

Preheat oven to 325 degrees.

Mix all crust ingredients and pat evenly over the bottom of a 9-inch springform pan.

To make filling, combine Kahlúa, chocolate chips and butter in a small saucepan. Cook over low heat, stirring constantly, until chocolate melts and mixture is smooth; set aside to cool slightly. Beat eggs in a medium bowl. Beat in sugar, salt and 1 cup sour cream. Beat in cream cheese, a few pieces at a time, until smooth. Gradually beat in chocolate mixture. Pour filling over crust in pan. Bake 40 minutes or until filling is just barely set in the center. Remove from oven and let stand at room temperature 1 hour. Spread ½ cup sour cream over top. Refrigerate several hours.

For chocolate sauce, heat chocolate chips, Kahlúa and corn syrup over low heat until chocolate is melted and mixture is smooth.

To serve, release and remove sides of pan. Cut chilled cheesecake into small slices with a thin, sharp knife dipped in cold water. Dip knife before each cut and wipe clean between cuts. Pour a bit of sauce over top of each slice.

Serves 12.

*Can use any coffee liqueur.

Port can be a dessert in itself, with some great nuts and candied papaya.

Experiment with the different types, a 10-year old tawny can be awesome, and a good vintage port is unbeatable.

From France, you can try Sauternes, from Italy, Vin Santo, from California, late harvest Zinfandel, late harvest Riesling, Muscat de Glacier are all good wines to seek out.

Pumpkin Cheesecake with Bourbon Sauce Ⓓ

Crust

1½	cups graham cracker crumbs	1	teaspoon nutmeg
¼	cup sugar	⅓	cup unsalted butter, melted
1	tablespoon orange zest		

Filling

3	packages (8 ounces each) cream cheese, softened	1½	cups canned pumpkin
1	cup sugar	½	teaspoon cinnamon
3	eggs	½	teaspoon ground ginger
½	cup sour cream	¼	teaspoon nutmeg
		½	teaspoon salt

Sauce

½	cup unsalted butter	2	tablespoons bourbon whiskey, or 1 tablespoon vanilla
1	cup dark brown sugar		
½	cup heavy cream		

Preheat oven to 350 degrees.

Spray bottom of a 9-inch springform pan with cooking spray; do not spray sides of pan. Wrap outside of pan with heavy-duty aluminum foil.

To make crust, combine cracker crumbs, sugar, orange zest and nutmeg. Stir in melted butter until well moistened. Press crust evenly over bottom and ½ inch up the sides of prepared springform pan. Bake 10 minutes or until golden brown.

For filling, beat cream cheese in a large bowl on medium-low speed until smooth. Beat in sugar until smooth. Add eggs, one at a time, beating just until combined. Beat in sour cream, pumpkin, cinnamon, ginger, nutmeg and salt. Do not overbeat. Pour filling over crust in pan.

Place springform pan in a large, shallow roasting pan or broiler pan. Fill outer pan with enough hot water to come ½ inch up sides of springform pan. Bake 65 minutes or until edges are puffed and top looks dull and is dry to the touch. Center should be less set than the edges and will move when pan is tapped, but not ripple as if liquid. Remove from oven; remove from water bath. Cool completely on a wire rack. Refrigerate at least 4 hours or overnight.

To make sauce, melt butter in a medium saucepan over medium heat. Whisk in sugar until mixture is smooth. Whisk in cream and bourbon and bring to a boil. Pour sauce into a medium bowl and cool completely. Serve sauce with cheesecake.

Serves 10 to 12.

Bountiful Apple Cake ⓓ ⓟ

This is a cross between a pie and a cake and is very moist. It's made with a dozen apples.

To prevent cut fruit from turning brown, toss with fresh lemon juice.

12	Granny Smith apples, peeled and sliced	1	cup butter or margarine
2	tablespoons fresh lemon juice	2	cups flour
1	teaspoon cinnamon	1	teaspoon cinnamon
		1¼	cups brown sugar

Preheat oven to 350 degrees.

Combine apple slices, lemon juice and 1 teaspoon cinnamon. Set aside while preparing a crust.

Cut butter into flour and 1 teaspoon cinnamon until mixture crumbs are the size of peas. Press two-thirds of crust mixture into bottom and up sides of a 10-inch springform pan. Place pan on a baking sheet. Pack apple slices into pan and press down until all fit into pan.

Mix brown sugar with remaining crust mixture and pat onto apples. Bake 90 minutes. If browning too quickly, cover loosely with foil during the first hour of baking. Cool in pan at least 2 hours before cutting. Cake may be made a day ahead.

Serves 12 to 14.

Apple Pecan Coffee Cake Ⓓ Ⓟ

Batter

½	cup butter or margarine, softened	1	teaspoon baking soda
1	cup sugar	¼	teaspoon salt
2	eggs	1	cup sour cream or non-dairy sour cream substitute
1	teaspoon vanilla	2	cups peeled and finely chopped apples
2	cups flour		
1	teaspoon baking powder		

Topping

½	cup chopped pecans	2	tablespoons butter or margarine, melted
½	cup brown sugar		
1	teaspoon cinnamon		

Preheat oven to 350 degrees.

Cream butter and sugar. Add eggs and vanilla and beat well. Sift together flour, baking powder, baking soda and salt. Add dry ingredients to creamed mixture, alternating with sour cream. Fold in apples. Pour batter into a greased 9-inch springform pan.

Combine all topping ingredients and sprinkle over batter. Bake 35 to 40 minutes.

Serves 8 to 10.

14-Carat Cake Ⓟ

2	cups flour	1½	cups oil
2	teaspoons baking powder	4	eggs
1½	teaspoons baking soda	2	cups grated carrots
1	teaspoon salt	1	can (8½-ounces) crushed pineapple
2	teaspoons cinnamon	½	cup chopped nuts
2	cups sugar		

Preheat oven to 350 degrees.

Sift together flour, baking powder, baking soda, salt and cinnamon. Add sugar, oil and eggs and beat well. Add carrot, pineapple and nuts and mix well. Pour batter into an 8-inch springform pan. Bake 35 to 40 minutes. Cool completely before frosting with Cream Cheese Frosting.

Cream Cheese Frosting

2	tablespoons margarine or butter, softened	½	teaspoon vanilla
4	ounces cream cheese, softened	½	(1-pound) package confectioners' sugar

Cream all ingredients together thoroughly. Spread over cooled cake.

The cake is also delicious with a dusting of confectioners' sugar instead of frosting.

Apricot Meringue Kuchen D

You may use 3 large peaches as a substitute for the apricots.

½	cup unsalted butter, softened and cut into 1-inch pieces	1	cup flour
½	cup sugar	1	teaspoon baking powder
	Dash of salt	⅓	cup apricot jam
2	eggs, separated	1½	pounds fresh apricots, halved and pitted
	Zest of half a lemon	¼	cup sugar
1	tablespoon lemon juice		

Preheat oven to 350 degrees.

Place butter, ½ cup sugar, salt, egg yolks, lemon zest and lemon juice in a food processor. Blend until smooth. Combine flour and baking powder in a small bowl and mix. Slowly add dry ingredients to lemon mixture, pulsing with each addition, just until ingredients are blended. Refrigerate 1 hour or until dough is firm.

Turn dough, flouring fingers if needed, into a greased 9-inch springform or a pan with a removable bottom. Press dough into the bottom and up the sides. Flute the sides. Smear apricot jam over dough. Press apricots, skin-side down, into the dough. Place pan on a baking sheet. Bake 40 minutes or until Kuchen is golden.

Meanwhile, beat egg whites with an electric mixer on high speed until frothy. Beat in ¼ cup sugar and beat 3 to 4 minutes or until whites form stiff peaks.

Remove Kuchen from oven and spoon egg white mixture evenly over the apricots, spreading with the back of the spoon. Reduce oven to 325 degrees and bake 15 to 20 minutes longer or until top of cake is golden.

Serves 8.

MANGO-GINGER DESSERT SAUCE

This rich tasting sauce is excellent over vanilla frozen yogurt and is low in calories.

2¾ cups finely chopped peeled pitted mangoes (about 2 mangoes)

2 tablespoons sugar

¼ cup chopped crystallized ginger

2 teaspoons fresh lime juice

Place 1 cup chopped mangoes in a medium bowl. Combine remaining 1¾ cups mangoes and sugar in a food processor. Purée until smooth. Add to bowl with chopped mangoes. Stir in ginger and lime juice. Let stand at least 30 minutes. Can be prepared the day before serving and stored, covered, in the refrigerator.

Banana Walnut Bundt Cake Ⓓ

Sprinkle confectioners'
sugar through a doily
for a pretty design on
a plain cake.

1¾ cups sugar
¾ cup vegetable shortening
3 cups flour
2 cups mashed ripe banana
    (about 4 large bananas)
½ cup sour cream
1 tablespoon baking powder
1 teaspoon vanilla
½ teaspoon salt
½ teaspoon baking soda
4 eggs
1 cup chopped walnuts, or
    chocolate chips
Confectioners' sugar or
    Glaze (recipe below)

Preheat oven to 350 degrees.

In a large bowl of an electric mixer, beat sugar and shortening on low speed until blended. Add flour, banana, sour cream, baking powder, vanilla, salt, baking soda and eggs. Beat until well mixed, constantly scraping bowl with a rubber spatula. Increase speed to high and beat 2 minutes, occasionally scraping bowl. Stir in walnuts.

Spoon batter into a greased and floured 10-inch Bundt pan. Bake 65 to 70 minutes or until a pick inserted in the center of cake comes out clean. Cool cake in pan on a wire rack 10 minutes. Remove from pan and cool completely on rack. Sprinkle with confectioners' sugar or drizzle with glaze.

Glaze (optional)

2 tablespoons butter, melted
1¼ cups confectioners' sugar
½ teaspoon vanilla
4-5 teaspoons milk

Combine all ingredients, using enough milk to reach desired consistency. Glaze should be thick enough to cling to cake but thin enough to pour.

Serves 12 to 14.

Flourless Chocolate Cake with Chocolate Glaze Ⓓ

Cake

12 ounces bittersweet or semisweet chocolate, chopped

¾ cup unsalted butter, cut into small pieces

6 eggs, separated

12 tablespoons sugar, divided

2 teaspoons vanilla

Glaze

½ cup heavy cream

½ cup dark corn syrup

9 ounces bittersweet or semisweet chocolate, finely chopped

Shaved chocolate curls (optional)

Preheat oven to 350 degrees.

Line bottom of a greased 9-inch springform pan with parchment or waxed paper cut to fit. Grease paper. Wrap outside of pan with foil. Stir chocolate and butter in a heavy medium saucepan over low heat until melted and smooth. Remove from heat and cool to lukewarm, stirring often.

Using an electric mixer, beat egg yolks with 6 tablespoons sugar in a large bowl for 3 minutes or until mixture is very thick and pale. Fold in lukewarm chocolate mixture. Fold in vanilla. Using clean, dry beaters, beat egg whites in a separate bowl until soft peaks form. Gradually add remaining 6 tablespoons sugar, beating to medium-firm peaks. Fold whites into chocolate mixture in 3 additions. Pour batter into prepared pan.

Bake 50 minutes or until top is puffed and cracked and a cake tester inserted into the center comes out with some moist crumbs attached. Cool cake in pan on a rack; cake will fall - don't worry! Gently press down crusty top to make an evenly thick cake. Using a small knife, cut around pan sides to loosen cake. Remove pan sides. Place a 9-inch tart pan bottom or cardboard round on top of cake. Invert cake onto tart pan bottom. Peel off parchment paper.

To make glaze, bring cream and corn syrup to a simmer in a medium saucepan. Remove from heat. Add chocolate and whisk until melted and smooth. Place cake on rack set over a baking sheet. Spread ½ cup glaze smoothly over top and sides of cake. Freeze 3 minutes or until almost set. Pour remaining glaze over cake and smooth sides and top. Place cake on a platter. Chill in refrigerator 1 hour or until glaze is firm. Cake can be made 1 day ahead and refrigerated. Garnish with curled chocolate shavings. Serve at room temperature.

Serves 10 to 12.

For a dessert wine, try a black Muscat wine with Flourless Chocolate Cake.

To decorate a flourless chocolate cake, sprinkle with confectioners' sugar, decorate with 5 or 6 strawberries and a handful of blueberries and top with a sprig of mint and a few strands of orange zest.

Prize-Winning Chocolate Fudge Cake Ⓓ
Dark and wonderfully dense.

To make chocolate curls, quickly draw a vegetable peeler down a block of chocolate. Chocolate curls melt at the slightest touch, so use tweezers to place them on a cake or pie.

1½ cups cake flour, plus more for preparing pan	11 tablespoons butter, softened, plus more for greasing pan
¾ cup cocoa	
1½ teaspoons baking soda	2 eggs
½ teaspoon salt	1 teaspoon vanilla
1¾ cups sugar	
2 cups sour cream, regular or low fat	

Preheat oven to 350 degrees.

Sift together flour, cocoa, baking soda and salt into a large mixer bowl. Stir in sugar. Add sour cream, butter, eggs and vanilla and combine on low speed of an electric mixer. Increase to medium speed and mix 3 minutes. Grease a 13 x 9-inch baking pan with butter and lightly dust with flour. Pour batter into prepared pan and use a spatula to smooth surface.

Bake about 40 minutes or until a pick inserted in the center comes out clean. Cool completely on a wire rack. Cake can be made a day ahead and frosted on the day of serving.

Frosting

1½ cups sugar	½ cup butter, softened
1 cup heavy cream	1 tablespoon vanilla
6 ounces unsweetened chocolate, cut into small pieces	

To decorate dessert plates, just put caramel or chocolate sauce in a plastic squeeze bottle and create some squiggly lines before placing your dessert on top.

Stir sugar and cream in a heavy 3-quart saucepan over medium heat for 3 minutes or until sugar is dissolved. Bring to a boil. Reduce heat and simmer gently 6 minutes. Remove from heat. Stir in chocolate and butter and mix until smooth. Stir in vanilla.

Refrigerate in a covered container until chilled and somewhat set, but not solid. Place in a food processor fitted with a metal blade and process briefly until light and fluffy. Spread over cake.

Serves 12.

Flourless Chocolate Soufflé with Raspberry Cream ⓓ

½ cup heavy cream
2 tablespoons confectioners' sugar
2 cups frozen raspberries, thawed
2 teaspoons butter
1 tablespoon granulated sugar
2 ounces semisweet chocolate, finely chopped
1 ounce unsweetened chocolate, finely chopped
¼ cup whole milk
3 egg whites
   Pinch of salt
2 tablespoons granulated sugar
2 egg yolks

Preheat oven to 400 degrees.

Whip cream in a chilled bowl until semi-stiff. Add confectioners' sugar and whip until stiff. Refrigerate. Purée raspberries in a food processor and pass through a sieve. Fold raspberries into whipped cream and reserve in refrigerator.

Grease four ½ cup ramekins with 2 teaspoons butter and dust lightly with 1 tablespoon granulated sugar; set aside.

Combine both chocolates and milk in a small saucepan. Melt over low heat, stirring constantly. The minute chocolate is melted, remove from heat and transfer chocolate to a small bowl. Cool to room temperature.

Whip egg whites with salt until soft peaks form. Add 2 tablespoons granulated sugar and whip until stiff but not dry. Whisk egg yolks into the cooled chocolate. Fold one-fourth of egg whites into the chocolate mixture, then fold chocolate mixture back into the egg whites. Spoon mixture into the ramekins. Bake 10 to 12 minutes. The soufflés should remain moist in the center.

Serve soufflés with raspberry cream on the side. Each diner should break into the center of the soufflé and add a dab of raspberry cream.

Serves 4.

To make chocolate leaves, wash and dry unsprayed, nonpoisonous leaves, such as ivy, lemon, rose or camellia. Paint the veiny side with melted chocolate. Chill 1 hour, then carefully peel away the leaf.

When baking a chocolate cake, don't use flour to dust the pan. Use cocoa instead. This way, the white flour "dust" won't cling to the sides of the cake.

European Chocolate Sponge Cake

Special occasion Hungarian family favorite, with two choices for frosting.

Batter

12 eggs, room temperature, separated
1½ cups sugar
6 ounces bittersweet or unsweetened chocolate, melted and cooled

8 ounces walnuts, ground
3 tablespoons matzo cake flour or regular flour for non-Passover use

Cream Frosting

2 egg yolks
1 cup confectioners' sugar
3 tablespoons freshly brewed coffee, cooled

6 ounces bittersweet or unsweetened chocolate, melted and cooled
1 cup butter or margarine, cut into pieces

Eggless Chocolate Buttercream Frosting

1 cup unsalted butter or margarine, softened
½ cup unsweetened cocoa powder, measured, then sifted

2-3 cups confectioners' sugar
2-4 tablespoons warm water, brewed coffee or cola

Preheat oven to 350 degrees.

Beat egg whites with a little of the sugar until stiff. Refrigerate. Beat egg yolks with remaining sugar. Add nuts and flour and beat well. Very slowly mix in cooled, melted chocolate. Fold in egg whites. Grease a 10-inch springform pan and line with waxed paper cut to fit bottom of the pan. Pour batter into pan. Bake 1 hour.

To make Cream Frosting, cream yolks while adding sugar, a little at a time. Add cooled coffee and cooled, melted chocolate. Add butter and blend thoroughly. When cake is completely cooled, spread frosting over top and sides of cake.

To make Chocolate Buttercream Frosting, cream butter with cocoa and 2 cups sugar using an electric mixer on medium speed, adding more sugar as needed. Increase to high speed, stopping to scrape bowl occasionally, and whip, mixing well. Add liquid, 1 tablespoon at a time, to achieve a spreading consistency. Whip 2 to 4 minutes longer for a fluffy texture.

Serves 10 to 12.

Hungarian Coffee Cake 🌸

Filling

⅓ cup dark brown sugar
2 teaspoons cocoa
⅓ cup semisweet chocolate, coarsely chopped
1 teaspoon cinnamon

⅓ cup dark raisins, plumped, drained and chopped
⅓ cup golden raisins, plumped, drained and chopped*
½ cup walnuts, chopped (preferably toasted)

Batter

¾ cup unsalted butter, softened
1 cup brown sugar
⅓ cup granulated sugar
½ package (8 ounce) cream cheese, softened
5 eggs
1½ teaspoons vanilla

1 cup plain yogurt or sour cream
3¼ cups all-purpose flour
¼ teaspoon salt
1 tablespoon baking powder
½ teaspoon baking soda

Preheat oven to 350 degrees.

Combine all filling ingredients and set aside.

To make batter, cream butter and both sugars together until fluffy. Add cream cheese and mix until blended. Add eggs and vanilla and mix thoroughly. Blend in yogurt. Fold in flour, salt, baking powder and baking soda. Mix well on low speed, scraping down sides and bottom occasionally.

Spread one-third of filling in a greased 9- or 10-inch tube or angel food cake pan. Top with some of batter. Continue layering until all batter is used. Bake 50 to 60 minutes or until done. Cool in pan 10 minutes before removing.

Serves 12 to 16.

*To plump raisins, cover with hot water and let them stand for a couple of minutes. Drain. You can also use hot orange juice, rum, or wine or any other liquid whose flavor will marry well with the recipe and the raisins.

BAKING POWDER

Think you have stale baking powder? Test by putting 1 teaspoon of the powder in a cup of hot water. If it bubbles a lot, it's good. If not, throw it out.

Upside-Down Cranberry Cake Ⓓ

An award-winning cake.

To make a richer cake, substitute 2 egg yolks for each whole egg.

Topping

½	cup butter	1	teaspoon cinnamon
1½	cups sugar	4	cups cranberries, at room
2	tablespoons water		temperature

Batter

1½	cups cake flour	½	cup light brown sugar
½	teaspoon baking soda	2	eggs
½	teaspoon salt	¾	cup sour cream
6	tablespoons butter, softened	1	teaspoon vanilla
½	cup granulated sugar		

Preheat oven to 350 degrees.

Generously grease a 9-inch springform pan and wrap outside of pan with foil to prevent leakage. Place on a baking sheet and set aside.

For topping, melt butter in a medium saucepan. Add sugar, water and cinnamon. Cook and stir over medium-low heat for 3 minutes or until sugar dissolves. Stir in cranberries. Pour topping into springform pan and spread evenly. Set aside.

To make batter, sift together flour, baking soda and salt; set aside. Beat butter and both sugars with an electric mixer on medium speed for 1 minute or until smooth and fluffy. Add eggs, one at a time, beating well after each addition. On low speed, mix in half of dry ingredients until combined. Add sour cream and vanilla and mix until combined. Add remaining dry ingredients and mix until smooth. Pour batter over topping in pan and spread evenly.

Bake 45 to 50 minutes or until golden brown, edges just begin to pull away from sides and a pick inserted in the center comes out clean. Cool in pan on a rack for 10 minutes. Run a knife around the edge to loosen cake and invert onto a plate. Remove foil, outer ring and bottom of pan. Replace any cranberries that fall. Cut into wedges and serve. Cake can be kept at room temperature, in an airtight container, for up to 2 days.

Serves 14 to 16.

Sour Cream Lemon Pound Cake

Very nice for brunch!

3	tablespoons bread crumbs	1½	tablespoons lemon zest (about 2 lemons)	
3¼	cups flour	2	tablespoons fresh lemon juice	
½	teaspoon baking soda	1	cup low fat sour cream	
¼	teaspoon salt	1	cup confectioners' sugar	
¾	cup butter or margarine, softened	2	tablespoons fresh lemon juice	
2¼	cups sugar			
2	teaspoons lemon extract			
3	eggs			

Preheat oven to 350 degrees.

Grease a 10-inch tube pan and dust with bread crumbs. Combine flour, baking soda and salt in a large bowl and stir with a wire whisk; set aside. Beat butter in a large bowl with an electric mixer on medium speed until light and fluffy. Gradually add sugar and extract, beating well until blended. Add eggs, one at a time, beating well after each addition. Add lemon zest and 2 tablespoons lemon juice. Beat 30 seconds. On low speed, beat in dry ingredients alternately with sour cream, beginning and ending with dry ingredients.

Spoon batter into prepared pan. Bake 70 minutes or until a pick inserted in the center of cake comes out clean. Cool in pan on a rack for 10 minutes. Remove from pan and cool completely on rack. Combine confectioners' sugar and 2 tablespoons lemon juice to make a glaze. Drizzle glaze over top of cake.

Serves 18.

Use paper coffee filters to line 8-inch cake pans. Just flatten one into a large circle and lay it on the bottom of the pan.

Lemonade Cake with Lemon Icing

This luscious cake starts out using a white cake mix. How easy can it be?

1 package (18 ounces) white cake mix	1 package (3 ounces) cream cheese, softened
1 container (8 ounces) sour cream	3 eggs
1 can (6 ounces) frozen lemonade concentrate, thawed	Lemon Icing (recipe below)

Preheat oven to 350 degrees.

In a large mixing bowl, blend all ingredients together, adding ingredients in order listed, beating with an electric mixer until combined. Beat blended mixture exactly 4 minutes on medium speed, scraping down sides of bowl as needed. Do not shorten beating time or final product will separate.

Spread batter in a greased 12-cup Bundt pan. Bake 1 hour or until a pick inserted in the center of cake comes out clean. Cool in pan upright on a rack for about 15 minutes. Meanwhile, prepare icing.

Invert cake onto a serving plate and drizzle icing over slightly warm cake. Refrigerate cake at least 2 to 3 hours before slicing.

Lemon Icing

1 teaspoon lemon extract	Dash of salt
2 tablespoons light corn syrup	1/3 cup buttermilk
4 tablespoons butter or margarine, softened	1 tablespoon lemon zest
Dash of nutmeg	2 cups confectioners' sugar

Combine all icing ingredients in order listed in a blender or food processor. Blend on high speed for 30 seconds or until smooth. Drizzle icing over warm cake.

Serves 12, makes 1½ cups icing.

Margarita Cake ⚜

Instead of drinking your margarita, eat it as a cake.

Batter

1	package (18.25 ounces) orange cake mix	½	cup vegetable oil
1	package (3.4 ounces) instant vanilla pudding	⅔	cup water
		¼	cup lemon juice
4	eggs	¼	cup tequila
		2	tablespoons triple sec liqueur

Glaze

1	cup confectioners' sugar	2	tablespoons triple sec liqueur
1	tablespoon tequila	2	tablespoons lime juice

Preheat oven to 350 degrees.

Combine all batter ingredients in a large bowl. Beat with an electric mixer for 2 minutes. Pour batter into a greased and floured 10-inch Bundt pan. Bake 45 to 50 minutes or until a pick inserted into the center comes out clean. Cool in pan 10 minutes. Remove cake from pan to a rack. Glaze cake while still warm.

To make glaze, combine all ingredients in a small bowl and mix until smooth. Pour over warm cake.

Serves 12.

Use cold coffee instead of water when making a chocolate cake mix. It gives the cake a rich mocha flavor.

*An orange Muscat
will go well with an orange
pound cake.*

Orange-Apricot
Buttermilk Bundt Cake Ⓓ

Batter

1	cup sugar
½	cup unsalted butter, softened
2	eggs, room temperature
2	teaspoons vanilla
1	cup chopped currants
½	cup chopped dried apricots

½	cup chopped walnuts
1	tablespoon orange zest
2	cups all-purpose flour
½	teaspoon baking soda
¼	teaspoon salt
¾	cup buttermilk

Syrup

½	cup sugar
1	tablespoon orange zest

⅓	cup fresh orange juice
1	tablespoon lemon juice

Preheat oven to 325 degrees.

Beat sugar and butter in a large mixing bowl with an electric mixer on high speed for 5 minutes or until light and fluffy. Add eggs, one at a time, beating well after each. Scrape down side of bowl. On low speed, mix in vanilla, currants, apricots, walnuts and orange zest until blended.

In a medium bowl, combine flour, baking soda and salt. Add dry ingredients and buttermilk to batter, alternately, with mixer on low speed, beginning and ending with dry ingredients. Mix until blended. Pour batter into a greased and floured 6-cup Bundt pan or ring mold. Bake 45 to 55 minutes or until a pick inserted in the center of cake comes out clean. Cool in pan on a rack for 10 minutes while preparing syrup.

Combine all syrup ingredients in a small saucepan. Bring to a boil and cook, stirring constantly, for 3 minutes or until mixture thickens and orange zest is lightly glazed.

Invert cake onto rack placed over a rimmed baking sheet. Remove pan and prick top with a long fork or skewer at 1-inch intervals. Spoon hot syrup slowly over cake. Cool completely.

Serves 8 to 10.

*When a recipe calls
for buttermilk and you
don't have any on hand,
you can substitute with
low-fat or nonfat milk into
which you have added
1 tablespoon lemon juice
or vinegar per cup
of milk.*

Cranberry Orange Bundt Cake ⓓ

A perfect fall cake.

1	package (18 ounces) butter cake mix	1	package (8 ounces) cream cheese, softened
3	eggs		Zest of 1 medium orange (about 2 tablespoons)
⅔	cup orange juice	1½	cups dried sweetened cranberries
½	cup butter or margarine, softened	1	tablespoon flour
¼	cup sugar		Orange Glaze (recipe below)

Preheat oven to 350 degrees.

Combine cake mix, eggs, orange juice, butter and sugar in a large bowl. Beat on low speed to blend. Add cream cheese and orange zest and beat 2 minutes. In a medium bowl, toss cranberries with flour to coat. Stir cranberries into batter. Pour batter into a greased and floured 12-cup Bundt cake pan. Bake 50 to 55 minutes or until a pick inserted in the center comes out clean. Cool in pan 10 minutes before inverting onto a serving platter. When completely cool, top with Orange Glaze.

Orange Glaze

½	cup sugar	1½	tablespoons orange zest
½	cup water	1	tablespoon butter or margarine
1½	tablespoons cornstarch	½	cup orange juice
	Pinch of salt		

In a medium saucepan, combine sugar, water, cornstarch and salt over medium heat. Bring to a boil, stirring frequently. Boil 1 minute, stirring constantly. Remove from heat and stir in orange zest and butter. Gradually stir in orange juice. Return to medium heat and bring to a simmer. Cook 3 to 4 minutes or until thickened. Remove from heat and cool. Spoon over cooled cake.

Serves 12.

To keep dried fruit, nuts or chocolate chips from sinking to the bottom of a cake batter, toss them in flour before adding to the batter.

Fresh California Peach Cake ⒹⒶ

The batter will puff up as it bakes.

1	cup sifted flour	3	tablespoons granulated sugar
1½	teaspoons baking powder	¾	cup slivered almonds
½	teaspoon salt	3	tablespoons unsalted butter
¼	cup granulated sugar	¼	cup unsifted flour
4	tablespoons unsalted butter	¼	cup light brown sugar
1	egg	¼	cup apricot preserves
¼	cup milk	1	tablespoon water
½	teaspoon lemon zest		
10	large ripe peaches, peeled and quartered		

Preheat oven to 400 degrees.

Sift together 1 cup sifted flour, baking powder, salt and ¼ cup granulated sugar in a bowl. Using fingers or a pastry blender, work in 4 tablespoons butter until mixture resembles coarse meal. Beat egg and milk in a separate bowl. Add egg mixture and lemon zest to flour mixture and stir until just blended. Spread batter evenly in a greased and floured 11- or 12-inch springform pan. Arrange peaches on batter, rounded-side up. Sprinkle 3 tablespoons granulated sugar on top. Bake 35 minutes.

While cake bakes, whirl almonds in a blender or food processor to a fine powder consistency. Mix almonds with 3 tablespoons butter, ¼ cup unsifted flour and brown sugar. After baking 35 minutes, remove cake from oven. Border top of cake with the almond mixture. Bake 10 minutes longer.

Meanwhile, press apricot preserves through a sieve into a small saucepan. Add 1 tablespoon water and cook 1 to 2 minutes or until preserves are melted. Immediately upon removing cake from oven, brush peaches with preserves.

Serves 12 to 14.

Poppy Seed Cake ⓓ

This has a lively lemony taste

1	cup poppy seeds	1	cup sour cream
⅓	cup honey	1	teaspoon salt
¼	cup water	2½	tablespoons lemon juice
¾	cup butter, softened	2¼	cups flour
¾	cup sugar	1	teaspoon baking soda
1	tablespoon lemon zest	½	teaspoon baking powder
2	teaspoons vanilla		Lemon Glaze (recipe below)
2	eggs		

Preheat oven to 325 degrees.

Combine poppy seeds, honey and water in a saucepan and cook over low heat for 4 to 5 minutes or until water evaporates, stirring frequently. Cool.

Cream together butter, sugar, lemon zest and vanilla. Add eggs, one at a time, beating well after each addition. Add sour cream, salt, lemon juice and poppy seed mixture. Sift together flour, baking soda and baking powder. Add dry ingredients to batter and beat on low speed until thoroughly combined.

Pour batter into a greased and floured 10-inch angel food tube pan. Bake 60 to 75 minutes or until cake pulls away from sides of pan and a pick inserted in the center of cake comes out clean. Cover with foil if cake browns too quickly. Cool 15 minutes. Invert and cool to room temperature. Pour hot Lemon Glaze over cooled cake.

Lemon Glaze

6	tablespoons lemon juice	¾	cup confectioners' sugar

Combine lemon juice and sugar in a saucepan. Bring to a boil and cook 1 to 2 minutes or until a thin syrup is formed.

Serves 10 to 12.

To prevent a freshly baked cake from sticking to the serving platter, dust the platter with confectioners' sugar.

WHY ADD SALT TO A CAKE RECIPE?

Salt heightens its flavor; otherwise your cake would have a flat taste.

Grandma's Apple Pastry Squares

"A family favorite made every Rosh Hashanah with apples from the tree that Grandpa planted."

¾ cup sugar
½ cup oil
½ cup orange juice
2 eggs
1 teaspoon vanilla
3¼ cups flour
2 teaspoons baking powder

Dash of salt
5-6 pounds cooking apples, peeled and thinly sliced
½ cup unsalted margarine
Strawberry preserves
Cinnamon sugar mixture for topping

Preheat oven to 350 degrees.

Combine sugar, oil, orange juice, eggs and vanilla in a bowl. Add flour, baking powder and salt and mix well until it can be handled. Knead dough into a ball on a floured board until it can be rolled out. Divide into 2 pieces, with one piece being slightly larger than the other. Roll larger piece between 2 pieces of wax paper until it fits into a 13 x 9-inch glass baking dish with a small overlap. Arrange apple slices in pan. Dot with margarine. Top apples with small spoonfuls of preserves. Roll out second piece of dough as the first, just to fit baking dish. Crimp edges together. Pat top of cake with warm water and sprinkle with cinnamon sugar mixture. Cut several small slashes in top crust to allow steam to escape.

Bake 1 hour or until apples are soft and top is browned. Cover with foil if top is browning too fast.

Serves 16 to 20.

Chocolate 'N Caramel Bars

Let's start with a cake mix.

1 package (18 ounces) German chocolate cake mix
⅓ cup margarine or butter, melted
⅓ cup milk

1 cup semisweet chocolate chips
1 cup chopped nuts
1 cup caramel ice cream topping

Preheat oven to 350 degrees.

Combine cake mix, margarine and milk. Mix well. Press half of dough evenly in a greased 13 x 9-inch baking pan. Sprinkle chocolate chips and nuts evenly over top. Drizzle evenly with caramel topping. Crumble remaining dough over caramel. Bake 25 to 30 minutes or until caramel starts to bubble. Cool completely before cutting into bars.

Makes 36 bars.

Deluxe Lemon Squares ⒹⓅ

2 cups sifted flour	½ cup lemon juice
½ cup sifted confectioners' sugar	2 tablespoons lemon zest
1 cup butter or margarine	¼ cup sifted flour
4 eggs, beaten	½ teaspoon baking powder
1½ cups sugar	Confectioners' sugar for dusting

Preheat oven to 350 degrees.

Sift together 2 cups flour and confectioners' sugar. Cut in butter until mixture clings together. Press mixture into a 13 x 9-inch baking pan. Bake 25 minutes or until lightly browned. Beat eggs, sugar, lemon juice and lemon zest together. Sift together ¼ cup flour and baking powder. Stir dry ingredients into egg mixture. Pour mixture over baked crust. Bake 25 minutes longer. Cool. Dust with confectioners' sugar and cut into bars.

Makes 36 bars.

If using margarine, decrease baking time by 5 minutes.

Apricot Coconut Squares ⒹⓅ

Crust

½ cup butter or margarine, softened	¼ cup granulated sugar
	1 cup all-purpose flour

Filling

⅔ cup dried apricots	¼ teaspoon salt
1 cup water	1 teaspoon vanilla
2 eggs	1 teaspoon lemon juice
1 cup light brown sugar	1 cup chopped walnuts
⅓ cup all-purpose flour	¾ cup flaked coconut
½ teaspoon baking powder	⅓ cup confectioners' sugar

Preheat oven to 325 degrees.

Combine all crust ingredients in a medium bowl. Press mixture into the bottom of an ungreased 13 x 9-inch baking pan. Bake 25 minutes.

Meanwhile, prepare filling. Combine apricots and 1 cup water in a small saucepan. Bring to a boil and cook 10 minutes. Drain, chop and set aside to cool.

In a medium bowl, beat eggs and brown sugar. Stir in flour, baking powder, salt, vanilla and lemon juice. Fold in nuts and chopped apricots. Stir in coconut. Pour filling over baked crust. Bake 20 minutes or until firm. Cool. Dust with confectioners' sugar before cutting into squares.

Serves about 24.

Berry Pecan Squares ⓓ ⓟ

These European favorites traveled all the way to Palos Verdes.

Pecan Cookie Dough

1	cup pecans
3	egg yolks (freeze whites for another use)
½	cup sugar
¼	teaspoon salt
2	teaspoons vanilla

2	teaspoons lemon zest
1	cup unsalted butter or margarine, cut into small cubes while cold
1⅔	cups all-purpose flour

Berry Topping

½	cup raspberry or strawberry preserves
2	tablespoons sugar

¼	cup all-purpose flour
¼	cup coarsely chopped pecans

Preheat oven to 350 degrees.

Finely chop nuts in a food processor. Set aside.

Combine egg yolks, sugar, salt, vanilla, lemon zest and butter in a food processor until blended. Add flour and pecans and process about 2 seconds. Scrape down sides and process about 3 seconds or until dough begins to form sticky crumbs, but does not come together into a ball. Wrap dough and press together, shaping it into a rectangle. Refrigerate 1 hour. Cut off one-fourth of dough and reserve in refrigerator. Pat remaining dough into an ungreased 13 x 9-inch baking pan.

For topping, stir preserves and then gently spread over dough in pan with a spatula, leaving a 1½-inch border. Cut reserved dough into 10 pieces and place in cleaned food processor. Add sugar and flour and process a few seconds or until blended but still very crumbly. Crumble dough quickly between fingers to separate any lumps. Sprinkle dough evenly over preserves. Sprinkle pecans on top. Bake 30 minutes or until crumbs are firm and light brown. Cool in pan on a rack until slightly warm. Cut into 1½ x 2-inch bars. Store in an airtight container at room temperature for up to 3 days.

Makes 24 bars.

Lemon Cheesecake Bars Ⓓ

Shortbread Crust
½ cup butter, softened
¼ cup confectioners' sugar

1 teaspoon vanilla
1 cup all-purpose flour

Cream Cheese Filling
1 package (8 ounces) cream
   cheese, softened
1½ cups confectioners' sugar

1 egg
1 teaspoon lemon extract

Lemon Curd
4 egg yolks
1 tablespoon cornstarch
¾ cup water
¾ cup sugar

2 teaspoons lemon zest
¼ cup fresh lemon juice
   (2 medium lemons)
2 tablespoons butter, softened

Topping
2 tablespoons confectioners'
   sugar

Preheat oven to 425 degrees.

To prepare crust, cream butter and sugar in a medium bowl with an electric mixer on high speed. Mix in vanilla. Add flour and mix on low speed until fully blended. Press dough evenly into the bottom of an 8-inch square baking pan. Refrigerate 30 minutes or until firm. Prick crust with a fork and bake 30 minutes or until golden brown. Cool on a rack to room temperature.

Prepare filling while the crust bakes. Beat cream cheese and sugar until smooth in a medium bowl with an electric mixer on high. Add egg and lemon extract and beat on medium speed until light and smooth. Cover bowl and refrigerate.

For lemon curd, blend egg yolks with cornstarch, water and sugar in a medium non-aluminum saucepan. Place over medium-low heat and cook, stirring constantly, until mixture thickens enough to coat the back of a spoon. Remove from heat. Stir in lemon zest, lemon juice and butter. Cool 10 minutes.

To assemble, spread filling evenly with a spatula over cooled crust. Spread lemon curd evenly over filling. Bake in the center of the oven for 30 to 40 minutes or until the edges begin to turn light golden brown. Cool on a rack to room temperature. Chill in refrigerator 1 hour before cutting into bars. Dust top with confectioners' sugar, using a flour sifter for best results.

Serves 24.

Orange Marmalade Bars

Crust

2 cups flour	1 teaspoon baking powder
1 cup sugar	1 teaspoon vanilla (optional)
1 egg yolk (egg white reserved for second layer)	1 cup unsalted butter, melted over low heat and cooled

Filling

3 eggs	2 cups chopped walnuts
1 egg white	1 cup orange marmalade (see note below)
½ cup sugar	Zest of 1 to 2 oranges, ground very fine in a processor
¼ cup flour	
1 teaspoon baking powder	
2 cups flaked coconut	

Preheat oven to 350 degrees.

To make crust, combine flour, sugar, egg yolk, baking powder and vanilla and mix. Pour in cooled melted butter and mix until blended but still somewhat lumpy. Pat mixture on to a 14 x 9-inch baking sheet with sides. Bake 15 to 20 minutes or until lightly browned. Crust will be only partially baked.

Meanwhile, prepare filling. Beat, using an electric mixer, eggs and egg white with sugar until very light. Gradually add flour and baking powder on low speed until thoroughly mixed. Stir in coconut, walnuts, marmalade and orange zest by hand. Spread over partially baked crust.

Reduce oven to 325 degrees. Bake bars 30 minutes or until nicely browned and fairly firm to the touch. When cool, cut into 1 x 2-inch bars.

Makes 60 to 65 bars.

Use an imported European orange marmalade as American brands are too sweet.

Chocolate Truffle Brownies

1	pound semisweet chocolate, chopped	¾	cup flour
⅔	cup butter, softened	1½	cups coarsely chopped hazelnuts or walnuts, or as desired
1¼	cups sugar		
6	eggs		Confectioners' sugar

Preheat oven to 350 degrees.

Melt chocolate in the top of a double boiler over hot, but not boiling, water. Cool slightly.

Cream butter with an electric mixer until light. Add melted chocolate and beat on medium speed until a mousse-like consistency and light-colored. Slowly beat in sugar. Add eggs, 1 at a time, beating well after each addition.

Fold in flour, then nuts. Pour batter into a greased and parchment paper-lined jelly-roll pan. Smooth top. Bake 20 to 25 minutes or until slightly cracked on top. Chill. Sprinkle with confectioners' sugar. Cut into bars.

Makes 3 dozen brownies.

Increase or decrease amount of nuts used according to your preference.

Orange Cappuccino Brownies

¾	cup unsalted butter	3	eggs
2	ounces semisweet chocolate, coarsely chopped	¼	cup orange flavored liqueur or orange juice
2	ounces unsweetened chocolate, coarsely chopped	1	tablespoon orange zest
		1	cup flour
1¾	cups sugar	1	package (12 ounces) semisweet chocolate chips
1	tablespoon instant espresso powder or instant coffee granules	2	tablespoons vegetable shortening

Preheat oven to 350 degrees.

Melt butter, 2 ounces semisweet chocolate and 2 ounces unsweetened chocolate in a large heavy saucepan over low heat, stirring constantly. Stir in sugar and espresso powder. Remove from heat and cool slightly. Beat in eggs, 1 at a time, with a wire whisk. Whisk in liqueur and orange zest. Beat in flour until blended. Spread batter evenly in a greased 13 x 9-inch baking pan. Bake 25 to 30 minutes or until center is set.

Meanwhile, melt chocolate chips and vegetable shortening in a small heavy saucepan over low heat, stirring constantly. Immediately after removing brownies from oven, spread hot chocolate over warm brownies. Cool completely. Cut into 2-inch squares.

Makes 24 brownies.

TIPS ON COOKING WITH CHOCOLATE

Use the microwave when melting chocolate on medium to low setting. It's much faster than using a double boiler.

It is best not to use a blender to produce chunks of chocolate. For best results, use a large serrated knife.

Wonderful Walnut Pecan Brownies

This brownie features a large amount of nuts, so if you love nuts with chocolate, you won't be able to resist this treat.

Walnut Pecan Topping

¾	cup brown sugar, packed	1	teaspoon vanilla
¼	cup margarine or butter	2	cups chopped walnuts
1	egg, beaten	2	cups chopped pecans
2	tablespoons all-purpose flour		

Batter

¾	cup margarine or butter	1	teaspoon vanilla
4	ounces unsweetened baking chocolate	4	eggs, beaten
2	cups sugar	1	cup all-purpose flour

Preheat oven to 350 degrees.

To make topping, heat brown sugar and margarine in a 2½-quart saucepan over low heat, stirring occasionally until margarine is melted. Remove from heat and cool slightly. Stir in egg, flour and vanilla. Mix in walnuts and pecans.

For batter, heat margarine and chocolate in a 3-quart saucepan over low heat, stirring constantly until melted. Cool slightly. Stir in sugar, vanilla and eggs. Stir in flour. Spread batter in a greased 13 x 9-inch baking pan. Spoon topping evenly over batter.

Bake 45 minutes; do not overbake. Cool in pan on a wire rack. Cut into 2 x 1-inch bars. Cover with plastic and refrigerate overnight.

Makes 32 brownies.

Date-Oatmeal Cookies

1	cup margarine or butter, softened	¾	teaspoon baking soda
1	cup sugar	1	teaspoon cinnamon
1	teaspoon vanilla	½	teaspoon salt
2	eggs	2	cups dry quick-cooking oats
1¾	cups flour	1	package (8-ounces) chopped pitted dates
1	teaspoon baking powder	1	cup finely chopped pecans

Preheat oven to 375 degrees.

Cream margarine and sugar together until fluffy. Add vanilla. Beat in eggs, one at a time. Sift together flour, baking powder, baking soda, cinnamon and salt. Add dry ingredients to butter mixture. Stir in oats, dates and pecans. Mix well and chill 1 hour.

Drop chilled dough by rounded teaspoonfuls 2 inches apart onto greased baking sheets. Bake 10 minutes or until cookies are golden. Cool on wire racks.

Makes 8 dozen cookies.

Mama's Toffee Squares

"This is one of Mother's favorite recipes. She always made them when she had company, just in case her guests didn't like the other desserts she had made."

1 cup butter, softened	1 teaspoon vanilla
¾ cup sugar	1 egg, separated
2 cups flour	2½ cups chopped walnuts

Preheat oven to 350 degrees.

Cream butter and sugar. Add flour, vanilla and egg yolk. Spread mixture in a greased 15½ x 10½-inch jelly-roll pan. Beat egg white with a fork and spread over butter mixture. Sprinkle walnuts on top. Bake 35 minutes or until golden brown. Cool slightly and cut into small diamonds.

Makes about 36 squares.

Use a clear plastic ruler as a measure to evenly cut bar cookies and phyllo dough.

Chocolate Raspberry Crumb Bars

1 cup unsalted butter, softened	1 can (14 ounces) sweetened condensed milk
2 cups flour	1 package (12 ounces) semisweet chocolate chips
½ cup light brown sugar	½ cup chopped nuts (optional)
¼ teaspoon salt	½ cup seedless raspberry jam

Preheat oven to 350 degrees.

Beat butter in a bowl until creamy. Add flour, sugar and salt and beat until well mixed. With floured fingers, press 1¾ cups of crumb mixture into the bottom of a greased 13 x 9-inch baking pan. Reserve remaining crumb mixture. Bake crust 10 to 12 minutes or until edges are golden brown.

Meanwhile, combine milk and half of chocolate chips in a small heavy saucepan. Melt over low heat, stirring until smooth. Spread chocolate mixture over hot crust.

Mix nuts with reserved crumb mixture and sprinkle over chocolate filling. Drop teaspoonfuls of jam over crumb mixture. Sprinkle remaining chocolate chips on top. Bake 25 to 30 minutes longer or until center is set. Cool completely before cutting.

Makes 32 bars.

Roly Poly Cookies Ⓟ

An heirloom recipe, from Canada to California.

A new favorite: Invite some friends to tea in the garden. Ask everyone to wear a fun hat. Bake some goodies. Brew some iced tea. Enjoy!

Dough

4	eggs	1	teaspoon vanilla
1	cup sugar	¼	teaspoon salt
1	cup vegetable oil	2	teaspoons baking powder
¼	cup orange juice	4¾-5	cups all-purpose flour
	Zest of 1 orange		

Filling

1	cup, or more, apricot jam	1	cup golden raisins
1	cup, or more, blackberry/ raspberry jam	1	cup dried cranberries
		1	cup chopped nuts

Egg Wash Topping

1	egg, beaten	Cinnamon sugar

Preheat oven to 350 degrees.

Stack 2 baking sheets lined with parchment paper or foil.

In a large mixing bowl, stir together eggs and sugar. Stir in oil, orange juice and zest, vanilla and salt. Fold in baking powder and 4¾ cups flour to make a soft dough. Chill 2 hours. Divide chilled dough into 4 sections.

Knead each section on a well floured surface until smooth enough to handle, adding more flour as needed. Roll one section at a time into a 10x12-inch rectangle. Spread ½ cup jam, ½ cup raisins or cranberries and ¼ cup nuts over dough. (Pair apricot jam with raisins for 2 rolls and pair blackberry/raspberry jam with cranberries for 2 rolls.) Starting at end nearest you, gently roll up pastry lengthwise like a jelly roll. Paint with beaten egg and sprinkle with cinnamon sugar.

Repeat for remaining 3 sections of dough. Place rolls on baking sheets seam side down. Bake 40 to 45 minutes or until golden brown. Remove from oven and cool on baking sheets before transferring to a cutting board. Cut into ¾- to 1-inch slices. If desired, whole baked rolls may be frozen for later use.

Makes 4 rolls, 16 slices per roll.

Orange Cranberry Biscotti

These biscotti are unique in appearance. They are baked in a loaf pan.

1-2 small seedless oranges (Clementines preferred)	¼ teaspoon salt
½ cup oil	1½ teaspoons baking powder
1½ cups sugar	¼ teaspoon cinnamon
2 eggs	2¾ cups flour
1 teaspoon vanilla	1½ cups dried cranberries

Preheat oven to 350 degrees.

Wash oranges well and cut into quarters. Purée oranges, with peel, in a food processor or coffee grinder to the consistency of baby food. Measure out ½ cup for use in biscotti.

In a mixing bowl, blend oil, sugar and eggs. Stir in ½ cup orange purée. Add vanilla and mix well. In a separate bowl, combine salt, baking powder, cinnamon and flour. Fold dry ingredients into orange mixture. Fold in cranberries. Transfer batter to a generously greased 9 x 5-inch loaf pan. Bake 45 to 55 minutes or until top seems set and dry. If loaf is browning too quickly, reduce oven temperature to 325 degrees and lengthen baking time. Allow to cool 15 minutes before removing from pan and wrapping tightly in aluminum foil. Freeze about 2 hours or overnight.

Thaw bread just until softened enough to cut. Cut into ⅛-inch slices. Arrange on a parchment paper-lined baking sheet. Bake at 325 degrees, turning once, for 20 to 30 minutes or until cookies are just lightly browned. Store in an airtight container.

Makes 20 to 28 slices.

Lemon Thins

½ cup vegetable shortening, softened
2 tablespoons unsalted butter or margarine, softened
1 cup sugar
½ teaspoon vanilla
½ teaspoon lemon extract
1½ tablespoons lemon zest
¼ cup fresh lemon juice
1½ cups all-purpose flour
1½ teaspoons baking powder
½ teaspoon baking soda
¼ teaspoon salt
Confectioners' sugar for dusting

Preheat oven to 350 degrees.

In the bowl of an electric mixer, cream shortening, butter and sugar. Add vanilla, lemon extract, lemon zest and lemon juice and beat until smooth. Sift in flour, baking powder, baking soda and salt and blend well.

Form dough into a 1½-inch diameter log on a piece of wax paper, using the paper as a guide. Wrap in wax paper and foil and chill 2 hours, or freeze up to 3 months.

Cut log into ⅛-inch thick slices using a sharp knife. Arrange cookies 2 inches apart on an ungreased baking sheet. Bake in center of oven for 8 to 10 minutes or until edges are just golden. Transfer cookies immediately with a metal spatula to racks to cool. Sift confectioners' sugar lightly over cookies.

Makes about 50 cookies.

Auntie's Mandelbrot

3 cups flour
2 teaspoons baking powder
¾ cup sugar
¾ cup oil
3 eggs
½ teaspoon vanilla
½ teaspoon lemon juice
¼ teaspoon almond flavoring
1 cup chocolate bits, walnuts or pecans, or combination to equal 1 cup
¾ cup black coffee, cooled
1 teaspoon sugar

Preheat oven to 350 degrees.

Mix flour, baking powder, ¾ cup sugar, oil, eggs, vanilla, lemon juice, almond flavoring and chocolate bits. Dough will be soft. Divide dough into 4 portions. Shape each portion into a high and narrow log crosswise on a baking sheet. Bake 30 minutes.

With a teaspoon, pour a little coffee on each log. Sprinkle 1 teaspoon sugar on top. Slice logs diagonally into ⅓-inch thick slices. Place cookies, cut-side down, on a baking sheet. Bake 15 minutes or until golden brown.

Makes 70 to 80 cookies.

A wonderful tip from a Hawaiian chef: For a sweeter pineapple, twist off the top green leaves, turn it over so that it stands upright, and let stand this way for 24 to 48 hours. Prepare your usual way.

Maple-Flavored Mandelbrot ⓟ

A favorite of many of our Sisterhood Members.

5	eggs	1	tablespoon baking powder
1½	cups vegetable oil	1	teaspoon baking soda
1½	cups sugar	4½	cups sifted flour
	Juice (about ⅓ cup) and zest	1½	cups ground nuts
	of 1 small orange		Apricot-pineapple preserves
1	teaspoon maple flavoring		Chocolate chips

Preheat oven to 350 degrees.

Beat eggs. Add oil, sugar, orange juice, orange zest and maple flavoring and beat until blended. Sift baking powder, baking soda and flour together and add to orange mixture. Mixture will be loose. Chill in refrigerator overnight.

The next day, place a handful of dough on a well-floured board. Shape into a short roll and transfer to a lightly greased baking sheet. Make an indent down the center of roll and place some nuts, preserves and chocolate chips in it. Pinch together and lengthen to form into a 10- to 12-inch roll. Repeat with remaining dough, placing 2 rolls on each baking sheet. This mixture should yield 6 to 8 rolls.

Bake 20 minutes. Remove from oven and cut into slices. Arrange slices on a baking sheet. Reduce oven temperature to 325 degrees. Bake until slices are dried out and crisp.

Serves a crowd.

Poppy Seed Cookies ⓓ

1	cup sugar	½	teaspoon nutmeg
	Zest of 1 orange	¼	teaspoon salt
1	egg yolk	1	cup unbleached flour
1	cup unsalted butter, softened	1	cup cake flour
	and cut into 8 pieces	¼	cup poppy seeds

Preheat oven to 350 degrees.

Combine sugar and orange zest in a medium bowl. Add egg yolk and beat until light. Add butter, nutmeg and salt and mix until light and fluffy. Add both flours and poppy seeds and mix thoroughly; do not overbeat.

Divide dough into 4 equal portions and place each on a separate sheet of plastic wrap. Using plastic as an aid, shape dough into 2 x 4-inch logs. Seal and refrigerate 1 hour or until firm, or freeze until ready to use.

Cut dough into ¼-inch slices and arrange 1½ inches apart on an ungreased baking sheet. Bake 8 minutes or until edges are slightly brown. Transfer to a wire rack and cool.

Makes 50 to 60 cookies.

Rugelach

Our favorite rugelach.

1	cup unsalted butter, chilled	⅓	cup sour cream
1	package (8 ounces) cream cheese, regular or low fat, chilled	½	cup sugar
		1	tablespoon cinnamon
2	cups all-purpose flour	1	cup finely chopped walnuts
¼	teaspoon salt	½	cup finely chopped raisins, or mini chocolate chips

Preheat oven to 350 degrees.

Cut chilled butter and cream cheese into bits and place in a food processor. Add flour, salt and sour cream and pulse until crumbly. Shape crumbly mixture into 4 equal disks and wrap each disk in plastic wrap. Chill 2 hours, or up to 2 days.

Roll each disk into a 9-inch round, keeping other disks chilled until ready to roll. Combine sugar, cinnamon, walnuts and raisins. Sprinkle round with sugar mixture and press lightly into dough. With a chef's knife or pizza cutter, cut each round into 12 wedges. Roll wedges from wide to narrow, ending up with points on the outside of cookie. Place cookies on ungreased baking sheets and chill 20 minutes.

Once chilled, bake in center of oven for 22 minutes or until lightly golden. Cool on wire racks. Store in airtight containers.

Makes 48 cookies.

Spread a thin layer of jam (any flavor) on dough before adding filling.

When making rugelach, roll dough in granulated sugar instead of flour for a sweeter cookie.

Low Fat Classic Rugelach Ⓓ

1 package (8 ounces) low fat cream cheese, softened	1 cup apricot preserves, as thick as possible
½ cup unsalted butter, softened	Confectioners' sugar
1⅓ cups unbleached all-purpose flour	

Preheat oven to 350 degrees.

Combine cream cheese and butter in the bowl of an electric mixer fitted with a paddle. Cream on low speed for 2 minutes or until combined. Add flour and mix 2 minutes longer or until a very soft dough forms. Cover with plastic wrap and refrigerate at least 2 hours.

Divide dough into 3 balls. Roll balls on a lightly floured board into four ⅛-inch thick, 9-inch diameter circles. Using a spoon or a dull knife, spread apricot preserves over each circle of dough, covering almost to the edges.

Using a dull knife, cut each circle into 12 pie-shaped pieces. Roll up each piece, starting from the wide side to the center. Place rugelach on 2 greased baking sheets. Bake on middle and top racks of oven for 30 minutes or until golden brown. Cool on wire racks. Sprinkle with confectioners' sugar just before serving.

Makes 36 cookies.

Rugelach ~ An Easy Way Ⓓ

1 package (8 ounces) cream cheese, softened	Pinch of salt
1 cup butter, softened	Filling
2 egg yolks	8 ounces walnuts, chopped
2 cups flour	1 cup sugar
¼ teaspoon baking powder	Cinnamon to taste

Preheat oven to 350 degrees.

Cream together cream cheese and butter. Mix in egg yolks, flour, baking powder and salt. Refrigerate for a few hours. Meanwhile, combine all filling ingredients; set aside.

Divide chilled dough into 4 equal parts and shape into balls. Roll each ball into a 10-inch circle. Spread ¼ of filling onto each circle and cut each circle into 12 wedges. Roll up wedges starting at wide end and place on a greased baking sheet. Bake 30 minutes.

Makes 48 cookies.

Chocolate Mexican Wedding Cookies

A chocolate version of the Mexican Wedding Cookie.

Dough

1	cup butter, softened	1	cup ground pecans
⅓	cup sifted confectioners' sugar	½	cup grated German sweet chocolate
2	teaspoons vanilla	¾	teaspoon cinnamon
1¾	cups all-purpose flour		Pinch of salt

Coating

½	cup sifted confectioners' sugar	¼	cup grated German sweet chocolate

Preheat oven to 325 degrees.

For dough, cream butter and sugar in a large bowl until light and fluffy. Add vanilla. In a separate bowl, combine flour, pecans, chocolate, cinnamon and salt and mix well. Gradually add dry ingredients to creamed mixture. Wrap dough in plastic wrap and chill 1 to 2 hours or until firm.

Shape dough into 1-inch balls and place 1-inch apart on an ungreased baking sheet. Bake 15 to 18 minutes or until cookies are firm to the touch. Cool 1 minute on baking sheet before transferring to a wire rack.

To prepare coating, combine sugar and chocolate in a shallow bowl. While cookies are still warm, roll them in coating.

Makes 16 cookies.

Malted Milk Ball Chocolate Chip Cookies

1	package chocolate chip dry cookie mix	1	egg
½	cup butter or margarine, softened	1	cup malted milk balls, crushed
		½	cup chopped pecans

Preheat oven to 350 degrees.

Combine dry cookie mix, butter and egg in a medium bowl and mix well. Stir in malted milk balls and pecans and blend well. Drop by heaping teaspoonfuls onto greased baking sheets. Bake 12 to 15 minutes. Cool on sheet 1 minute. Transfer to wire racks to cool completely.

Makes 2½ to 3 dozen cookies.

Apples and Sour Cream Crumb Pie 🏛️

Cinnamon Pastry Shell

1¾ cups flour
¼ cup sugar
1 teaspoon cinnamon

½ teaspoon salt
⅔ cup butter, chilled
2-3 tablespoons cold water

Filling

1½ cups sour cream
1 egg
1 cup sugar
¼ cup flour

2 teaspoons vanilla
½ teaspoon salt
3 pounds apples, peeled, cored
   and cut into thin wedges

Streusel Topping

½ cup flour
⅓ cup granulated sugar
⅓ cup brown sugar, firmly
   packed
1 tablespoon cinnamon

¼ teaspoon salt
½ cup butter
1 cup coarsely chopped
   walnuts

Preheat oven to 450 degrees.

For pastry, combine flour, sugar, cinnamon and salt in a bowl. Cut in butter until particles are the size of small peas. Sprinkle with cold water, 1 tablespoon at a time, tossing with a fork until all flour is moistened and pastry almost cleans side of bowl. Gather dough into a ball. On a lightly floured board, roll pastry out 2 inches larger than an inverted 10-inch pie pan. Ease pastry into pie pan and crimp edges in a decorative fashion.

To make filling, combine sour cream, egg, sugar, flour, vanilla and salt in a large bowl. Add apples and toss to mix well. Turn filling into pastry shell. Cover and crimp foil lightly around edges. Bake 10 minutes. Reduce temperature to 350 degrees and bake 35 to 40 minutes longer.

Meanwhile, prepare topping. Combine flour, both sugars, cinnamon and salt in a bowl. Cut in butter until crumbly. Stir in walnuts. Set aside.

After baking period, remove pie from oven. Gently, but thoroughly, stir apple filling. Remove foil from around edges. Spoon topping evenly over pie. Bake 15 to 20 minutes longer. Serve warm, at room temperature or cold.

Serves 8 to 10.

Blackberry Crisp

A Palos Verdes Havurah favorite.

Crust Topping

1	cup flour	1	teaspoon baking powder
1	cup sugar	1	egg, beaten

Berry Filling

2	tablespoons flour	½	cup unsalted butter or
¾	cup sugar		margarine, melted
4-5	cups fresh or frozen blackberries, or frozen mixed berries		

Preheat oven to 375 degrees.

Combine flour, sugar and baking powder in a medium bowl. Make a well in the center of dry ingredients and blend in egg, mixing until topping is crumbly. Set topping aside.

To prepare filling, mix flour and sugar in a small bowl. Place berries in a large bowl and sprinkle with flour mixture. Toss gently to evenly coat berries. Transfer berry mixture to a well-greased 13 x 9-inch baking dish. Sprinkle topping over berries. Drizzle melted butter evenly over topping. Place dish on a baking sheet. Bake 45 minutes.

Serves 6 to 8.

FIGS

Dessert: Slice figs and sprinkle with cinnamon sugar.

Slice black figs and place next to a scoop of vanilla ice cream. Drizzle with balsamic vinegar.

Or, you can do what we enjoy and that's to pop a fresh fig right into a waiting mouth.

Rum Balls ℗

3	cups ground vanilla wafers	½	cup rum
1	cup ground nuts	1½	teaspoons cocoa powder
1	cup confectioners' sugar		(optional)
3	tablespoons light corn syrup		

Combine vanilla wafers and nuts in a bowl. Mix sugar, corn syrup and rum together and add to wafer mixture. Knead dough until smooth. Form into smooth walnut-size balls. Roll in confectioners' sugar.

Makes about 40 balls.

Variation: Add cocoa to ½ the dough for Chocolate Rum Balls.

If wrapped in foil, cookies can keep indefinitely.

Lemon Meringue Pie with Pecan Crust

Crust

1	cup all-purpose flour	3	tablespoons vegetable shortening, chilled and cut into ½-inch pieces
⅓	cup cake flour		
⅔	cup finely chopped pecans		
3	tablespoons light brown sugar	3	tablespoons ice water, or as needed
½	teaspoon salt		
5	tablespoons unsalted butter, chilled and cut into ½-inch pieces		

Filling and Topping

1¾	cups sugar	5	eggs, separated
⅓	cup cornstarch	2	tablespoons lemon zest
1½	cups water	½	teaspoon cream tartar
½	cup lemon juice	⅓	cup sugar

Preheat oven to 375 degrees.

To make crust, combine both flours, pecans, sugar and salt in a bowl. Add butter and shortening. Using an electric mixer, beat on low speed until mixture resembles coarse meal. Add 2 tablespoons ice water. Beat until dough holds together, adding more water by ½ tablespoons if dry. Gather dough into a ball, then flatten into a disk. Wrap disk in wax paper and chill at least 1 hour, or up to 1 day, or until firm enough to roll.

Roll out dough between sheets of wax paper to a 12-inch round. Peel off top sheet and invert dough into a 9-inch glass pie dish. Peel off paper and press dough gently into dish. Trim overhang to ¾ inch. Turn under edge and crimp decoratively. Freeze 30 minutes or until crust is firm.

Line crust with foil and fill with dried beans or pie weights. Bake on center rack for 15 minutes or until edges are golden. Remove foil and beans and continue to bake 12 minutes or until crust is pale golden, piercing with fork if crust bubbles. Cool completely on a rack. Reduce oven temperature to 325 degrees.

For filling, whisk 1¾ cups sugar and cornstarch in a heavy medium saucepan to blend. Gradually add water and lemon juice, whisking until cornstarch dissolves and mixture is smooth. Add egg yolks and lemon zest and whisk to blend. Cook over medium-high heat, whisking constantly, for 8 minutes or until filling comes to a boil and thickens. Pour into baked crust.

Using an electric mixer, beat egg whites and cream of tartar in a large bowl until soft peaks form. Gradually add ⅓ cup sugar, beating until stiff and shiny. Mount meringue on top of filling and spread to edges to seal in filling. Bake at 325 degrees for 20 minutes or until meringue is golden. Cool 1 hour at room temperature. Transfer to refrigerator for 6 hours or until cold.

Serves 8.

Peach Pie with a Crunch

Crust
1   pie crust (9-inch), unbaked   1   egg yolk, beaten

Filling
4   heaping cups sliced fresh   2   dashes of nutmeg
      peaches   Juice of 1 large lemon
2   tablespoons flour   ¼   cup honey
½   teaspoon cinnamon

Topping
5   tablespoons butter   ½   cup chopped almonds
3   tablespoons honey   ¼   cup flour
2   cups raw rolled oats   ½   teaspoon salt
½   teaspoon cinnamon

Preheat oven to 400 degrees.

Brush pie crust with egg yolk. Set aside.

To prepare filling, toss peaches with flour, cinnamon and nutmeg until evenly coated. Drizzle lemon juice and honey over peaches and gently mix. Let stand while preparing topping.

For topping, melt butter and honey together. Combine butter mixture with oats, cinnamon, almonds, flour and salt. Mix well.

Pour filling into pie crust. Sprinkle topping evenly over filling and pat firmly into place. Bake 10 minutes. Reduce temperature to 375 degrees and bake 25 to 35 minutes longer. If top browns too quickly, cover pie with foil. Serve warm or cold.

Serves 6.

Plunge fruits or vegetables into boiling water for 2 to 3 minutes to either maintain the bright color of vegetables or to remove the skins of stone fruits and tomatoes.

Southern California
Fresh Peach Cobbler ⒟

Pastry

1¾	cups all-purpose flour
½	teaspoon salt
⅓	cup vegetable shortening, chilled in freezer

5	tablespoons unsalted butter, chilled and cut into 5 pieces
4	tablespoons ice water

Filling

6-7	ripe peaches (about 2 pounds total)
⅔	cup light brown sugar, loosely packed
¼	teaspoon nutmeg

2	tablespoons all-purpose flour
	Dash of salt
4	tablespoons unsalted butter, softened

Preheat oven to 400 degrees.

To make pastry, combine flour and salt in a food processor fitted with a metal blade, or in a medium bowl using a pastry blender or fingertips. Add shortening and butter and pulse until mixture resembles coarse meal. Sprinkle ice water over dough and mix just until pastry hold together when pinched between your fingers. Do not form into a ball. Flatten pastry into a disk, wrap in plastic wrap and refrigerate 30 minutes or until firm enough to roll. Pastry can be refrigerated up to 5 days.

For filling, peel peaches by plunging them into a large pot of boiling water for 20 seconds. Run under cold water. When cool enough to handle, slip off peel. Cut peaches into ½-inch thick slices, discarding pits, and place in a large bowl, yielding about 5 cups. Add sugar, nutmeg, flour and salt and toss with your hands until well combined. Pour into a greased 11 x 7-inch baking dish or 4- to 5-cup gratin dish. Dot with butter.

Roll out pastry onto a lightly floured board into a rectangle about 1 inch larger than baking dish and about ⅓-inch thick; it should be slightly thicker than a pie crust. Place pastry over filling and press against side of dish, forming a border and sealing the edges. Cut 4 to 6 slits in the top to allow steam to escape.

Bake 35 minutes or until pastry is golden and fruit is bubbling. Cool 15 minutes before serving. The cobbler is best served warm. Serve with vanilla ice cream, if desired.

Serves 6 to 8.

Apples in Phyllo Dough Ⓓ Ⓟ

⅔ cup sugar
½ teaspoon cinnamon
½ cup unsalted butter or
   margarine
½ cup vegetable oil

1 package (1 pound) phyllo
   dough, thawed if frozen
8 medium apples, peeled and
   cored

Preheat oven to 375 degrees.

Mix sugar and cinnamon in a small bowl and set aside. In a small saucepan, melt butter with oil, set aside.

Remove 20 sheets of phyllo from the package and, using a scissors, cut stack of sheets into quarters. Leave out 10 of the quartered sheets and cover with plastic wrap. Place remaining sheets in a sealed plastic bag.

Gently peel off 1 phyllo sheet and lay on a work surface. Brush with melted butter mixture. Remove second sheet, rotate slightly and lay, diagonally, on top of first sheet. Brush with butter mixture. Continue layering the sheets, rotating and brushing with butter mixture each time, until all 10 sheets are on the stack.

Place an apple in the center of the stack and spoon a heaping tablespoon of cinnamon-sugar mixture into apple's center. Bring edges of phyllo up around the apple and pinch closed on top. Transfer to a greased baking sheet. Repeat process with remaining ingredients making 8 desserts total.

Bake 40 to 45 minutes or until dough is deep golden, the apples are soft and the center is bubbly. Let stand 10 minutes. Serve with vanilla ice cream, if desired.

Serves 8.

Cherry Goat Cheese Strudel ⓓ

A most unusual delicious strudel for brunch.

5	ounces goat cheese, such as Montrachet, softened	½	teaspoon cinnamon
2	packages (3 ounces each) cream cheese, softened	12	sheets phyllo dough
		½	cup unsalted butter, melted
⅓	cup sugar	14	tablespoons sugar
2	egg yolks	1	can (16 ounces) tart pie cherries, well drained

Preheat oven to 375 degrees.

Combine goat cheese, cream cheese, ⅓ cup sugar, egg yolks and cinnamon in a medium bowl of an electric mixer or in a food processor fitted with a metal blade. Beat on low speed, or process, until blended. Refrigerate until chilled.

Stack 6 phyllo sheets, long side facing you, on a damp towel, brushing each sheet with melted butter and sprinkling each with 1 tablespoon sugar. Spread half of cheese filling along one long end of phyllo stack, leaving a 2-inch border. Sprinkle half of cherries over cheese. Fold narrow ends of phyllo over filling. Using a towel as a guide, gently roll up jelly-roll fashion. Place strudel, seam-side down, on a foil-lined rimmed baking sheet. Brush top with melted butter and sprinkle with 1 tablespoon sugar. Repeat with remaining ingredients to make second strudel on a separate foil-lined baking sheet. Strudel may be refrigerated on baking sheet up to 4 hours.

Bake 25 to 30 minutes or until golden brown. The filling may leak out slightly. Cool at least 1 hour to allow cheese to set up before cutting. Serve lukewarm or at room temperature.

Makes 2 strudels, 8 pieces each.

If melons are not as sweet as you would like, drizzle some Muscatel wine over cut melon.

Mini Nut Strudels Ⓓ Ⓟ

Tiny rolls of shallow, nut-filled, rich, flaky pastry.

1¼	cups flour	2	egg whites
½	cup butter or margarine	⅓	cup sugar
2	egg yolks, beaten	⅔	cup ground walnuts
1	teaspoon lemon zest		Confectioners' sugar
1	tablespoon lemon juice		

Preheat oven to 350 degrees.

Sift flour into a medium bowl. Cut in butter using a pastry blender. Combine egg yolks, lemon zest and lemon juice in a separate bowl. Add yolk mixture to flour and blend lightly with a fork to form a dough. Divide and shape dough into 24 balls. Place dough balls in a shallow pan and chill at least 4 hours.

Beat egg whites until foamy in a medium bowl. Beat in granulated sugar, 1 tablespoon at a time, until mixture forms stiff peaks. Fold in walnuts.

Roll out each dough ball to a 4-inch round on a lightly floured pastry cloth or board. Spread 2 tablespoons nut mixture over each round and roll up jelly-roll fashion. Place, seam-side down, on an ungreased baking sheet. Bake 15 minutes or until golden brown. Cool on wire racks. Slice each roll diagonally into 3 pieces. Sprinkle with confectioners' sugar.

Makes 6 dozen.

Alsatian Plum Tart

This tart is served traditionally at the high holidays. The tart is lined with bread crumbs and then apricot preserves, which protect the dough during baking, leading to a crispy crust. This is easy to prepare and is simply delicious.

1	cup unbleached all-purpose flour	2	teaspoons dried bread crumbs
	Dash of salt	⅓	cup apricot preserves
1	tablespoon granulated sugar	1	tablespoon brandy
½	cup unsalted butter or pareve margarine, cut into small pieces	2	pounds Italian plums, pitted and quartered
1	egg yolk	½	teaspoon cinnamon
		3	tablespoons granulated sugar
			Confectioners' sugar

Preheat oven to 400 degrees.

To make the crust using a food processor, fitted with a metal blade, pulse flour, salt and 1 tablespoon granulated sugar together. Add butter and process until crumbly. Add egg yolk and process until a ball is formed, adding more flour if necessary.

To make crust by hand, use your fingers or a pastry blender to work butter into flour, salt and 1 tablespoon granulated sugar until mixture resembles coarse bread crumbs. Add egg yolk and work dough into a ball.

Remove dough from bowl, dust with flour and pat into a flattened circle on a plate. Cover with plastic wrap and refrigerate at least 30 minutes. When ready to make crust, dust hands and dough with flour. Place dough in the center of a 9-inch tart pan and gently pat out with fingers to cover bottom and up sides of pan. Prick crust with a fork in several places and bake on center rack for 10 minutes. Remove from oven and cool slightly. Reduce oven to 350 degrees.

Sprinkle bread crumbs over crust. Spoon apricot preserves on top and drizzle with brandy. Arrange plum quarters over crust in a circle so that each overlaps the next and eventually forms a spiral into the center. Sprinkle with cinnamon and 3 tablespoons granulated sugar. At this point, tart can be wrapped and frozen to bake later. Remove from freezer 1 hour before baking.

Bake at 350 degrees for 30 to 40 minutes or until crust is golden brown and plums are juicy. Remove from oven. Just before serving, sprinkle with confectioners' sugar.

Serves 6 to 8.

Warm Chocolate-Walnut Tart

Here is the dark, fudgy, warm chocolate tart you've been looking for all your life. If there is any left over, it is unbelievably good served cold.

Short Crust Tart Dough

1½	cups flour	¾	cup unsalted butter, chilled and cut into ½-inch pieces
2	tablespoons sugar		
¼	teaspoon salt		
1½	teaspoons lemon zest	1-1½	tablespoons ice water

Filling

2	cups walnuts	1	cup heavy cream
5	ounces bittersweet chocolate, chopped	2	tablespoons confectioners' sugar
¼	cup unsalted butter, cut into 8 pieces	¼	teaspoon vanilla
1	cup dark corn syrup	1	tablespoon confectioners' sugar
¼	cup granulated sugar		Toasted walnut halves for garnish
3	eggs		
2	tablespoons brandy or cognac		

Preheat oven to 400 degrees.

Combine flour, sugar and salt in a food processor. Whirl briefly to blend. Add lemon zest and butter. Pulse machine until mixture resembles coarse meal. With machine on, add water, a few drops at a time, just until dough begins to form a ball. Flatten dough into a 6-inch disk, wrap in plastic wrap and refrigerate 30 minutes or until firm.

Press dough evenly into bottom and up the sides of a lightly greased 10-inch tart pan with a removable bottom. Freeze 30 minutes or until firm. Prick bottom and sides of dough all over with a fork. Fit a 12-inch square of parchment paper (or double thickness foil with a few holes poked in it) snugly against pastry in pan. Bake 10 to 15 minutes or until edges of pastry are light golden brown. Carefully remove parchment and reduce oven to 375 degrees. Bake 15 to 20 minutes longer or until tart shell is evenly golden brown.

To prepare filling, reduce oven temperature to 350 degrees. Spread walnuts on a baking sheet or in a shallow pan. Bake, stirring once or twice, for 10 to 12 minutes or until lightly browned and fragrant. Cool.

In the top of a double boiler, with the bottom containing 2 inches of hot water, melt chocolate and butter, stirring until smooth. Remove from heat. In a medium saucepan, combine corn syrup and granulated sugar. Cook and stir over medium-high heat until mixture boils. Stir in chocolate mixture.

In a medium bowl, whisk eggs with brandy until foamy. Stir into chocolate mixture. Add cooled walnuts. Scrape filling into prepared tart shell. Bake at 350 degrees for 35 to 40 minutes or until filling is set and a pick inserted into the center comes out clean. Cool 15 to 20 minutes on a rack or just until warm.

Meanwhile, in a large bowl, combine cream, 2 tablespoons confectioners' sugar and vanilla. Whip until soft peaks form. Dust tart with 1 tablespoon confectioners' sugar and garnish with walnut halves. Serve with sweetened whipped cream.

Serves 8 to 10.

Amaretto Bread Pudding with Sauce

Can use nonfat milk and eggbeaters as a substitute. You can bake the bread pudding until it is almost done, cool it and freeze it. When ready to serve, defrost and finish baking and pour sauce over top.

1	pound egg bread (challah), broken into 1-inch pieces	3	eggs, room temperature
1	quart half-and-half	2	tablespoons almond extract
2	tablespoons unsalted butter	¾	cup golden raisins
1½	cups sugar	¾	cup sliced almonds

Amaretto Sauce

1	cup confectioners' sugar	1	egg, well beaten
½	cup unsalted butter	¼	cup amaretto liqueur

Preheat oven to 325 degrees.

Combine bread pieces and half-and-half in a large bowl. Cover and let stand about 1 hour, stirring occasionally. Grease a 13 x 9-inch glass baking dish with 2 tablespoons unsalted butter.

Whisk together sugar, eggs and almond extract and stir into bread mixture. Gently fold in raisins and almonds. Spoon pudding into prepared dish. Bake on center rack for 50 minutes or until firm. Cool. Pudding can be prepared up to 6 hours ahead; do not refrigerate.

Meanwhile, prepare sauce. Combine sugar and butter in the top of a double boiler that has been set over simmering water. Cook and stir until butter melts, sugar dissolves and the mixture is very hot. Remove from heat and whisk in egg. Continue whisking until cooled to room temperature. Mix in liqueur. Sauce can be prepared up to 4 hours ahead.

Cut cooled pudding into squares. Spoon sauce over pudding. Broil until sauce bubbles.

Serves 8 to 10, makes 1½ cups sauce.

Rustic French Apple Tarts 🄳

These are delicious served with lightly sweetened whipped cream or scoops of vanilla ice cream.

Use an ice cream scoop to scoop the seeds out of a melon.

1 package (17.3 ounces) frozen puff pastry (2 sheets), thawed
2 Golden Delicious apples (6 to 7 ounces each), peeled, quartered and quarters cut into 8 slices each
4 tablespoons light brown sugar
4 teaspoons unsalted butter, melted
1 egg, beaten

Preheat oven to 400 degrees. (Position baking rack in top third of oven.)

Unfold 1 pastry sheet on a lightly floured surface. Using a 9-inch tart pan bottom as an aid, cut out a 9-inch round from pastry sheet. Leaving a 1-inch border, overlap slices from 1 apple on pastry round. Sprinkle 2 tablespoons sugar and drizzle 2 teaspoons butter over slices. Fold border over edge of apples, pressing so pastry will stay in place. Brush pastry edge with beaten egg. Transfer to an ungreased baking sheet. Repeat with remaining pastry sheet, apple, sugar and butter.

Bake tarts 28 minutes or until apples are tender and pastry browns, piercing with a toothpick if pastry bubbles. Serve warm.

Serves 8.

Croissant Pudding 🄳

Rich, but so delicious.

1 tablespoon butter
6 large croissants, cut into ½-inch rounds
8 eggs, lightly beaten
2 cups sugar
3 cups milk
1 teaspoon almond extract
2 teaspoons vanilla
¼ cup almond paste, cut into bits
½ cup chopped almonds (chopped in a blender)

Preheat oven to 350 degrees.

Use 1 tablespoon butter to grease a 13 x 9-inch baking dish. Place croissant rounds in prepared dish, arranging rounds next to each other and stacking until even. Whisk together eggs, sugar, milk, almond extract and vanilla and pour over croissants. Put almond paste over each croissant. Pat down with a spoon and let soak 10 minutes. Sprinkle almonds on top. Bake 35 to 40 minutes or until golden and puffed.

Serves 8 to 10.

Poached Peach Dessert

A simply refreshing taste of summer. You can also use pears, nectarines or large plums.

8	fresh peaches, still slightly firm	6	whole cloves
1	cup apple juice		Zest of 1 orange
	White wine to cover fruit while poaching		Vanilla or cinnamon ice cream
1½-2	cups sugar, to taste		Brandy (optional)
3	cinnamon sticks		Whipped cream for topping

To remove skin from peaches, thinly peel; or plunge into boiling water for 30 seconds, then remove peel. Cut in half and remove pit.

Place peach halves in a large pot. Add apple juice and enough wine to cover peaches. Add sugar, cinnamon sticks, whole cloves and orange zest. Poach peaches, with liquid in a gentle rolling boil, for 10 to 15 minutes or until soft. Cooking time will depend upon ripeness of fruit. Remove fruit to a container, cut-side down.

Cook 2 cups of poaching liquid until reduced to a syrup consistency. Pour syrup over peaches and refrigerate in syrup until chilled.

To serve, place a fruit half on each individual plate, cut-side up. Spoon syrup over fruit. Using a mini-scooper, place a small scoop of ice cream on top of peach half. Sprinkle a few drops of brandy over fruit and top with whipped cream.

Serves 16.

The above recipe can be enjoyed in autumn, substituting juice from 4 tangerines for apple juice and 1 vanilla bean, split lengthwise, as well as ¼ teaspoon ground nutmeg for the cinnamon and cloves. Eliminate ice cream and serve with whipped cream. Garnish with tangerine peel. Comice or Seckel pears are nice.

Poached Pears in Raspberry Sauce

Fresh pears poached in raspberry juice are then dressed in a bright raspberry sauce enhanced with cognac and kirsch.

2	tablespoons fresh lemon juice	1	cup sugar
8	ripe pears	2	tablespoons fresh lemon juice
3	packages (10 ounces each) frozen raspberries in syrup, thawed	¾	cup seedless raspberry preserves
6	cups water	2	tablespoons cognac or kirsch
			Mint sprigs for garnish

Fill a medium bowl with water. Add 2 tablespoons lemon juice. Peel pears, leaving stems intact. Working from the base of the pears, use a melon baller to scoop out the cores, leaving top of pears intact. Cut a small slice from the bottom of each pear so they will stand upright. Place peeled and cored pears in lemon water to prevent browning.

Drain raspberries, reserving syrup and setting raspberries aside. Combine raspberry syrup, 6 cups water, sugar and 2 tablespoons lemon juice in a 4-quart saucepan. Bring to a boil. Reduce heat and simmer 5 to 7 minutes or until sugar is completely dissolved.

Drain pears and add to syrup mixture. Cover and simmer slowly, turning pears occasionally, until they are tender when pierced with a knife. Poaching time will depend on type, size and ripeness of pear, from 10 to 40 minutes. When tender, remove pears from syrup and place in a bowl. When syrup is cool, pour over pears. Cover and refrigerate overnight, turning pears occasionally.

Heat drained raspberries and preserves in a medium saucepan until boiling. Press mixture through a strainer twice to produce a clear sauce without seeds. Stir in cognac and refrigerate in a covered bowl.

To serve, remove pears from syrup and blot with paper towels. Spoon a small amount of sauce onto each dessert plate. Place a pear in center of each plate and carefully pour remaining sauce over the top. Garnish with mint sprigs.

Serves 8.

Traditional & Holidays

Traditional & Holidays

Traditional Challah

1	package active dry yeast		2	eggs, well beaten,
1	teaspoon sugar			1 tablespoon reserved for
¼	cup warm water			brushing on top
3½	cups all-purpose flour		¾	cup boiling water
1	tablespoon honey		¼	cup vegetable oil
2	teaspoons salt			Poppy or sesame seeds for
				topping

In a small bowl, combine yeast, sugar and warm water. Set aside for 10 minutes.

In the large bowl of an electric mixer, using beaters or a dough hook on low speed, combine flour, 1 cup at a time, honey and salt. Add eggs. Add yeast mixture, boiling water and oil and mix on medium speed for 5 minutes. Continue to knead with a dough hook for 8 to 10 minutes or until dough is smooth and shiny. (This releases the gluten.)

Remove dough from bowl and shape into a ball. Use ¼ cup oil to grease a large bowl. Place ball in greased bowl, coating entire surface of dough with oil. Cover with a slightly dampened cloth and place in a warm, draft-free place for 1 to 2 hours.

Punch dough down and place on a floured board. Knead 2 to 3 minutes or until smooth and shiny. Heat oven to 250 degrees and then turn oven off.

Divide dough into 3 pieces, rolling each with your hands into a long, smooth rope about 20 inches long by ¾-inch wide. Braid ropes tightly together and pinch and tuck ends under. Transfer bread onto a greased baking sheet and cover with greased wax paper. Place baking sheet in warmed oven for 1 hour to rise. Remove from oven.

Heat oven to 375 degrees. Brush top of dough with reserved tablespoon of beaten egg. Sprinkle with seeds. Bake 30 to 45 minutes or until loaf is golden brown. When cool, place in a plastic bag and seal tightly. If not being used within a day, freeze.

Makes 1 loaf.

To reheat challah, preheat oven to 400 degrees. Spray bread with water using a spray bottle, then place loaf on a baking sheet and bake about 10 minutes.

**A NOTE ON
CHICKEN SOUP:**

*Simmer soup for
no more than 2 hours,
as the longer it cooks,
the cloudier it can get.*

Chicken Soup

"Authentic Jewish Penicillin".

4	pounds stewing chicken with giblets (without the liver), cut into several pieces, excess fat discarded
4	quarts water
1	large onion, chopped

2	large carrots, diced or sliced
2	stalks celery, chopped
1	parsnip, peeled and chopped
	Salt and pepper to taste
	Fresh dill (optional)

Place chicken and 4 quarts water in a large stew pot. Bring to a quick boil. Reduce heat and simmer 30 minutes. Skim fat carefully from soup. Add onion, carrots, celery and parsnip and continue to simmer until chicken is tender. Season with salt and pepper. Strain broth into a clean pot. Reserve chicken for another use, or chop meat and return to broth. Serve soup hot with Matzo Balls (Knaidlach), rice, noodles or kasha.

Serves 8 to 10.

Matzo Balls (Knaidlach) (P)

You will get the lightest matzo balls by using club soda.

4	eggs, separated
½	cup cold club soda
1	teaspoon salt, or to taste
⅛	teaspoon white pepper, or to taste

⅓	cup vegetable shortening, melted, kosher for Pesach
1	cup matzo meal

Beat egg yolks until lemon colored. Mix in club soda. Add salt, pepper and melted shortening. In a separate bowl, beat egg whites until foamy. Fold whites into yolk mixture. Stir in matzo meal. Refrigerate several hours or overnight, or 20 minutes in the freezer. Dip both hands in ice water before forming mixture into balls the size of golf balls. Drop each ball into a pot of boiling salted water. Cook about 30 minutes. Drain and add balls to hot chicken soup.

Makes 16 to 18 balls.

Easy Brisket for Shabbat

4-5 pounds brisket
1½ cups water, or as needed
½ cup ketchup

1 package dry onion soup mix
½ can (12 ounces) cola

Preheat oven to 350 degrees.

Rinse brisket and place in a roasting pan, fat-side up. Add about 1½ inches of water. Pour ketchup over entire brisket. Sprinkle soup mix over the brisket and mix into the ketchup. Pour cola on top. Cover tightly with foil. Bake 3 hours or until tender. Cool completely before slicing against the grain. Pour pan gravy over sliced brisket and reheat about 30 to 45 minutes.

Serves 6 to 8.

Easy Apple Strudel Ⓓ

5-6 tart medium apples, peeled and thinly sliced
1 tablespoon fresh lemon juice
½ cup sugar
2 teaspoons cinnamon
2 tablespoons flour

½ cup raisins, plumped in hot water and drained
8-10 sheets phyllo dough
½ cup butter, melted and clarified
¼ cup bread crumbs
Confectioners' sugar

Preheat oven to 375 degrees.

Toss apples with lemon juice. Add sugar, cinnamon, flour and raisins. Set aside.

Use 4 or 5 sheets phyllo dough per strudel. Place 1 sheet on a work surface and brush with butter. Sprinkle with bread crumbs. Stack 3 phyllo sheets on top of first, brushing each with butter. Place half the apples on the lower third of phyllo stack. Roll dough from the side nearest you over the apples and fold in from both the right and left edges about 1-inch, making a jelly roll. Brush top with butter. Repeat for second strudel.

Bake 40 minutes or until golden brown. Cool and dust with confectioners' sugar. Cut into diagonal slices. Strudel can be wrapped tightly and frozen.

Makes 2 strudel rolls.

To lower calorie count, omit butter and spray phyllo sheets with cooking spray.

Round Apple-Filled Egg Challah
Made in a bread machine for Rosh Hashanah.

Filling

3	apples, peeled and diced	2	tablespoons honey
	Juice of 1 lemon	½	teaspoon cinnamon

Dough

¾	cup water	4	tablespoons margarine
3	cups white bread flour	2	eggs
⅓	cup sugar	1¼	teaspoons rapid-rise yeast
¼	teaspoon salt		

Preheat oven to 350 degrees.

Combine all filling ingredients in a bowl and chill. Drain before using.

Place all dough ingredients into a bread machine pan. Spray pan lightly with cooking spray. (Yeast should be placed in separate yeast container.) Set machine to dough cycle. When dough is ready, remove and spray dough with cooking spray.

Roll and stretch dough into a long, thin rope. Place drained apple filling inside rope and brush edges with water. Pull edges around filling and seal to enclose filling and form a long tube. Coil tube into a spiral and transfer to a greased glass baking dish. (A glass dish allows viewing of bottom of bread while baking.)

Bake 30 minutes or until golden brown on top and bottom. If the bottom browns before the bottom, place a sheet of aluminum foil lightly over top of bread and bake until done. To serve, dip challah in honey – for a sweet New Year.

Makes 1 loaf.

Fragrant Chicken with Figs Ⓜ

1	chicken (3½ to 4 pounds), cut into pieces	1	teaspoon ground coriander
12	fresh figs	1	teaspoon salt, or to taste
1½	cups Muscat wine	½	teaspoon freshly ground black pepper
¼	cup honey	2	bay leaves
1	teaspoon cinnamon		

Preheat oven to 375 degrees.

Rinse chicken and place in a bowl. Pour boiling water over chicken to cover and let stand 2 to 3 minutes. Using a sharp knife, scrape the skin to remove excess surface fat. Pat dry and set aside.

Rinse figs, trim stems and slice in half lengthwise. Place chicken and figs in a single layer in a large heavy roasting pan.

In a small bowl, mix wine, honey, cinnamon, coriander, salt, pepper and bay leaves and pour over chicken. Cover and marinate 1 to 4 hours in refrigerator, turning occasionally. Remove figs and set aside.

Roast chicken, basting and turning occasionally. Add figs after 20 minutes. Roast 50 minutes or until chicken is tender and brown. Serve chicken and figs with a little pan juice poured on top accompanied by herbed rice. May be prepared in advance and reheated in the oven.

Serves 6.

FIGS

They have been described as the fruit of the gods. We are fortunate to have access to fresh figs in Southern California.

Kasha Varnishkes Ⓜ Ⓟ

1	cup medium buckwheat groats	2	onions, chopped
1	egg, beaten	½	pound bow-tie or shell pasta, cooked and drained
1¾	cups boiling water or chicken broth	½	teaspoon freshly ground black pepper
1	teaspoon salt	1	teaspoon salt
6	tablespoons oil		

Mix groats and egg in a saucepan over low heat until each grain is separated. Add boiling water and 1 teaspoon salt. Cover and cook over low heat for 12 minutes.

Heat oil in a skillet over medium heat. Add onions and sauté 10 minutes, stirring frequently. Add groats, pasta, pepper and 1 teaspoon salt. Mix together lightly and heat before serving.

Serves 4 to 5.

Crowned Apple Cake P

The perfect apple cake for Rosh Hashanah.

4   large green apples (about 2½ pounds), such as Granny Smith or Pippin
⅓   cup honey
1   tablespoon cinnamon
3   cups all-purpose flour
2   cups sugar
1   cup vegetable oil
4   eggs
⅓   cup orange juice
1   tablespoon baking powder
2½ teaspoons vanilla
1   teaspoon salt
½   cup chopped walnuts or pecans (optional)
½   cup walnut or pecan halves (optional)

Preheat oven to 350 degrees.

Peel, quarter and slice apples ¼-inch thick. Combine apple slices with honey and cinnamon in a bowl and toss to coat. Set aside while preparing cake.

In a large bowl using an electric mixer on medium speed, combine flour, sugar, oil, eggs, orange juice, baking powder, vanilla and salt. Increase speed to medium-high and mix 2 minutes or until well-blended. Pour one-third of batter into a greased 10-inch tube pan with a removable bottom. Arrange a third of apple slices over top and sprinkle with all the chopped nuts. Cover with half of the remaining batter. Arrange half of remaining apples over batter. Top with remaining batter and spread top evenly. Overlap remaining slices around tube of the pan, extending out like petals. Pour any juices that remain in bowl over apples. Arrange nut halves along the outer edge to encircle top of cake.

Place cake on a rimmed baking sheet. Bake 80 to 90 minutes or until a pick inserted in the center comes out clean. If top gets too brown, cover loosely with foil. Remove cake from oven and cool 10 minutes. Run a knife around the edges of pan to loosen sides but do not remove cake from pan. Cool cake to room temperature. Lift cake from pan to a serving plate. Cake can be stored, covered, at room temperature for up to 2 days, or frozen.

Serves 14.

Majestic and Moist Honey Cake Ⓟ

The ultimate honey cake.

3½ cups all-purpose flour
1 tablespoon baking powder
1 teaspoon baking soda
½ teaspoon salt
4 teaspoons cinnamon
½ teaspoon ground cloves
½ teaspoon allspice
1 cup vegetable oil
1 cup honey
1½ cups granulated sugar
½ cup brown sugar

3 eggs
1 teaspoon vanilla
1 cup warm coffee or strong tea
½ cup fresh orange juice
¼ cup whisky, rye if possible
    (if preferred, can substitute
    same amount of extra
    coffee or orange juice)
½ cup slivered or sliced
    almonds (optional)

Preheat oven to 350 degrees.

In a large bowl, whisk together flour, baking powder, baking soda, salt, cinnamon, cloves and allspice. Make a well in the center and add oil, honey, both sugars, eggs, vanilla, coffee, orange juice and whisky. Using a strong wire whisk or with an electric mixer on low speed, stir together to make a thick, well-blended batter, making sure no ingredients are stuck to the bottom.

Spoon batter into a lightly greased 9-inch angel food cake pan, lined on the bottom with lightly greased parchment paper, cut to fit. Sprinkle evenly with almonds. Place on 2 baking sheets stacked together to ensure proper baking with the bottom baking faster than the interior and top. Bake 60 to 70 minutes or until cake springs back when cake center is gently touched. Let stand 15 minutes before removing from pan.

Serves 12 to 15.

This cake is best baked in a 9-inch angel food cake pan, but you can also make it in the following:

   One 9- or 10-inch tube or Bundt pan
      (line tube pan with greased parchment paper)

   One 13 x 9-inch sheet cake

   Two 9-inch square or round cake layer pans

   Two 9 x 5-inch loaf pans

When baking, bake 60 to 70 minutes for tube pan, 45 to 55 minutes for loaf pans. For sheet cake, bake 40 to 45 minutes.

When measuring sticky ingredients such as honey or corn syrup, spray the measuring cup with cooking spray. Voila! It slides right out.

Break-the-fast recipes can be found in Breads and Brunch on p. 69.

Hanukkah

Potato Latkes 🅿

The authentic classic recipe for the Chanukah Celebration.

1½	pounds baking potatoes, peeled (about 4 large)	2	eggs, lightly beaten
	Ice water	1	teaspoon salt
	Juice of ½ lemon or 1 tablespoon salt	¼	teaspoon baking powder
1	onion, peeled	2	tablespoons flour or matzo meal
			Vegetable oil

Using the metal blade of a food processor or a hand shredder, shred potatoes into a bowl of ice water into which lemon juice has been added. Shred or finely chop onion. Drain potatoes thoroughly and mix in onion. Stir in eggs, salt, baking powder and flour until mixed. Use immediately.

In a large skillet, heat ½-inch of oil over medium-high heat. Using a slotted spoon, spoon about 2 tablespoons batter into hot oil for each pancake. Do not crowd. Flatten slightly with the back of the spoon. Fry pancakes until golden on both sides, turning once. After frying, remove pancakes to paper towels to drain. Pancakes may be kept warm in a low temperature oven on a baking sheet in a single layer for 1 hour. Turn oven to 450 degrees for 5 minutes to ensure crispiness. Serve with applesauce and sour cream, if desired.

Pancakes may be frozen and reheated. Freeze on baking sheets in single layers. When solid, layer in an airtight container with wax paper between each layer. Before reheating, return the frozen pancakes to baking sheets. Reheat at 450 degrees in a single layer without crowding for 5 to 10 minutes if thawed, 15 to 20 minutes if frozen, or until crisp.

Makes 24 pancakes.

Placing shredded potatoes in ice water and lemon juice prevents browning.

Veggie Pancakes 🄳

2	potatoes, peeled	1½	teaspoons dried sage
2	carrots, peeled	1½	teaspoons dried thyme
2	zucchini, trimmed	½	cup freshly grated Parmesan cheese
2	summer squash, trimmed		
1	medium onion (optional)	1¼	cups flour
2	eggs, beaten		Salt and pepper to taste
¼	teaspoon baking powder		Oil for frying

Grate potatoes, carrots, zucchini, squash and onion in a food processor. Mix vegetables thoroughly with eggs, baking powder, sage, thyme, cheese and flour in a bowl. Season with salt and pepper.

Drop batter into oil over medium-high heat in a skillet. Fry until lightly browned.

Makes 32 (3-inch) pancakes, serves 8.

No Fry Potato and Spinach Latkes

2	teaspoons canola or vegetable oil	3	medium baking potatoes, peeled and cut into chunks
1	package (10 ounces) frozen chopped spinach, thawed and squeezed dry	2	eggs, lightly beaten
		2	egg whites, lightly beaten
1	medium onion, cut into chunks	2	teaspoons canola or vegetable oil
1	carrot, cut into chunks	¼	cup white or whole wheat flour
2	tablespoons minced fresh dill, or 2 teaspoons dried	½	teaspoon baking powder
		¾	teaspoon salt
		¼	teaspoon black pepper

Preheat oven to 450 degrees.

Place oven racks on the lowest and middle positions in oven. Line 2 baking sheets with aluminum foil. Spray each lined sheet lightly with nonstick cooking spray. Brush each with 1 teaspoon oil.

Using the steel blade of a food processor, process spinach, onion, carrot and dill until fine. Add potatoes, eggs, egg whites and 2 teaspoons oil. Process until finely ground. Blend in flour, baking powder, salt and pepper.

Drop batter by rounded tablespoons onto prepared baking sheets. Flatten batter slightly with the back of spoon to form latkes. Bake, uncovered, for 10 minutes or until bottoms are golden brown and crisp. Turn latkes over. Transfer pan on the upper rack to the lower rack and vice versa. Bake 8 to 10 minutes longer or until golden brown. Serve immediately.

Latkes can be prepared a day in advance. Cool, cover and refrigerate. To reheat, arrange in a single layer on a baking sheet. Bake at 350 degrees, uncovered, for 8 to 10 minutes.

Makes about 2 dozen latkes.

BLUE AND WHITE ICING FOR HANUKKAH COOKIES

1 tablespoon lemon juice

1 tablespoon heavy cream, milk or non-dairy creamer

2 cups confectioners' sugar

2-3 drops blue food coloring

Blend lemon juice, cream and sugar in a bowl until creamy. Add more cream if needed to thin icing. Divide icing in half. Add food coloring to half of icing and mix until blended. Place each color icing into separate pastry bags fitted with a star tip and pipe onto cooled cookies.

Makes about 2 cups.

Ner Tamid Sisterhood Hanukkah Cookies Ⓓ Ⓟ

1	cup sugar	2	teaspoons baking powder
½	cup margarine or butter, softened	¼	teaspoon salt
2	eggs, well beaten	1	tablespoon orange juice
2	cups flour	1	teaspoon vanilla

Preheat oven to 400 degrees.

Cream together sugar and margarine. Add eggs. In a separate bowl, mix together flour, baking powder and salt. Slowly add dry ingredients to creamed mixture. Add orange juice and vanilla and mix well. Chill dough 1 hour. Roll out dough and a lightly floured or powder sugared board, using Hanukkah cookie cutters.

Bake 10 minutes on ungreased baking sheets. When cool, decorate with blue and white icing using a pastry bag with a star tip.

Makes about 40 cookies.

Hanukkah Brown Sugar Shortbread Cookies Ⓓ Ⓟ

This recipe has only 4 ingredients and is very tasty. Rolled out, they make delicious holiday cookies, ready to decorate if desired.

1	cup butter or margarine, softened	1	teaspoon vanilla
1¼	cups brown sugar, packed	2½	cups flour

Preheat oven to 300 degrees.

Beat butter and sugar in a bowl until creamy. Add vanilla. Gradually beat in flour. Gather dough into a ball and wrap tightly with plastic wrap. Refrigerate 1 hour or until firm.

Divide dough into 4 parts. Working with 1 part at a time, roll out dough to about ¼-inch thick on a lightly floured (or powder sugared) board. Cut out with cookie cutters. Place 1-inch apart on lightly greased baking sheets. Bake about 15 minutes or until firm to the touch. Cool. Decorate with icing if desired.

Makes about 3 dozen cookies.

Stained Glass Cookie Pops

A Hanukkah cookie project for children.

⅓ cup vegetable oil or softened margarine	½ teaspoon baking soda
⅓ cup sugar	½ teaspoon salt
1 egg	Lollipops or hard candies of different colors
⅔ cup honey	12 craft sticks
3 cups flour	

Preheat oven to 350 degrees.

Mix oil, sugar, egg, honey, flour, baking soda and salt in a bowl until a soft dough forms. Divide dough into 12 portions.

To outline the cookies, roll dough between hands into a ¼-inch thick rope. Form rope into a design and place on a baking sheet that has been foil-lined and sprayed with vegetable spray. You can make shapes like dreidels, 6-sided stars, faces of the Maccabbees or latke shapes. Let the children's imagination run wild. Make sure the dough ends are completely pinched together, as these will form the outline of the stained glass picture.

Cover lollipops or candies with a kitchen towel and crush into small pieces using a light-weight hammer. Sprinkle crushed candies inside the dough outlines, filling spaces completely and heaping slightly. Carefully insert a craft stick into cookies, forming a "lollipop".

Bake 8 to 10 minutes, watching carefully that the sticks don't burn. Remove baking sheet from oven and cool on a rack. When cooled, gently peel off foil from each cookie pop. Wrap each separately in plastic wrap and tie with a colorful ribbon if giving as a gift.

Makes 12 cookie pops.

Make chocolate cake mix and frost. Press gold Chanukah coins all around bottom, pressing flat into cake. Stand gold coins on top of cake in a small circle. Or, make cupcakes and place a gold coin standing up on each cupcake.

Purim

Sisterhood's Hamantaschen

A small army of Synagogue volunteers have been baking these desserts as a fundraising project for many years and tens of thousands have been enjoyed by all of our members and our friends.

¾	cup vegetable shortening	½	teaspoon salt
1	cup sugar	⅓	cup orange juice or
2	eggs		nondairy liquid creamer
½	teaspoon vanilla		Filling of choice
3	cups plus 4 teaspoons flour		(recipes below)
3½	teaspoons cornstarch		Egg yolk, thinned with water
1	tablespoon baking powder		

Preheat oven to 375 degrees.

Cream shortening and sugar together. Mix in eggs and vanilla. In a separate bowl, combine flour, cornstarch, baking powder and salt. Add dry ingredients alternately with orange juice to creamed mixture. Mix well to form a smooth dough. Roll out dough onto a floured board to about ⅛-inch thickness. Cut with a 3-inch round cutter (size of a tuna can). Place 1 teaspoon filling in center of each round. Press 3 edges together to form a triangle. Brush sides and top with egg yolk.

Place on greased baking sheets. Bake 15 to 20 minutes or until golden brown, making sure triangles do not touch. Remove from baking sheets and cool before handling.

Makes 3½ to 4 dozen cookies.

Prune and Raisin Filling

1½	pounds pitted prunes	1	cup chopped nuts
½	pound raisins, plumped in		Juice and zest of 1 lemon
	hot water for 20 minutes		Pinch of salt
	and drained		Sugar to taste

Mix all ingredients well in a food processor.

Date Filling

1	pound dates, pitted and cut	1	scant cup water
	into small pieces		Juice and zest of 1 lemon
⅔	cup sugar		

Place dates in a saucepan. Add sugar and water and cook over medium heat until thick. When cool, mix in lemon juice and zest.

Poppy Seed Filling

1	can (20 ounces) poppy seed filling	½	cup white raisins, plumped in hot water for 20 minutes and drained
		½	cup chopped nuts
		2	tablespoons orange marmalade

Mix all ingredients well.

Ready-prepared fillings may be purchased.

Crisp Hamantaschen ⓟ

2	cups flour	1	egg, beaten
½	cup margarine, softened	2	tablespoons orange juice
⅔	cup sugar		Fillings (see "Sisterhood's Hamantaschen" recipe)
1½	teaspoons baking powder		

Preheat oven to 375 degrees.

Combine flour, margarine, sugar and baking powder and mix well. Add egg and orange juice. Mix well. Refrigerate dough 30 minutes.

Roll out dough onto a floured board to about ⅛-inch thickness. Cut with a 3-inch round cutter (size of a tuna can). Place 1 teaspoon filling in center of each round. Press 3 edges together to form a triangle. Place on a baking sheet. Bake 20 to 25 minutes.

Makes 24 hamantaschen.

Artichoke Matzo Brei

It's wonderful any time of the day.

¾ pound onions, very thinly sliced (3 cups)	1 tablespoon balsamic vinegar or red wine vinegar (kosher for Passover)
5 tablespoons olive oil, or 4 tablespoons olive oil and 1 tablespoon butter	4 whole plain or egg matzos
1 package (8 ounces) frozen artichoke hearts, thawed, patted dry between layers of paper towels and sliced	5 eggs
	3 tablespoons finely chopped fresh dill, plus more for garnish
½ teaspoon minced garlic (optional)	1 teaspoon dried oregano
Salt and freshly ground pepper to taste	Plain yogurt (optional)
	Chopped scallions (optional)
	Freshly chopped mint (optional)

Sauté onions in 2 tablespoons oil in a 10- to 12-inch heavy cast iron or nonstick skillet over medium heat, lifting and turning occasionally, for 10 to 15 minutes or until soft and golden at the edges. Add artichokes and garlic and continue lifting and scraping 5 to 7 minutes or until artichokes are cooked through and onions are dotted and dark gold. Generously season with salt and pepper and add vinegar. Cook a few minutes over high heat, stirring, until vinegar is completely evaporated and just a soft, acidic sparkle remains. Taste again for seasoning, then remove from heat and let cool to room temperature.

Break matzos into 2- or 3-inch pieces and place in a bowl. Cover with cold water and soak 5 minutes. Meanwhile, beat eggs in a large bowl until light and foamy. Drain matzo in a colander, pressing out water with your hands or the back of a spoon. Add drained matzo to eggs. Add dill and oregano and season with salt and pepper to taste. Stir in artichokes and onions and combine thoroughly.

Wipe out skillet thoroughly and heat remaining 3 tablespoons oil over medium-high heat until sizzling. Add matzo batter all at once and cook, either frittata-style (in 1 piece, waiting until whole is golden brown before turning, 4 to 5 minutes per side, or break it into sections with the spatula in order to turn it) or scrambled egg-style (lifting and turning pieces as different egg-soaked matzos begin to set, 6 to 8 minutes total). You can also drop by heaping tablespoons, like pancakes, onto skillet and fry over medium heat until golden brown on bottom. Turn and fry until done to taste on the other side, (either golden and fluffy or more well-done and crisp), about 3 to 4 minutes per side. Serve immediately with yogurt mixed with chopped scallions and garnished with dill and chopped mint.

Serves 4.

Cottage Cheese Pancakes for Passover Ⓓ

For each serving, use the following ingredients.

1	egg	⅓	cup matzo meal
⅓	cup milk	⅓	cup cottage cheese

Combine all ingredients. Pour batter onto a hot lightly greased griddle and cook until bubbles form and burst. Turn over and brown on second side. Serve with sour cream or jam.

Serves 1.

Passover Cupcake Blintzes Ⓓ

Children and adults alike love these.

1	pound creamed cottage cheese, regular or low fat	½	cup sugar
		½	cup cake meal
2	ounces butter or margarine, melted	1	tablespoon potato starch
		4	eggs, beaten

Preheat oven to 350 degrees.

Combine cottage cheese, butter, sugar, cake meal and potato starch. Beat well. Add eggs and beat until well mixed. Pour batter into greased muffin tins, filling each three-fourths full. Bake 40 to 45 minutes. Serve with sour cream or preserves.

Makes 12 cupcakes.

Cupcakes can be made ahead of time and reheated in the microwave for about 20 seconds each.

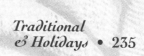

Sephardic Spinach-Mushroom Matzo Pie

1	tablespoon olive oil	⅛	teaspoon freshly ground black pepper
1	cup coarsely chopped onion	6	squares matzos
1	teaspoon minced garlic	1	teaspoon margarine or butter
8	ounces fresh mushrooms, finely chopped	5	extra large eggs, beaten
2	packages (10 ounces each) frozen spinach, thawed and squeezed dry	1	red bell pepper, cut into strips
6	ounces feta cheese, crumbled	2	tablespoons finely minced fresh parsley
¾	teaspoon salt		Oil-cured black olives

Preheat oven to 375 degrees.

Heat oil in a large skillet. Add onion and garlic and sauté 3 minutes, stirring frequently. Add mushrooms and cook over medium-high heat, stirring frequently, 3 to 5 minutes longer or until most of liquid released by mushrooms has evaporated. Remove from heat and stir in spinach, feta, salt and pepper.

Place matzos in a 12 x 7-inch baking dish. Pour ample water over matzos. Gently press matzos down into water for about 30 seconds or just long enough to moisten surfaces. Remove matzos. Discard water and dry out baking dish. Grease dish with margarine.

Beat eggs in a large, flat dish that has sides. Soak each matzo in beaten eggs for about 1 minute on each side. Set 2 egg-dipped matzos, side by side, in bottom of greased dish, overlapping slightly. Evenly distribute half of vegetable filling on top. Add a second layer of matzos and then remainder of filling. Top with remaining matzos. Reserve any remaining beaten egg.

Tightly cover with foil. Bake 20 minutes. Remove foil and brush top with remaining egg. Continue to bake 5 to 10 minutes or until top is lightly browned. Arrange red pepper strips on top. Sprinkle with parsley and dot with olives. To serve, cut like lasagna.

Serves 6 to 8.

Gourmet Charoses ℗

½	pound walnuts	½	cup sweet red wine
¼	pound dried apricots	2	tablespoons Passover brandy
¼	pound pitted prunes, diced	½	teaspoon cinnamon
¼	pound pitted dates	⅛	teaspoon ground cloves
3	apples, peeled and quartered	⅛	teaspoon nutmeg
1	large seedless orange, unpeeled and quartered	1	tablespoon lime juice

Using the steel blade of a food processor, chop, in batches if necessary, walnuts, apricots, prunes, dates, apples and oranges very fine, but not to a paste. Add wine, brandy, cinnamon, cloves, nutmeg and lime juice.

Makes 6 cups.

The Best Baked Gefilte Fish ℗

3	small onions, chopped	2¼	cups ice water
	Vegetable oil	2	teaspoon salt
3	pounds whitefish, skinned, boned and ground	½	teaspoon white pepper
5	eggs	½	cup sugar
½	cup matzo meal	4	large carrots, finely grated

Preheat oven to 350 degrees.

In a large skillet, cook onions in oil until softened but not browned. In a large electric mixer bowl, mix ground fish with eggs, adding eggs one at a time and beating well after each addition. Add matzo meal, ice water, salt, pepper, sugar and onions. Beat 20 minutes. Stir in carrots.

Spread mixture in a greased 10-inch tube pan and place on a foil-lined baking sheet. Bake 1 hour. Tent with foil and bake 90 minutes longer. Cool before inverting onto a platter. Cover with plastic wrap and refrigerate. Slice and serve.

Serves 20.

PEAR AND RAISIN CHAROSES

This is a great variation while still keeping the traditional feeling and message behind Charoses.

2 small pears, peeled, cored and coarsely chopped

1 teaspoon lemon juice

12 dried apricots, chopped

¼ cup golden raisins

1½ teaspoons cinnamon

2 tablespoons sweet wine or grape juice

Place chopped pears in a medium bowl and immediately toss with lemon juice to prevent browning. Add apricots, raisins, cinnamon and wine and mix well. Cover and refrigerate at least 1 hour. Spoon into a large serving dish or individual dishes. Serve chilled.

Serves 8.

Classic Gefilte Fish Ⓟ

A traditional Passover and Shabbat recipe.

Stock

	Bones, heads and skin from fish used in recipe	¾	teaspoon ground white pepper
4	medium onions, sliced	3-4	parsley roots, well scrubbed
1-1½	teaspoons salt, or to taste	3	large carrots, sliced

Fish Balls

2	pounds pike, filleted and ground by kosher shop	7	eggs, well beaten
2	pounds white fish, filleted and ground by kosher shop	2-4	tablespoons matzo meal, or enough to make a pasty fish mixture
1½	pounds carp, filleted and ground by kosher shop	¾	teaspoon salt
3	large onions, chopped	¾	teaspoon ground white pepper
		¼	cup sugar

Prepare stock before making fish balls, using the bones, heads (with the eyes removed) and skin from the fish used for the fish balls. Add fish parts to a stock pot filled two-thirds full with water. Bring to a boil. Reduce to a simmer. Add onions, salt, pepper, parsley roots and carrots. Cook 60 to 90 minutes. Strain stock, discarding solids. Return stock to pot and return to a simmer.

To make fish balls, mix all ingredients well, cover and refrigerate at least 1 hour or until stock is ready. Dip a large serving spoon in the fish mixture and, with wet hands, form a ball. Flatten ball slightly to create an oval shape. With a slotted spoon, carefully lower each fish ball into the simmering stock. Cover pot loosely after making sure the fish is fully submerged in the stock. Simmer 2 hours, shaking pot gently to loosen fish balls occasionally.

Cool in the stock, then carefully lift each ball from the stock with slotted spoon. Cover and refrigerate until ready to serve. Serve each portion on a bed of lettuce garnished with 1 or 2 cooked carrot slices on top. Serve with horseradish.

Makes 30 balls.

The remaining fish stock can be strained and frozen to be used for fish chowders. It is quite delicious and you won't be throwing away the flavorful broth.

Lamb Shanks with Prauses and Apricots Ⓜ

This makes a delicious Passover main course.

6	lamb shanks	1	can (14½ ounces) tomatoes, diced
	Salt and pepper to taste		Fresh rosemary sprigs
½	cup olive oil	¼	cup chopped parsley
6	cloves garlic, minced	6	ounces dried prunes, plumped in sweet Passover wine
2	large onions, finely chopped in a food processor		
8	carrots, finely chopped in a food processor	6	ounces dried apricots, plumped in sweet Passover wine
6	stalks celery, finely chopped		
1½	cups dry white wine (kosher for Passover)		Parsley sprigs for garnish

Have the butcher cut lamb shanks in halves or thirds. Wash and pat dry. Sprinkle with salt and pepper.

Heat oil in a large heavy skillet over medium heat. Brown shanks on all sides for about 5 minutes and remove to a platter. To the same skillet, add garlic, onions, carrots and celery and sauté until lightly browned. Place shanks on top of vegetable mixture. Add wine and cook 3 to 4 minutes or until reduced. Add tomatoes, rosemary sprigs and chopped parsley. Cover and simmer over low heat for 1 hour.

Drain plumped fruit and add to skillet. Continue to cook 30 to 60 minutes or until meat is tender enough to fall away from the bones. Garnish with parsley and serve with couscous (or matzo farfel for the Passover meal).

Serves 6.

Traditional Potato Kugel Ⓟ

6	medium potatoes, grated	1½	teaspoons salt
1	large onion, grated	¼	teaspoon black pepper
1	large carrot, grated	2	eggs, beaten
¼	cup matzo meal	¼	cup oil

Preheat oven to 375 degrees.

Combine all ingredients and place in a greased 11 x 8-inch casserole dish. Bake 1 hour or until golden brown and a knife inserted in the center comes out clean.

Serves 8 to 10.

Passover Peach Farfel Soufflé

1	box matzo farfel, soaked in warm water and drained	¾	teaspoon salt
2	cans (15 ounces each) sliced peaches, 2 cups juice reserved	1	teaspoon vanilla
		¾	cup butter or margarine, melted
7	eggs		Sugar for sprinkling
1	cup sugar		Cinnamon for sprinkling

Preheat oven to 350 degrees.

Combine drained farfel, 2 cups reserved peach juice, eggs, 1 cup sugar, salt, vanilla and butter. Layer farfel mixture with peaches in a greased 13 x 9-inch glass baking dish, reserving enough peaches to garnish top of soufflé. There will be a small amount of ingredients left over to fill a small casserole dish.

Sprinkle top with sugar and cinnamon. Bake 1 hour. Garnish with reserved peaches. Delicious anytime.

Serves 10 to 12.

Passover Layered Zucchini Potato Kugel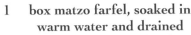

1	carrot, cut into chunks	1	teaspoon chopped garlic
1½	pounds potatoes, peeled and cut into chunks	4	ounces zucchini, unpeeled
		2	egg whites
1	small onion, cut into chunks	¼	cup chopped fresh dill
½	cup matzo meal	½	cup matzo meal
2	eggs	⅛	teaspoon black pepper
2	tablespoons oil	½	teaspoon salt
⅛	teaspoon black pepper	1	tablespoon oil
1	teaspoon salt		

Preheat oven to 375 degrees.

Finely chop carrot, potatoes and onion in a food processor. Add ½ cup matzo meal, eggs, 2 tablespoons oil, ⅛ teaspoon pepper, 1 teaspoon salt and garlic. Spread half of mixture over the bottom of a greased 9-inch square baking dish.

Grate zucchini in food processor. Add egg whites, dill, ½ cup matzo meal, ⅛ teaspoon pepper and ½ teaspoon salt. Spread zucchini mixture over potato layer in baking dish. Top with remaining potato mixture. Drizzle 1 tablespoon oil on top.

Bake 75 minutes or until nicely browned and firm in the center. Cool thoroughly. If freezing, cover with wax paper and wrap tightly in aluminum foil.

Serves 8.

Passover Sponge Cake

9 eggs, separated	1 cup sifted cake meal
1½ cups sifted sugar	¼ cup sifted potato starch
1½ teaspoons lemon zest	Dash of salt
3 tablespoons lemon juice	Fresh strawberries

Preheat oven to 350 degrees.

Using an electric mixer, beat egg yolks for 2 minutes at high speed. Add sugar, lemon zest and lemon juice and mix on medium speed for 2 minutes. Gradually add cake meal, potato starch and salt and continue beating 2 minutes longer. In a separate bowl, beat egg whites with clean beaters until stiff but not dry. Fold whites gently, but thoroughly, into batter.

Pour batter into an ungreased 2-piece, 10-inch tube pan. Bake 55 to 65 minutes or until cake springs back when firmly touched with fingers. Remove from oven and immediately invert pan onto a towel. Cool thoroughly before removing cake pan, using a slender sharp knife to loosen sides. Serve with strawberries.

Passover Apricot Walnut Squares

⅔ cup dried apricots	2 eggs
Water	1 cup brown sugar
½ cup margarine or butter,	⅓ cup sifted cake meal
softened	1 tablespoon potato starch
1 cup sifted cake meal	¼ teaspoon salt
¼ cup granulated sugar	1 tablespoon orange juice
1 egg white, beaten	¾ cup chopped walnuts

Preheat oven to 350 degrees.

Boil apricots in water for about 10 minutes. Drain and cut into small pieces. Set aside to cool.

Combine margarine with 1 cup cake meal and granulated sugar until mixture is crumbly. Press mixture into a greased 8-inch square glass baking dish. Bake 25 minutes or until edges begin to lightly brown; do not burn. Cool. Brush beaten egg white over entire cooled crust to allow filling to adhere.

Beat together eggs and brown sugar. Add ⅓ cup cake meal, potato starch and salt. Stir in orange juice, walnuts and cooled apricots. Combine well. Carefully spread filling over baked layer. Bake 25 to 30 minutes or until done. Cool and cut into squares. Can be frozen.

Makes 16 squares.

When a recipe calls for separating whites from yolks, do so when the eggs are cold, but let the eggs come to room temperature before adding to recipe. Be certain that no yolk spills into the whites as the fat will prevent the whites from whipping up to their maximum volume. If a small amount of yolk does get into the egg whites, removing it with a paper towel works well. Remember, for maximum volume when beating egg whites, you will want stiff mounds that are still shiny.

Orange-Apricot Layer Cake with Chocolate Frosting

Apricot Purée
6 ounces dried apricots	6 tablespoons sugar
1½ cups orange juice	

Cake
½ cup sugar	½ cup potato starch
6 eggs, separated	½ cup matzo cake meal
⅓ cup vegetable oil	½ teaspoon salt
1 tablespoon orange zest, plus 1 tablespoon for garnish	½ cup sugar

Frosting
1 pound bittersweet or semisweet chocolate, chopped	½ cup unsalted pareve margarine

Preheat oven to 325 degrees.

To prepare apricot purée, combine dried apricots and orange juice in a small saucepan. Bring to a boil. Reduce heat to low and cover tightly. Simmer 15 minutes or until apricots are very tender. Transfer mixture to a food processor. Add sugar and purée until smooth. Apricot purée can be prepared a day or 2 ahead and refrigerated in a covered container.

To make cake, beat ½ cup sugar, egg yolks, oil, orange zest and ⅓ cup apricot purée in a large bowl with an electric mixer for 5 minutes or until batter is thick. Beat in potato starch and cake meal. In a separate large bowl using clean, dry beaters, beat egg whites and salt until soft peaks form. Gradually add ½ cup sugar, beating until whites are stiff but not dry. In 4 additions, fold large spoonfuls of egg whites into batter.

Transfer batter to an ungreased 10-inch diameter springform pan. Bake in bottom third of oven for 40 to 45 minutes or until a pick placed in the center comes out clean. Cool on a rack. Cake will sink slightly.

Meanwhile, prepare frosting. Stir chocolate and margarine in a saucepan over low heat until melted and smooth. Whisk in 3 tablespoons apricot purée. Remove from heat. Let stand 2 hours or until thickened but still spreadable.

When cake is cooled, cut around sides and remove rim. Cut cake horizontally in half to form 2 layers, leaving bottom layer on pan bottom. Place top layer, cut-side up, on a plate. Spread bottom layer with ⅔ cup apricot purée. Spread ½ cup chocolate frosting on cut side of top layer. Place top layer, chocolate-side down, on apricot filling. Spread remaining frosting over top and sides of cake. Refrigerate 1 hour or until frosting sets. Cake can be made a day ahead; keep refrigerated and let stand at room temperature 1 hour before serving. Garnish with orange peel, if desired.

Serves 12.

I Can't Believe They Are Passover Brownies ⓟ

6	ounces pareve bittersweet or semisweet bar chocolate, broken into small pieces	¼	teaspoon salt
½	cup canola or safflower oil	2	eggs
1	cup sugar	2	egg whites
		¾	cup matzo cake meal

Preheat oven to 350 degrees.

Combine chocolate and oil into a 4-cup microwave-safe bowl or in a medium saucepan. Melt on high in microwave for 1½ minutes, or over very low heat on the stove. Remove mixture from heat and stir until combined. Allow to cool until mixture is tepid.

By hand, use a sturdy spoon to stir the sugar and salt into the chocolate mixture until combined. Beat eggs and egg whites together in a small bowl until well blended. Add beaten eggs to chocolate mixture and stir until completely incorporated. Add cake meal and gently stir 2 to 3 minutes. The batter will be very thick. Let batter rest 5 minutes.

Line an 8-inch square shiny metal pan, or two 8-inch square disposable foil pans nestled together for increased sturdiness, with a piece of aluminum foil large enough to reach top of all sides. Press foil into corners and grease foil. The foil will be used to lift out the baked brownies, leaving behind a clean pan. Stir batter briefly and spread into prepared pan, smoothing the top. Bake 35 to 40 minutes or until the center top is puffed and a wooden pick comes out clean. For the fudgiest brownies, do not overbake.

Remove from oven and cool in pan on a wire rack. Use foil to lift cake completely out of pan and leave it on the foil. When the cake is cooled to room temperature, use a metal spatula to loosen the foil, then lift entire cake off foil and place on a cutting board. Use a large, sharp knife to evenly cut the cake into 16 brownies, wiping the knife after each cut. Store brownies in an airtight container for up to 4 days, or freeze for longer storage.

Makes 16 brownies.

Chocolate Nut Meringue Cookies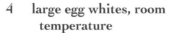

They are light and delicious.

4   large egg whites, room
      temperature
1   cup sugar
      Zest of 1 orange
2   squares unsweetened
      chocolate, finely grated

6   ounces semisweet chocolate
1-2   teaspoons oil
      Chopped nuts or shredded
      coconut

Preheat oven to 275 degrees.

Beat egg whites until stiff. Gradually add ⅔ cup sugar and continue beating. Add remaining ⅓ cup sugar, orange zest and unsweetened chocolate. Beat a few minutes longer.

Drop batter from a teaspoon onto a nonstick baking sheet or a parchment paper- or brown paper-lined baking sheet, allowing space for cookies to spread. Bake 45 to 50 minutes. When cool, remove from baking sheet.

Melt semisweet chocolate and oil together. Dip top of cookies in melted chocolate, then dip in nuts.

Makes 2½ to 3 dozen cookies.

Date and Chocolate Bit Squares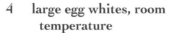

Irresistible.

1   cup pitted dates, diced
1½   cups boiling water
1½   teaspoons baking soda
2   eggs
1   cup sugar
¾   cup oil
¾   teaspoon baking soda
½   teaspoon salt

1½   cups cake meal
2   tablespoons potato starch
      Oil and cake meal for pan
3   ounces semisweet chocolate,
      chopped into small pieces
¼   cup sugar
1   cup finely chopped nuts

Preheat oven to 350 degrees.

Combine dates, boiling water and 1½ teaspoons baking soda in a small saucepan. Bring to a boil. Remove from heat and set aside to cool. In a medium bowl, cream eggs with 1 cup sugar and oil until well blended. Add cooled date mixture.

Sift together ¾ teaspoon baking soda, salt, cake meal and potato starch into a small bowl. Add dry ingredients to date mixture. Blend thoroughly.

Use oil and cake meal to grease and dust a 13 x 9-inch baking pan. Pour batter into pan. Sprinkle chocolate over the batter. Sprinkle ¼ cup sugar and nuts on top. Bake 40 to 45 minutes. Cool and cut into 2-inch squares.

Makes 24 squares.

Passover Lemon Bars

Crust

1	cup margarine	1	cup matzo cake meal
½	cup confectioners' sugar (see sidebar)	1	cup potato starch

Filling

4	eggs, beaten	½	cup fresh lemon juice
2	cups sugar	1	teaspoon lemon zest
2	tablespoons matzo cake meal		Confectioners' sugar for sprinkling
2	tablespoons potato starch		

Preheat oven to 350 degrees.

To make crust, cream margarine and sugar. Add cake meal and potato starch and mix until well blended. Pat into a 13 x 9-inch pan. Bake 20 minutes.

For filling, beat eggs until light. Continue beating and slowly add sugar. Add cake meal, potato starch, lemon juice and zest. Beat well. Pour filling over baked crust. Bake 15 to 20 minutes longer or until golden brown. Sprinkle confectioners' sugar over hot bars. Cool before cutting into bars. Bars can be frozen before cutting.

Makes about 36 bars.

PASSOVER CONFECTIONERS' SUGAR

1 cup less ½ tablespoon granulated sugar

1½ teaspoons potato starch

Pulverize sugar in a blender or food processor. Sift pulverized sugar with potato starch.

Passover Mandelbrot

4	eggs	½	teaspoon salt
¾	cup vegetable oil	1½	cups chopped nuts
1	cup sugar		Chocolate chips (optional)
¾	cup matzo meal		Cinnamon sugar for sprinkling
¾	cup potato starch		

Preheat oven to 350 degrees.

Combine eggs, oil, sugar, matzo meal, potato starch, salt and nuts and mix 5 minutes. Add chocolate chips during last 30 seconds of mixing. Form dough into two 1-inch high loaves and place on a greased baking sheet with sides. Bake 30 minutes.

Remove from oven and sprinkle with cinnamon sugar while hot. Cut each loaf into ½-inch slices and place each on its side on a baking sheet. Bake 20 to 25 minutes longer or until golden brown.

Makes 6 to 7 dozen cookies.

To liven up the Seder for children, throw plastic frogs on the table when you read the 10 plagues. They will squeal with delight.

Blintzes with a Variety of Fillings

These blintzes are baked rather than fried.

Blintz Batter

4   eggs
1½ cups flour
¼   teaspoon salt
2   tablespoons butter or
      margarine

2   cups milk or water
3   tablespoons butter or
      margarine, melted, for
      brushing
      Filling (recipes follow)

Toppings

    Confectioners' sugar
    Sliced sweetened
      strawberries or berry
      preserves
    Sour cream

Preheat oven to 375 degrees.

Beat eggs with an electric mixer. Add flour and salt and beat well. Mixture will be thick. Add 2 tablespoons melted butter. Gradually beat in milk until smooth.

Heat a lightly greased 6-inch nonstick skillet over medium heat until just warm. Add 3 tablespoons batter using a small ladle or measuring cup. Tilt pan from side to side to cover bottom with batter. Cook over medium heat 20 to 30 seconds or until lightly brown on bottom. Invert onto a piece of wax paper. Repeat with remaining batter, greasing skillet as needed and stacking blintzes between pieces of wax paper.

Place a slightly rounded tablespoon of filling in center of browned side of each blintz. Fold over both sides in an envelope shape. Arrange blintzes in a single layer. Cool, then refrigerate until chilled. Blintzes can be well covered and refrigerated up to 2 days, or frozen for as long as 1 month.

Place blintzes in a single layer on a greased baking sheet, leaving a ½-inch space between each. Brush lightly with 3 tablespoons melted butter. Bake about 20 minutes (slightly longer if frozen; it is not necessary to thaw before baking) or until lightly browned.

Sprinkle with confectioners' sugar and serve hot with berries or preserves and sour cream.

Cheese Filling

½	cup small curd cottage cheese	2	tablespoons sugar
1½	cups farmer's cheese	1	teaspoon vanilla, or 1 to 2 tablespoons fresh lemon juice
1	egg yolk		
2	tablespoons butter or margarine, melted		

Combine all ingredients in a 1-quart bowl. Fill as directed.

Apple Filling

1	egg white	½	teaspoon cinnamon
1½	cups finely chopped peeled apple	3	tablespoons brown sugar
¼	cup sugar	3	tablespoons butter, melted

Beat egg white until it starts to stiffen. Fold in apple, sugar and cinnamon. Fill as directed above. Sprinkle brown sugar and butter over filled blintzes. Bake at 400 degrees for 20 minutes.

Vegetable Filling

½	cup shredded cabbage	¾	cup diced onion
½	cup grated carrot	3	tablespoons butter or oil
½	cup finely sliced green bell pepper	1	teaspoon salt
			Dash of cayenne pepper

Sauté cabbage, carrot, bell pepper and onion in butter for 10 minutes, stirring occasionally. Season with salt and cayenne pepper. Drop a slightly rounded tablespoon of filling into center of browned side of each blintz. Fill as directed above.

Makes 24 blintzes.

When buying acorn, butternut or other winter squash, choose those with dull skin, as shiny skin means the squash was probably picked too early.

Butternut Squash and Potato Strudel

Garnish with seasoned olive oil, feta cheese and fresh marjoram or Italian parsley sprigs.

2	tablespoons butter	1¾	cups peeled and chopped butternut squash
1	cup chopped onion		
1	teaspoon salt	1¾	cups peeled and chopped new potatoes
½	teaspoon black pepper		
1	tablespoon fresh marjoram leaves, or 1 teaspoon dried, crushed	2	tablespoons crumbled feta cheese
		4	sheets phyllo dough, thawed
		4	tablespoons butter, melted

Preheat oven to 350 degrees.

Melt 2 tablespoons butter in a large skillet over medium heat. Add onion, salt, pepper and marjoram and sauté 5 minutes, stirring occasionally. Mix in squash and potatoes and cook 10 minutes, stirring occasionally. Cover and cook 5 to 10 minutes longer or until vegetables are soft and breaking apart. Cool. Stir in cheese.

Place a phyllo sheet on a work surface, covering remaining sheets with a damp towel. Brush phyllo sheet with melted butter, then fold in half lengthwise and brush with butter again. Spoon one-fourth of the filling at the bottom of the sheet and fold the sheet over into a triangle. Continue folding until you reach the end of the phyllo sheet. Place on a greased baking sheet. Repeat with remaining phyllo sheets and filling, making 4 triangles.

Bake 30 minutes or until golden brown.

Serves 4.

Quick & Easy

Quick & Easy

Brie Kisses Ⓓ

½-⅔	pound Brie cheese (wedges are fine)
1	package (17.3 ounces) frozen puff pastry

Hot pepper jelly

Preheat oven to 400 degrees.

Cut Brie into ½-inch squares; leave rind on if desired. Place on a dinner plate and freeze 30 minutes while thawing puff pastry at room temperature.

Unfold thawed pastry, press together at seams and roll lightly with a rolling pin to smooth out. Cut each sheet into fourths, then cut each fourth into quarters, resulting in 16 squares per sheet. Fit a square of dough into each of 32 lightly sprayed mini muffin cups, pushing into the cup but leaving the edges sticking up. Place a dab of jelly in each cup. Top with a piece of cheese. At this point, kisses can be refrigerated until ready to bake.

Bake 10 to 15 minutes or until golden. Serve warm.

Makes 32.

Recipe can be prepared ahead and refrigerated until ready to bake, or bake them and re-warm in a 350 degree oven for about 10 minutes before serving.

Apple-Roquefort Puffs Ⓓ

2	packages refrigerated crescent rolls
2	large Granny Smith apples, peeled and chopped into ¼-inch dice

1	package (8 ounces) crumbled Roquefort cheese

Preheat oven to 325 degrees.

Remove crescent rolls from package and smooth perforations to make 2 large rectangles. Cut each rectangle into 24 equal squares (2 down, 12 across). Press one square into each of 48 greased mini-muffin cups.

Combine apple and cheese. Spoon 1 to 2 teaspoons of mixture into each muffin cup. Bake 10 to 15 minutes or until dough is golden brown. Serve warm.

Makes 48 puffs.

PUFF PASTRY TIPS

Chill any filling before it makes contact with the pastry.

Use water or an egg wash to seal the edges of the dough. An egg wash (1 egg beaten with 1 teaspoon cold water) will help create a golden brown exterior.

Cut puff pastry with a sharp knife or pastry wheel. If you don't, the layers of fat and flour within the dough may "fuse", inhibiting rising.

Always bake puff pastry in a preheated oven at 400 or 425 degrees. A hot oven produces a high puff. Bake until the pastry is a golden brown with distinct layers that easily crumble.

Use pastry scraps to make decorative garnishes, or bake them with a little cinnamon and sugar for quick treats. Do not try rolling the pieces together.

Cheese Straws Ⓓ

A savory accompaniment to vegetarian soups.

1 sheet (8 ounces) frozen puff pastry, thawed	½ cup finely shredded Cheddar cheese
1 egg, beaten	1 teaspoon cayenne pepper
1 tablespoon milk	1 teaspoon paprika
1 cup freshly grated Parmesan cheese	

Preheat oven to 400 degrees.

Roll puff pastry to ¹⁄₁₆-inch thickness. Combine egg and milk and brush over both sides of pastry. Mix both cheeses, cayenne and paprika and press onto both sides. Cut pastry into ½ x 6-inch strips. Twist each strip 4 times and place on a dry rimmed baking sheet, pressing the ends down to hold the twists in place.

Refrigerate up to several hours or freeze up to several weeks. Bake 15 minutes. If frozen, thaw before baking.

Makes 48 straws.

Cranberry Herring Ⓓ

Everyone's favorite. Always requested. Guaranteed to be a hit!

1 jar (2 pounds) herring in wine sauce, drained	1 can (16 ounces) whole berry cranberry sauce
1 container (16 ounces) sour cream, regular or fat-free	1 large onion, thinly sliced

Combine all ingredients and refrigerate for a few days. Serve with cocktail rye or pumpernickel bread or crackers.

Serves 20 to 25.

Parmesan Puffs Ⓓ

These are so delicious served hot at a luncheon.

1 package (11 ounces) refrigerated biscuit dough	⅓ cup freshly grated Parmesan cheese
¼ cup butter, melted	

Preheat oven to 475 degrees.

Cut each biscuit into quarters. Roll each into a small ball. Dip balls into melted butter, then roll in cheese. Place on a greased baking sheet. Bake 8 minutes or until golden. Serve hot.

Makes 40 small balls.

Easy Potato Knish Appetizers 🅟

1   small onion, chopped
    Oil for sautéing
3   large potatoes, boiled, then
    peeled

Salt and pepper to taste
1   package (10 ounces) frozen
    puff pastry shells

Preheat oven to 450 degrees.

Sauté onion in a small amount of oil until golden brown. Mash potatoes with onion and season with salt and pepper.

Roll out each patty shell into a long rectangle and place one-sixth of potato mixture along the edge of one long side of the pastry. Roll up, long side to long side. Slice each roll into 4 pieces and pinch edges. Bake 35 minutes or until golden brown. Serve hot.

Makes 24 appetizers.

Grilled Artichoke-Mozzarella Sandwich 🅓

3-4 slices mozzarella
2   artichoke hearts, drained
     and thinly sliced

Pinch of black pepper
2   large slices sourdough bread
2   teaspoons butter

Arrange mozzarella cheese, artichoke hearts and black pepper between bread. Spread outside of bread with butter. Grill sandwich 3 to 4 minutes on each side or until lightly browned and cheese is melted.

Serves 1.

Asian Cucumber Salad 🅟

1   tablespoon rice wine vinegar
1   tablespoon soy sauce
2   teaspoons grated fresh ginger
1   teaspoon sesame oil

1   chopped shallot
1½   cucumbers, sliced
2   tablespoons chopped fresh
     cilantro

In a large bowl, whisk together vinegar, soy sauce, ginger, sesame oil and shallot.

Stir in cucumbers and cilantro. Refrigerate at least 30 minutes. Serve chilled.

Serves 4.

Broccoli Tarragon Soup

2	boxes (10 ounces each) frozen broccoli pieces	4	cups chicken broth
	Large pinch of dried tarragon		Salt and pepper to taste

In a saucepan over medium heat, combine broccoli, tarragon and broth and simmer 7 minutes. Purée mixture until smooth in a food processor or blender. Season with salt and pepper.

Reheat over low heat and serve.

Serves 4.

Instant Beet Borscht

1	jar (16 ounces) pickled beets, chilled and undrained	2	cups cold buttermilk
		1	cup ice water
		⅓	cup chopped fresh dill

Purée all ingredients in a blender. Serve cold.

Serves 4.

Cabbage Soup

1	large head cabbage, thinly sliced	1	bottle (1 liter) ginger ale
1	brown onion, diced	1	bottle (32 ounces) ketchup

Combine all ingredients in a large pot. Bring to a boil. Reduce heat, cover and cook 45 minutes.

Serves 6 to 8.

Can add protein to soup by adding chopped meat, chicken, hot dogs, etc.

Presto Minestrone

This is wonderful for a crowd. Kids love it. By leaving out the meat, you have a pareve soup.

½	pound ground beef or turkey	4	carrots, thinly sliced
½	cup chopped onion	½	package (10 ounces) frozen green beans, or fresh
½	cup chopped celery		
1	teaspoon salt	1½	cups coarsely chopped cabbage
1	jar (15½ ounces) spaghetti sauce	⅓	cup dry small macaroni pasta
1	can (15½ ounces) red pinto beans, drained	1	tablespoon Italian seasoning
		3	cups water

Sauté ground meat, onion and celery in a large saucepan or Dutch oven. Add salt, spaghetti sauce, pinto beans, carrots, green beans, cabbage, dry pasta, Italian seasoning and water. Simmer 30 minutes or until vegetables are tender.

Makes 2 quarts.

Double the recipe and freeze some for later use.

No-Crust Artichoke Quiche

1	jar (6 ounces) marinated artichoke hearts	1¼	cups milk
4	ounces mushrooms, sliced	½	teaspoon salt
8	ounces Muenster cheese, shredded	⅛	teaspoon black pepper
		6	eggs, or equivalent egg substitute

Preheat oven to 350 degrees.

Drain artichokes, reserving marinade. Dice artichokes; set aside.

Warm 2 tablespoons reserved artichoke marinade in a skillet over medium heat. Add mushrooms and cook 5 minutes or until tender, stirring occasionally. In the bottom of a quiche dish sprayed with vegetable spray, evenly distribute artichoke hearts, mushrooms and cheese; set aside.

In a large bowl, whisk together milk, salt, pepper, eggs and 2 tablespoons reserved artichoke marinade. Pour mixture into quiche dish. Bake 30 minutes or until a knife inserted in the center comes out clean.

Serves 6.

To get the best flavor from fresh herbs, add tender herbs, such as basil, parsley, cilantro and dill toward the end of cooking time, or sprinkle on top of the finished dish. Cooking these tender herbs rapidly diffuses their flavor. Add strong-flavored hardy herbs, such as thyme, marjoram or rosemary earlier in the cooking process so that they have time to mellow. Added at the end, these hardy herbs may be too overpowering.

Tomato and Basil Pie

1	packaged pie crust, unbaked	4	cloves garlic, peeled
½	cup shredded mozzarella cheese	1	cup shredded mozzarella cheese
5	Roma or 4 medium tomatoes, cut into wedges and drained on paper towels	½	cup mayonnaise
		¼	cup freshly grated Parmesan cheese
1	cup loosely packed fresh basil leaves, plus extra for garnish	⅛	teaspoon white pepper

Preheat oven to 375 degrees.

Unfold pie crust and place in a 9-inch quiche or pie dish sprayed with vegetable spray. Prebake according to package directions. Remove from oven and sprinkle with ½ cup mozzarella cheese.

Arrange tomatoes on melted cheese. In a food processor, combine 1 cup basil and garlic. Process until coarsely chopped and sprinkle over tomatoes.

In a medium bowl, combine 1 cup mozzarella cheese, mayonnaise, Parmesan cheese and pepper. Spoon cheese mixture over tomatoes and spread evenly to cover. Bake 35 to 40 minutes or until top is golden and bubbly. Serve warm. Garnish top with basil leaves.

Serves 4 to 6.

Pasta Florentine D

You'll be using a microwave with this one.

2	packages (10 ounces each) frozen leaf spinach	12	ounces part-skim mozzarella cheese, shredded
8-12	cloves garlic, finely chopped	2	tablespoons plus 2 teaspoons grated Parmesan cheese
12	ounces thin spaghetti, cooked al dente and drained		

Place frozen spinach and garlic in a 3-quart greased casserole dish. Cover and microwave on high for 2 minutes. Drain spaghetti and immediately add to the casserole along with the mozzarella and Parmesan cheeses. Stir to combine. Cover and microwave on high 2 minutes or until heated through. Serve immediately.

Serves 4.

Bow Tie Pasta à la Greek 🄳

This is a warm weather pasta dish that is so easy and quick to make. It zings with flavor.

1	package (16 ounces) bow tie pasta	¼	cup extra virgin olive oil
2	scallions, chopped	2	cups chopped fresh tomato or small grape tomatoes, if available
1	package (6 ounces) feta cheese, crumbled		
½	cup balsamic vinegar	½	cup sliced olives (optional)

Bring a large pot of lightly salted water to a boil. Add pasta and cook 8 to 10 minutes or until al dente. Drain and place in ice water until cool. Drain again.

Toss drained pasta with scallions, cheese, vinegar, oil, tomato and olives. Serve immediately or chill 1 hour if time permits.

Serves 8.

A variation served hot can be made by eliminating the vinegar, tomatoes and olives and substituting the following:

4 to 5 ounces roasted red bell pepper from a jar, chopped

1½ teaspoons lemon zest

1½ teaspoons chopped fresh oregano

Toss with oil and serve.

Ziti Pasta with Veggies and Pine Nuts 🄳

A taste of the Mediterranean, on the Palos Verdes Coast.

1	pound dry ziti pasta	2	tablespoons olive oil
2	cups fresh broccoli, broken into small florets; or fresh green beans, sliced and microwaved 2 to 3 minutes	½	cup vegetable broth, or more as needed
		8	ounces mozzarella cheese, cut into small cubes
1	tablespoon minced fresh garlic	¼	cup pine nuts, toasted
2	tablespoons chopped fresh basil		Salt and pepper to taste

Cook pasta in boiling water until al dente, or tender, but still firm to bite.

While pasta cooks, sauté broccoli or par-cooked beans, garlic and basil in oil for 2 to 3 minutes. Add broth and cook 3 to 4 minutes longer. Drain pasta and toss with vegetables, mixing well. Add cheese cubes and pine nuts and toss. Season with salt and pepper.

Serves 8.

Microwaved Salmon or Halibut Steaks Ⓓ Ⓟ

The use of lettuce leaves gives this easy dish a delicately-delicious flavor.

4	salmon or halibut steaks (1-inch thick, about 4 ounces each)		Lemon pepper to taste
		1	small onion, thinly sliced Paprika
2	tablespoons butter or margarine	8	lettuce leaves
2	tablespoons fresh lemon juice Salt to taste	1	lemon, thinly sliced for garnish

Arrange fish steaks in a 10-inch glass casserole dish, placing narrow ends toward center of dish. In a glass cup, melt butter in microwave on high for 30 seconds. Add lemon juice and pour over fish. Season with salt and lemon pepper. Scatter onion slices over steaks and sprinkle with paprika. Cover each steak with a damp lettuce leaf.

Microwave on high for 5 to 7 minutes, rotating dish a quarter turn halfway through cooking. (If using a carousel microwave, this step can be omitted.) Remove from microwave and let stand 5 minutes. Serve steaks hot or cold on the remaining lettuce leaves. Garnish with lemon slices.

Serves 4.

If preparing a 2-pound fish roast, follow directions as above, cooking 10 to 12 minutes, turning roast over and rotating as noted above.

Red Snapper Vera Cruz Ⓟ

This is a quick adaptation of a favorite Mexican classic.

1	can (15 ounces) green chile enchilada sauce	4	red snapper fillets, or other firm-flesh fish
1	can (15 ounces) diced tomatoes	4	cups hot cooked rice
½	cup chopped onion	1	can (4 ounces) sliced black olives for garnish

Combine enchilada sauce, tomatoes and onion in a deep skillet. Cook over medium heat until onion is softened. Add snapper fillets, skin-side down and cover pan. Simmer 15 minutes or until fish flakes easily with a fork.

To serve, place a cup of cooked rice on each plate. Top each with a fish filet. Divide sauce evenly among servings. Garnish with olives.

Serves 4.

Trout Stuffed with Scallions Ⓟ

1   bunch scallions (white part only), chopped
2   ounces Japanese pickled ginger, chopped
     Zest of 1 lemon
4   rainbow trout, cleaned and boned
     Juice of 1 lemon
1   teaspoon olive oil

Mix scallions, ginger and lemon zest. Stuff mixture into interior of trout. Close and douse trout with lemon juice.

Preheat broiler. Rub trout with olive oil and broil 4 inches from heat for 4 minutes on each side or until fish is opaque.

Serves 4.

Rare Yellowfin or Albacore Tuna Steaks Ⓟ

This preparation of fresh rare tuna is popular with California diners.

2   pieces (1 pound each) center-cut extremely fresh tuna
3-4 tablespoons olive oil
2   tablespoons coriander seeds
1   tablespoon fennel seeds
     Salt and freshly cracked black pepper to taste

Rub tuna with olive oil, coriander seeds, fennel seeds and salt and pepper. Refrigerate 1 hour or longer. Sear tuna on a hot grill for about 2 minutes on each side. Remove and cool slightly. Cut into thin slices with a sharp knife. Serve with Fennel, Cilantro and Radish Vinaigrette.

Fennel, Cilantro and Radish Vinaigrette
To be served with rare, seared tuna.

3   shallots, finely diced
     Juice of ½ lemon
3   tablespoons Champagne vinegar
     Salt
½   cup extra virgin olive oil
1   medium fennel bulb, trimmed
1   small bunch radishes, trimmed
1   small bunch cilantro, tough stems removed

Macerate shallots in lemon juice and vinegar with a pinch of salt for 10 minutes. Whisk in olive oil and adjust seasoning.

Lay slices of tuna on individual serving plates. Shave fennel bulb into ribbons with a mandolin and strew over the tuna. Shave radish slices over the fennel. Splash vinaigrette over tuna and vegetables. Chop cilantro and scatter over each plate.

Serves 6 to 8.

Cranberry Sweet 'N Sour Meatballs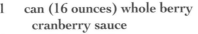

An old family recipe loved by young and old alike.

1	can (16 ounces) whole berry cranberry sauce	2	teaspoons seasoned salt
1	can (16 ounces) tomato sauce	¼	teaspoon white pepper
2	pounds ground turkey or beef	½	cup bread crumbs
1	egg	¾	cup water

Combine cranberry sauce and tomato sauce in a saucepan and bring to a simmer.

Meanwhile, mix ground turkey, egg, seasoned salt, pepper, bread crumbs and water. Form mixture into balls and drop into simmering sauce. Cook 1 hour. Serve over rice or noodles.

Serves 8 as a main dish, 16 as an appetizer.

For variety, add a can of drained pineapple chunks at end of cooking.

If using as an appetizer, form into very small balls.

Chicken Marsala

6	small, boneless, skinless, whole chicken breasts	6	tablespoons olive oil
	Salt and white pepper to taste	1	cup Marsala wine
	Flour for dredging	1	cup chicken broth
		1	cup sliced fresh mushrooms
		12	ounces dry flat pasta

Pound chicken breasts between 2 layers of plastic wrap until each is about ¼-inch thick. Season lightly with salt and white pepper and dredge in flour.

Heat olive oil in 2 large skillets over medium-high heat. Shake off excess flour from chicken breasts and sauté about 2 minutes per side or until lightly browned. Add wine, broth and mushrooms, divided between the 2 skillets. Reduce to a simmer and cook 5 minutes or until mushrooms soften and sauce thickens slightly. Serve with a side of freshly cooked pasta.

Serves 6.

Chicken Chili with Green Salsa

This chicken dish is quick to prepare – filled with the flavors from South-of-the-Border.

12-14	ounces chicken breast, cut into ½- to 1-inch pieces	1¾	cups mild or medium green salsa (about 16 ounce jar)
2	cans (15 ounces each) white kidney beans (cannellini), rinsed and drained	¼	cup chopped fresh cilantro
		½	cup water
		1	cup red or yellow cherry tomatoes, halved

Heat a nonstick 12-inch skillet over medium-high heat until hot. Add chicken and cook 2 to 3 minutes or just until chicken loses its pink color throughout, stirring constantly.

Add beans, salsa, cilantro and water and cook 5 minutes, stirring occasionally, to blend flavors. Top with tomatoes and serve.

Serves 4.

Green salsa is made with tomatillos, a Mexican fruit resembling a green tomato and covered with a loose papery husk. This can be found in the Mexican food section of your supermarket.

Baked Chicken Breasts with Mushrooms and Artichokes

4	chicken breasts Salt and pepper to taste	8	ounces fresh mushrooms, sliced
1	jar (6 ounces) marinated artichoke hearts	5	scallions, sliced
		1	cup dry white wine

Preheat oven to 350 degrees.

Season chicken with salt and pepper. Place, skin-side up, in a 13 x 9-inch baking dish. Drain artichokes, reserving marinade. Cut artichokes in half and place over chicken with mushrooms and onions. Mix reserved marinade with wine and pour over chicken.

Bake 45 minutes or until chicken is cooked.

Serves 4.

Easy Chicken Cacciatore

2	teaspoons olive oil	1	can (8 ounces) tomato sauce
1	chicken (2½ pounds)	1	medium bell pepper, sliced
½	envelope dry Italian salad dressing mix	4	ounces fresh mushrooms, sliced

Heat oil in a large skillet. Add chicken and brown well on all sides. Sprinkle dressing mix over chicken in skillet. Add tomato sauce, bell pepper and mushrooms to skillet. Cover and simmer 25 to 30 minutes, turning chicken once. Transfer chicken to a serving platter and top with sauce.

Serves 4.

Cranberry Chicken

1	can (16 ounces) whole berry cranberry sauce	1	package (1 ounce) dry onion soup mix
1	bottle (16 ounces) French salad dressing	2	chickens, cut into serving pieces

Preheat oven to 350 degrees.

Combine cranberry sauce, dressing and onion soup mix. Place chicken in a lightly greased dish. Pour cranberry mixture over chicken. Bake, uncovered, for 40 to 45 minutes or until cranberry gravy is bubbling. Serve over cooked rice or noodles.

Serves 6.

For a different flavor, substitute a 10 ounce jar apricot jam for the cranberry sauce.

Curried Honey-Mustard Chicken

This is our cantor's recipe that is often served at our Synagogue Shabbat dinners and enjoyed by all.

1	chicken, cut into serving pieces, rinsed and patted dry	⅓	cup lemon juice
⅓	cup grainy mustard	1	tablespoon curry powder
½	cup honey	1	tablespoon soy sauce
		1	bunch scallions, chopped

Preheat oven to 350 degrees.

Place chicken in a baking pan, skin-side up. Combine mustard, honey, lemon juice, curry powder and soy sauce and pour over chicken. Bake about 1 hour. Serve over brown rice or couscous with scallions sprinkled on top.

Serves 4 to 6.

Corn Spoon Pudding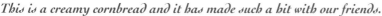

This is a creamy cornbread and it has made such a hit with our friends.

1   package (8½ ounces) corn muffin mix
1   can (7½ ounces) whole kernel corn
1   can (7½ ounces) creamed corn
1   cup sour cream (regular or light)
2   eggs, beaten
½   cup unsalted butter or margarine, melted
½   cup shredded Swiss cheese

Preheat oven to 350 degrees.

Combine all ingredients except cheese in a large bowl. Pour batter into a lightly greased 13 x 9-inch baking dish. Bake 35 minutes. Sprinkle with cheese and bake 10 minutes longer or until a pick inserted in the center comes out clean.

Serves 12.

Horseradish Smashed Potatoes

This is ideal served with a pot roast.

3-3½   pounds russet potatoes, peeled and cut into chunks
1-1½   cups chicken broth
2   tablespoons margarine
    Salt and pepper to taste
1-2   tablespoons prepared horseradish

Place potatoes in a 4- to 5-quart pan with 2½ quarts water. Bring to a boil over high heat. Reduce heat, cover and simmer 20 to 25 minutes or until potatoes mash easily when pressed.

When potatoes are done, heat chicken broth with margarine in a microwave until steaming. Drain potatoes and mash in pan until almost smooth. Add hot broth mixture a little at a time and mix until potatoes have the desired consistency. Stir in salt and pepper and horseradish to taste.

Serves 6 to 8.

Sherried Carrots with Ginger

2 tablespoons butter or margarine	3 tablespoons dry sherry, or more to taste
1½ pounds baby carrots	3 tablespoons water
½ cup crystallized ginger or ginger chips	1 teaspoon minced parsley
	Salt and pepper to taste

Melt butter in a 12- to 14-inch skillet over medium-high heat. Add carrots in a single layer and cook 8 to 10 minutes or until browned, turning as needed. Mix in ginger, 3 tablespoons sherry and water. Cover and reduce heat. Simmer 5 minutes or until carrots are crisp-tender. Stir in parsley and season with salt and pepper.

Arrange carrots on a platter. Top with ginger sauce, adding more sherry to taste.

Serves 4.

Sparkling Carrots

This unusual method of cooking carrots in a carbonated beverage came from a Southern California restaurant.

1 small onion, chopped	1 cup lemon-lime carbonated beverage
2 tablespoons butter or margarine	Salt and pepper to taste
1½ pounds carrots, sliced ⅛-inch thick	1 tablespoon sugar

Sauté onion in butter in large saucepan. Add carrots and carbonated beverage. Season with salt and pepper. Add sugar and cook over high heat 8 to 10 minutes or until liquid is absorbed and carrots are slightly glazed.

Serves 6.

Baked Apple Pizza

1	refrigerated ready-to-bake pie crust	1-2	tablespoons butter	
½	cup seedless raspberry jam	2-3	tablespoons sugar	
3-4	medium Granny Smith, Rome or Fuji apples, peeled and thinly sliced	¼	teaspoon cinnamon	
		¼	cup raisins (optional) Vanilla ice cream	

Preheat oven to 350 degrees.

Flatten pie crust onto a 9- or 10-inch pizza pan. Spread jam over crust, leaving a 1-inch border. Arrange apple slices over jam. Dot with butter.

In a small bowl, mix sugar and cinnamon and sprinkle over apples. Sprinkle with raisins. Bake 30 minutes. Serve warm with vanilla ice cream

Serves 6 to 8.

To core apples or pears easily, cut fruit in half lengthwise and scoop out centers with a melon baller.

Apple Pie, the Easy Way Ⓓ Ⓟ

All you need for this pie is a pie plate, a fork to combine ingredients and a knife to cut the apples. Don't bother to peel the apples.

5-6	apples, tart or sweet according to preference	1	cup flour
1	tablespoon sugar	1	cup sugar
1	tablespoon cinnamon	1	cup pareve margarine or butter, melted
1	egg, beaten		

Preheat oven to 350 degrees.

Slice unpeeled apples into a 9-inch pie plate. Combine 1 tablespoon sugar and cinnamon and sprinkle over apples. Blend egg, flour, 1 cup sugar and margarine until well mixed. Pour mixture over apples. Bake 35 to 40 minutes. A crust will form as pie bakes.

Serves 8.

Babe Ruth Bars

1	cup peanut butter	6	cups corn flakes cereal
1	cup light corn syrup	1	cup semisweet chocolate
½	cup brown sugar		chips
½	cup granulated sugar	⅔	cup peanuts

Combine peanut butter, corn syrup and both sugars in a large saucepan over medium heat. Cook, stirring occasionally, until smooth. Remove from heat and quickly mix in cereal, chocolate chips and peanuts until evenly coated.

Press mixture gently into a greased 13 x 9-inch baking dish. Cool completely before cutting into bars.

Makes 32 bars.

Lemon Glazed Pecan Bars

These bars resemble pecan pie with a sweet cookie crust.

1	package (17½ ounces) sugar cookie mix	1	cup flaked coconut
		2	teaspoons vanilla
3	eggs	½	cup confectioners' sugar, sifted
1	cup dark brown sugar, firmly packed		
1	cup chopped pecans, toasted	¼	cup fresh lemon juice
			Zest of 1 small lemon

Preheat oven to 350 degrees.

Prepare cookie dough as directed on package. Press dough evenly into a lightly greased and floured 13 x 9-inch baking pan. Bake 15 minutes or until lightly browned around the edges. Remove from oven and cool about 10 minutes.

While crust bakes, combine eggs, brown sugar, pecans, coconut and vanilla in a medium bowl. Mix well and pour over warm crust. Bake 15 to 20 minutes longer or until slightly browned on top.

If desired, make a glaze by combining confectioners' sugar, lemon juice and lemon zest. Mix well and drizzle over bars while still warm from the oven. Cool and cut into bars.

Makes 4½ to 5 dozen bars.

S'Mores Bars Ⓓ

This is so simple that you can have your children help out with the preparation as they will be the first to enjoy the results.

2	cups graham cracker crumbs	½	cup unsalted butter, melted
⅓	cup sugar	1	pound solid milk chocolate
¼	teaspoon salt	4	cups mini-marshmallows

Preheat oven to 350 degrees.

Combine cracker crumbs, sugar, salt and butter in a bowl. Mix well. Reserve 1 cup of mixture and press remaining mixture into a 13 x 9-inch baking dish. Bake 12 minutes or until golden. Cool on a rack.

In a double boiler over barely simmering water, melt chocolate, stirring until smooth. Pour chocolate over crust and spread evenly. Sprinkle with marshmallows, pressing them lightly. Sprinkle reserved crumb mixture on top.

Broil 2 inches from heat source for 30 seconds or until marshmallows are golden. Cool completely and cut into squares.

Makes 24 bars.

To make graham cracker crumbs, place crackers in a plastic bag and seal. Use a rolling pin to crush crackers into crumbs.

Caramel Crispy Treats Ⓓ

Chewy but crispy at the same time. Easy to make for casual gatherings.

4	milk chocolate covered caramel and nougat candy bars (2.05 ounces each)	3	cups crispy rice cereal
		1	cup milk chocolate chips
		¼	cup butter or margarine
½	cup butter or margarine		

In a microwave or the top of a double-boiler, melt candy bars and ½ cup butter, stirring occasionally until smooth. Stir in cereal until well blended. Press mixture into a greased 11 x 7-inch pan.

Melt chocolate chips with ¼ cup butter, stirring until smooth. Remove from heat and spread over top of bars. Refrigerate at least 2 hours.

Makes 32 bars.

Easy California picnic, which takes a few minutes to prepare: slice French bread in half lengthwise and scoop out some of the soft bread. Spread mustard on lower portion of bread. Arrange ¾ pound of sliced turkey evenly over mustard. Top with lettuce and sliced tomatoes. Add mayonnaise to the top half of bread. Put top and bottom of bread together and wrap tightly in foil. At your picnic, cut into pieces. Easy to double for a large group.

Blueberry Bundt Cake

This is a favorite summertime cake, which starts out with a cake mix. What a terrific way for a busy cook to create a delicious dessert.

1 tablespoon flour	1 cup sour cream or non-dairy
1½ cups fresh blueberries, well	sour cream
drained	4 eggs
1 package (16 ounces) lemon	
cake mix	

Preheat oven to 350 degrees.

Sprinkle flour over berries. Combine dry cake mix and sour cream with an electric mixer. Beat in eggs, 1 at a time, on low speed. Increase to medium speed and beat well, scraping bowl often. Fold in floured berries. Pour batter into a well-greased Bundt pan. Bake 35 to 40 minutes. Cool in pan 15 to 20 minutes before inverting onto a serving platter.

Serves 12.

Pumpkin Crunch Cake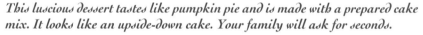

This luscious dessert tastes like pumpkin pie and is made with a prepared cake mix. It looks like an upside-down cake. Your family will ask for seconds.

1 can (28 ounces) pumpkin	1 package (18 ounces) yellow
1 can (12 ounces) evaporated	cake mix
milk	1 cup chopped nuts
1 cup sugar	1 cup butter, melted and cooled
3 eggs, beaten	Whipped cream or non-dairy
¼ teaspoon cinnamon	whipped topping

Preheat oven to 350 degrees.

Mix pumpkin, milk, sugar, eggs and cinnamon and pour into a greased and wax paper-lined 13 x 9-inch baking pan. Spread dry cake mix over pumpkin mixture. Sprinkle with nuts. Drizzle butter evenly over top.

Bake 1 hour. Cool 20 to 30 minutes. Invert onto a serving platter or tray and peel off wax paper. Refrigerate. Serve with whipped cream.

Serves 12 to 15.

Quick Walnut Tart

You can replace walnuts with pecans, almonds or pine nuts. Some dough will be left over, so you may bake a few cookies alongside the tart.

1	package (18 ounces) refrigerated sugar cookie dough	½	cup brown sugar, firmly packed
½	cup unsalted butter	¼	cup dark corn syrup
		2	tablespoons heavy cream
		2	cups walnuts (about 8 ounces)

Preheat oven to 350 degrees.

Cut cookie dough log crosswise into 3 equal pieces. Press 2 pieces of dough evenly into a 9-inch tart pan with removable bottom. Reserve remaining dough for another use. Bake crust 12 minutes. Using the back of a fork, press down bottom of crust, if necessary. Bake 3 minutes longer or until golden brown. Transfer to a rack.

Combine butter, sugar and corn syrup in a heavy medium saucepan over low heat. Stir until sugar dissolves. Increase to medium heat and boil 1 minute. Mix in cream. Stir in walnuts. Boil 4 minutes or until mixture thickens, stirring occasionally. Spoon filling over warm crust.

Bake 10 minutes or until filling is bubbling and color deepens slightly. Transfer to a rack and cool completely.

Serves 8.

Easy Peach Sherbet

1	can (28 ounces) peaches in heavy syrup	1	tablespoon finely chopped crystallized ginger and/or
⅛	teaspoon almond extract		¼ teaspoon raspberry vinegar

Freeze peaches in can until solid. Open can, dig out frozen contents, and purée in food processor along with almond extract, ginger and/or vinegar.

Serves 4.

Death by Chocolate Trifle

1   package (19.8 ounces) fudge
    brownie mix
3   packages (3½ ounces each)
    instant chocolate mousse

8   chocolate covered toffee
    candy bars (1.4 ounces each)
1   container (12 ounces) frozen
    whipped topping, thawed

Prepare brownie mix according to package directions. Cool. Meanwhile, prepare mousse according to package directions.

Break candy bars into small pieces in a food processor or by gently tapping wrapped bars with a hammer. Break up half of brownies into small pieces and place in the bottom of a large glass bowl or trifle dish. Cover with half the mousse. Layer half the candy on top. Spread half of whipped topping over all. Repeat layers with remaining ingredients.

Serves 24 (or 1 serving for the serious chocoholic).

A

Index • 279

R

T

KOSHER *on the* COAST

Sisterhood – Congregation Ner Tamid
5721 Crestridge Road
Rancho Palos Verdes, California 90275
(310) 377-6986

Kosher on the Coast Cookbook

Price $27.95 . . . . Quantity _____ $ _____

Postage & Handling for first book . . . . $5.00 $ _____

Each additional book . . . . $2.50 $ _____

Sales Tax (California only) . . . . 8.25% $ _____

Total Enclosed $ _____

Ship to:

Name _____

Address _____

City _____ State _____ Zip _____

Make checks payable to **CNT Sisterhood**

Charge to (circle one) Visa   MasterCard   Signature _____

Account number _____ Expiration date _____

Proceeds from the sale of this book contribute to the fulfillment of Sisterhood's commitments to sponsor scholarships and educational enrichment programs and to offer vital services and financial support to congregation and community projects.

Thank you for your order.

- -

KOSHER *on the* COAST

Sisterhood – Congregation Ner Tamid
5721 Crestridge Road
Rancho Palos Verdes, California 90275
(310) 377-6986

Kosher on the Coast Cookbook

Price $27.95 . . . . Quantity _____ $ _____

Postage & Handling for first book . . . . $5.00 $ _____

Each additional book . . . . $2.50 $ _____

Sales Tax (California only) . . . . 8.25% $ _____

Total Enclosed $ _____

Ship to:

Name _____

Address _____

City _____ State _____ Zip _____

Make checks payable to **CNT Sisterhood**

Charge to (circle one) Visa   MasterCard   Signature _____

Account number _____ Expiration date _____

Proceeds from the sale of this book contribute to the fulfillment of Sisterhood's commitments to sponsor scholarships and educational enrichment programs and to offer vital services and financial support to congregation and community projects.

Thank you for your order.